LAW & GRACE

Origin of Origins

BOOK FOUR

LAW & GRACE

Origin of Origins

Book Four

*Much is at stake,
there's no time for games!*

Judson McCawl

iii

Copyright

Law and Grace: Origin of Origins
Book Four

For information please visit www.thehumblesaint.com

Cover design by GERMANCREATIVE
(germancreative on Fiverr)

ISBN 978-1-990977-32-9

Duke of Valmary Publishing House

Dedication

To the LORD: who was, who is, and who always will be – the
Almighty.

Acknowledgement

I firstly have to acknowledge the help, encouragement and
inspiration that the Lord Most High afforded me. He kept me
going and provided the support that I needed.

To my parents, for their help and support where required.

Contents

Preface

BOOK One in the *Law & Grace* series, *Journey to Calvary*, clearly tackles the specific issue of Law and Grace. Book Two, *Divine Intervention*, does no less, with a number of twists and turns, and it raises many thought provoking issues that face us all too often. Book Three, *Revealing Love*, has a mixture of mystery and romance, yet keeps at its core the principle of salvation and biblical teachings. Book Four follows the thread with salvation and biblical teachings, yet it remains pointed, digging deep into the heart of man and faces the reality of deception and attempts by man to escape from God. It is for both a Christian and non-Christian audience, for it is relevant to core issues that both will face in their lifetime and the hereafter.

In essence, all the current books in the *Law & Grace* series challenge the status quo, challenge complacency, challenge current world views and challenge the heart of man towards God. They make plain the way of Salvation and present the saving grace of God, biblical principles and explain God's working.

The exaltation and praise of man's intellect has increased as man has gained in knowledge, yet his condemnation of God's existence and Sovereign authority has remained its opposite equal. Has increased knowledge made man wise or foolish? Is his denial of God based on understanding or self-opinion and delusion? Has man's worldly enlightenment also brought spiritual light, insight and freedom to his soul or is Scripture justified when it says in John 3:19 that men loved darkness rather than light, because their deeds were evil? Where does pride take a man? Where does defiance lead him? Can man emancipate himself through his efforts and through his beliefs or is true freedom, wisdom, understanding and knowledge gained solely through humility from the hand of Divine provision? Does man ultimately have a hope? These are questions the world tends to want to ignore or have answered from a one-sided point of view – man's view. However, does Scripture not have power and authority to answer it? Is there not a Man who can testify, and One who will also judge?

Man leaves no stone unturned in his effort to search out in detail the greatness of the unknown – from the depths of the dark sea to the heights of the tallest peaks and even beyond, from what is visible to the naked eye to that which can only be viewed with the aid of sophisticated and technologically advanced equipment and machinery. What then about the unsearchable riches of Christ? Shunning the very thought of seeking the truth about Jesus Christ may not be a wise choice, particularly when one considers that one's life and soul may depend on it – for all eternity. Enough said, it is now time for the fourth book in the series, *Law & Grace: Origin of Origins*.

Judson McCawl

Chapter 1

The reunion

'HI, James,' greeted Professor McKenzie Smyth, sitting on his black, cloth-covered, high-back executive chair. He was speaking on the phone in his comfortable office at Ailensbury University's faculty of biology. 'Has Dr Lang arrived yet?'

It was first thing on a Monday morning in early July, the bright summer sun piercing through the lace curtain gently swaying from the open window and lighting upon the papers lying strewn on the lecturer's large mahogany desk. The office was quite spacious, with an elongated feel as it stretched just more than twice its width. A large matching mahogany bookcase, packed with educational books and research volumes, covered one third of the left wall from floor to ceiling. A small mahogany counter-height cupboard on the right housed half a dozen mugs and a kettle. Two black, visitors' chairs were neatly positioned in front of the professor's desk, with an additional two placed against the wall behind the door. Family photos graced the mahogany shelf behind the professor, with a few sporting photos randomly dispersed on the two side walls amongst the learned man's certificates of qualification.

There was suddenly an interrupting knock at the professor's door.

'Looking for me?' asked Dr Loris Lang with a big smile as he peered round the door, causing the professor to look up startled.

'Don't worry, James,' interrupted Professor Smyth with a pleased look, 'there's no need to play the detective and track him down; the object of my interest has just shown his handsome face. Thanks anyway for your preparedness to assist.' Professor Smyth promptly hung up the phone. 'Come, come, Loris, my bright colleague,' continued the professor, beckoning with cordial manner for the younger man to enter, 'you cannot talk to me about your new venture from there!' He promptly stood up to warmly receive Dr Lang.

Professor McKenzie Smyth, whose grandparents were immigrants from the British Isles, was fondly known as Kenny. He was a tall, slim man, who carried himself well. Now in his early 60s, he had thinning wiry hair, with only small remnants of his hair's former red colour being noticeable from close up. It had been replaced with a light grey tint, and he wore with pride a matching beard. His thick, wiry eyebrows had lost none of their strong red colour though, and his piercing blue eyes were as bright and as strong as ever. His deep voice was penetrating, and his loud laughter could be heard all the way to the ends of the long corridor. He was the head professor of Ailensbury University's department of biological studies and responsible for all research projects undertaken.

Dr Loris Lang was a different character altogether. Fondly known as Lori, he was 35 years old and married to Sarah, the sweetheart of his youth. He was short and stocky, with a round face and dark eyes set deep in their sockets. He allowed his mop of curly, black hair to grow thick and wild, which seemed to contradict his usually composed manner. Loris was studious and hardworking, with a keen eye for detail and an interest in extending the sphere of microbiology in which he had received his doctorate. A challenge in the area of his interests was as inviting to him as honey to a bee.

'It truly is good to see you again,' commented Professor Smyth after heartily shaking Loris' hand and patting him on the back. 'How was the trip back to your homeland?'

'I had thoughts of misgiving when we left,' replied Loris, 'but once back home, I cannot tell you how quickly the flooding memories instilled a happiness to be back on native soil.'

'Five years across the pond is a long time,' mentioned Professor Smyth, gesturing Loris to take a seat. 'It's enough time to surely have influenced anyone – particularly if you were enjoying the task of lecturing on your favourite subject!'

'Indeed!' confirmed Loris as he pulled out one of the visitor chairs and sat down. 'Lecturing across the Atlantic at Bridgetown University was an opportunity I relished. It's not often that a young man like myself gets afforded such a bright opportunity, and being able to do so in the company of notable academics!'

'Before I enquire about the family,' asked Professor Smyth, who was now sitting on the edge of his desk, dangling his one leg, 'how is Duke?'

'Professor Kensington?' asked Loris enquiringly, to the Professor's nod. 'Dudley's doing fine – the same old conceited English intellectual that he always was during his doctoral studies here at Ailensbury! He was a Whig with his words when here, but back home, you can be sure that deep down he has a Tory's heart.'

'What you mean is,' joked Professor Smyth, 'that if this was the year 1745, Duke would have fought in a red coat alongside bonnie Prince Charlie!' The two men laughed heartily, with the professor's booming voice echoing down the corridor as usual. 'I expect we'll hear from him sometime in the future,' remarked the professor, still chuckling, 'when he eventually hears about the task that you'll be involved in! He'll be friend or foe, depending on his viewpoint.'

'Most likely,' confirmed Loris. 'He's not one to sit still or keep his mouth shut if he feels he has something to say. Whether it's a wisdom or folly, I'll leave that decision up to others! I'll cross that bridge when I come to it! Nevertheless, he's a great friend of mine and was an incredible support during my time there.'

'How's Sarah and the girls?' asked Professor Smyth, with more sober interest. 'The relocation going smoothly?'

'Smoothly enough for the moment,' replied Loris with a sigh, 'but there's still a lot of pressure on us to get things done, and I can see that Sarah's taking some strain in trying to co-ordinate all that she needs to do. We've only been back a week, so there's still much to do – schooling to arrange for the girls, furniture and household stuff to be sorted out. We really had it good with the already furnished apartment we were given the use of while at Bridgetown! Not to mention I've still got to set up my pottery studio in one of our back rooms, but thanks to your efforts, some things have already been sorted!'

'No doubt you refer to Sarah's new job,' assumed Professor Smyth, 'but that was not something great on my part. I owe that to Gloria Sparletti.'

'The name's not familiar to me,' commented Loris thoughtfully. 'Could you acquaint me with who she is?'

'Maybe if I use her maiden name, Gloria Nicholls, it would be better,' said Professor Smyth quickly. 'She recently remarried her former husband alongside her son's marriage. The university has used the events company that she works for, Irving & Baxter, to manage certain of our high profile events and conferences. I know her from that association and while co-ordinating your return, took a chance in asking her if Irving & Baxter perhaps had an opening for Sarah. Before the double wedding, just more than two weeks back now, she confirmed the half-day secretarial position in which Sarah will start next week.'

'We're much obliged for that, I assure you,' thanked Loris, gratefulness clearly noticeable in his voice. 'Half-day jobs aren't always easy to come by, and it suits Sarah perfectly so that she can still manage the kids.' 'Ah, Nicholls!' exclaimed Loris with lighted eyes after a moment's reflection. 'Just as I was leaving our rented apartment this morning, Sarah received a phone call from a July' – pronounced Julie – 'Nicholls. She told Sarah to contact her father, a Mister Harris, branch manager at Ottenger's department store, who would be able to help us sort out our household needs. A direct connection, I presume? Any relation to Timothy Nicholls, former Ailensbury University football player?'

'Tim is Gloria's son, and July is her new daughter-in-law,' confirmed the professor with a smile.

'Amazing!' said Loris, quite taken aback. 'Sarah also sent me a message to say that the catering company had confirmed that they would continue this week to help us out with meals, as they had done during last week. They've been so helpful. We would have struggled to manage otherwise, as we never realised how much there would be for us to do in the little time we had between ending my contract at Bridgetown and starting this new task.'

'It's good to hear such news,' responded Professor Smyth

with satisfaction, 'but please remember that you're free to call on the university for assistance too, so don't go round needlessly being stubborn and bull-headed. I'll pull strings and chains and whatever if need be!' With a smile, Loris nodded his appreciation. 'And if you hadn't realised it yet,' added the professor quickly, 'your lovely new house on the side of the hill overlooking the majestic coastline is just one street down from the Sparletti's and Nicholls' abode – Timothy and July have a private extension to the house. Practically neighbours, you and that family!'

'Wow!' exclaimed Loris as Professor Smyth's laughter once again caught the attention of the furthest extents of the connecting corridor. 'Small world we live in, indeed!'

'Maybe it's just Ailensbury,' managed the professor before settling down again, 'and to add to the whole scene—' Professor Smyth stopped mid-sentence, having heard a gentle knocking at his door once again. 'Show your face, man,' he called jestingly, 'let me see if you are friend or foe!' With a look of self-approval at his own joking, the professor raised his wiry eyebrows and nodded to Loris.

A shy face tentatively peered round the door standing slightly open and promptly beheld the professor and Loris, who had swivelled his torso so that he could face the door, looking intently at him.

'My dear lad, no need to be hesitant!' exclaimed Professor Smyth loudly, getting up and making his way to the door. 'Do come in, do come in – I'm expecting you. What a joy, what a reunion. I haven't seen you since you were a student here!'

Chapter 2

A noble task

'LORIS,' beckoned Professor Smyth, turning towards him for a split second, 'let me introduce you to another whom I've not seen for three years at least, maybe even four – I cannot fully recall. This truly is a pleasant reunion!'

Loris got up energetically from the chair and promptly joined Professor Smyth and the new arrival in the middle of the office.

'It's been three years now, sir,' said the bright young man, who seemed to lose his shyness upon entering.

'Indeed!' exclaimed the professor while shaking the young man's hand with energy and looking at him with approval. 'Maybe I've missed your presence around these parts that it seems longer to me. Anyhow, it's such a pleasure for an old man like myself!'

'Thank you kindly,' responded the young man, his formal clothing enhancing his neat and tidy presentation, 'it's good to be back – particularly not in the roll of a student.'

The other two gentlemen laughed quietly, fully comprehending his meaning.

'Loris,' said Professor Smyth heartily, 'allow me to introduce to you Andrew Renshaw, your assistant for the duration of this praiseworthy task that you'll be undertaking. Andy, meet Dr Loris Lang – Lori for short, for which I'm sure he'll not mind at all!'

'Not at all,' confirmed Loris enthusiastically, liking the look of his new assistant and shaking his hand in friendly gesture. 'As long as we're to be working together, there's no need for undue formalities, just hard, diligent and conscientious work. I may be in charge of proceedings but the rest is inconsequential, for besides, it's clearly evident that there's less than a decade of age separating us.'

Andrew Renshaw was the son of George and Kelly Renshaw, Kelly being Gloria's younger sister. He was relatively tall, slim but well-built, quite athletic looking and had neat, honey-brown hair. He was a microbiologist working alongside his father at Microlab Industries, a laboratory located in the heart of the Ailensbury CBD. He was one for the outdoors and when the opportunity afforded him, would not be found anywhere else. Andrew was 26-years old and a young man of sound upbringing and steady character.

'Okay, Dr Lang,' responded Andrew positively, 'it's appreciated. I haven't been fully briefed as to what the task is or what will be required of me, but diligent work I can commit myself to.'

'Good lad,' said Professor Smyth, stepping round Andrew on his way to close the office door. 'Are Timothy and July back yet from honeymoon?'

'Yes,' replied Andrew, swivelling round to look at the professor, 'I fetched them yesterday from Ailensbury National Airport.'

'I presume they had a pleasant time?' enquired the professor as he shut the door.

'You presume correctly, sir,' answered Andrew. 'How could they not! They went to the holiday destination of their dreams! July had hoped more than three years back of going there on honeymoon!'

'Where would that be?' enquired Loris, listening thoughtfully to the present conversation.

'Angels Delight Resort,' replied Andrew, 'in the mountain area of Baroncorra.'

'Indeed I know it well,' mentioned Professor Smyth. 'Our family have often vacationed there.'

'I have to confess,' said Loris, 'I'm not familiar with the area but will look it up the next time we want to spend some time away.'

'You don't know what you've missed,' added the professor with conviction, 'it certainly is a delightful place! Can I offer you both coffee before we get down to business?'

'For me, that would be much appreciated,' answered Loris. 'Even after being back a whole week, the pace of activity seems to have kept me in jetlag – I'm continually tired at the moment. Hopefully it will be gone by next Monday when the real action starts! One sugar and a splash of milk, thanks Kenny.'

'I'm fine, thank you, sir,' replied Andrew politely. 'My wife, June, has the coffee pot on the boil before the sun rises in the morning. I've already had my "boost" quota for the day.'

'You may soon learn to "boost" more often,' chirped Professor Smyth jestingly, then quickly made two cups of steaming coffee.

The air of the office filled swiftly with the delightfully rich and intense aroma from a strong brew of South American beans.

The professor placed the two white, ceramic mugs on cork coasters lying on his desk, shifted some of the papers he was working with and sat down in his chair opposite Loris and Andrew, who had already seated themselves. Andrew was sitting quite upright, waiting in eager anticipation for the finer details of the brief, having only been informed in general that very morning of the task to which he would be assigned over the coming months, year or even two years if the research stretched out that long.

'Andy,' began Professor Smyth, his demeanour having changed to a more serious and intense one, 'just short of a year ago, Lori telephoned me one evening from across the Atlantic – he was there lecturing at Bridgetown University under a 5-year contract. He still had a year to fulfil but wanted to run past me some of his thoughts – rather interesting thoughts by my observation. He wasn't looking to renew his lecturing commitment there, even though the university had indicated that they were willing to make him a permanent member of staff with even the possibility of him heading one of the departments.'

'By all accounts,' interjected Loris, 'the professorship and financial incentives were certainly appealing!'

'However,' continued Professor Smyth, 'as Loris confided in me, there was something plaguing his interests, and he wanted to establish the viability of pursuing it. Loris' information was certainly private and confidential and I dare say held a high level of fresh interest in the area of microbiological studies. He, in fact, took me by surprise with his insight and the bold venture he wanted to pursue but placed the prospect in my hands to see what influence and muscle I could wield, if I felt it warranted the merit of pursuit.'

The professor calmly took a sip of his coffee while Andrew

continued to sit glued to his seat in suspense, waiting anxiously for all to be clearly revealed.

'I mused over Lori's details for some time,' continued Professor Smyth, carefully placing his mug back on the cork coaster. 'I felt that what he wanted to do would be an adventurous undertaking in the world of microbiology and daunting too, as it would require certain apparatus to be created or still invented as the technology at the time was only a speculative prospect of mere boastful talk, no hard, real product that one could comfortably back.'

At this point, the professor stopped and looked directly at Loris momentarily, almost as though he was reliving the experience.

'However,' said the professor, 'Loris' conviction soon became mine, and I think he knew that it would! I felt compelled to act in favour of it and seek its unanimous approval, having first done some investigations as to the feasibility of obtaining what we needed. It's a risk, I admit, but we have strong backing, and those backing, which for the most part is this university, are aware of the risks of failure. I say this without intent to flatter, but if it had been anyone other than Loris, I wouldn't have given it a second thought. Such a task, with such high risks of failure attached, I would not have put in the hands of anyone else!'

Andrew was almost sitting on the edge of his seat with interest, and his heart was beating strongly with excitement, yet somehow still managed to present a face of calm as he took in what was being told to him.

'Before I reveal to you the nature of the task,' continued Professor Smyth, 'there's another aspect attached to it and that is immediate secrecy. Due to the nature of the task, we have had to obtain co-operation from certain other parties before committing to pursuing this avenue. One such major player is Bramford University, in the heart of aristocracy that still flies the flag of ancient times and stirs the embers from time to time of the near-forgotten band of once exalted civility. They have an incredible design faculty headed by the acclaimed, and rightly so, Professor Stanley Berg. They haven't only agreed to work alongside us regarding required apparatus but for the past six months have already been working on technological advancements on our behalf. I can see from your facial expression, Andrew, that you already know where I'm headed and understand the position.'

'Indeed,' affirmed Andrew promptly, 'I think I'm catching on. The prestige of universities, competition, breakthroughs, bragging rights and the world of intellectual property should it ever arise.'

'That's a rather cold assessment,' concluded Loris, he and the professor amused at Andrew's frank but true observation.

'Absolutely so,' confirmed Professor Smyth, quickly reverting back to his serious manner. 'The ultimate goal is to the benefit of mankind and the progression of science as a whole, but those aspects that you mentioned are, nonetheless, a reality that needs to be factored in, particularly when a lot of money is part of the program. It's not that we want to keep everything for ourselves, just protect our interests, and at this point in time we need to gain an advantage – a head start, if you will.'

'I understand,' said Andrew, sitting back in his chair a little, feeling that a clear disclosure may still be a moment in waiting.

'One such concern is Bridgetown University,' said the professor, 'from which Loris has just returned, as we have partnered with Bramford, who is one of their close rivals. Annoying nonsense but nevertheless a reality!'

'In other words,' concluded Andrew, 'the less said, the easiest mended.'

'Absolutely!' agreed Loris. 'That's the bottom line. We need to maintain secrecy for a period of time, until we're off the ground and don't make ourselves out to be fools. Generalisations are fine, specifics are not, but at this point still only to close family such as your wife and father. I believe he's working at Microlab Industries and will partly assist us from time to time.'

'Understood,' confirmed Andrew, 'I have no problem with that, but could you please clear the air as to what it is that we'll be researching or trying to research as the case may seem to be?'

'It seems we've unintentionally created an air of anticipation, Loris,' remarked Professor Smyth amusedly. 'Sorry, Andrew. I'll brief you forthwith. Firstly though, for the purposes of secrecy, Ailensbury University have decided not to attempt using our facilities for the research but keep it off campus and out of our labs. Right or wrong, it's just a decision we have taken. Therefore, Microlab Industries was approached for assistance. Your boss, Dr Llewellyn Whyte, has been most accommodating, and an agreement was easily reached. We have confidence in him and the work of the lab. I'll be heading the overall project; Loris will be heading the overall research and process thereof. You will be assisting him fulltime. There will be no others, that's it, so it will be hard, exacting work. Your father will play a supportive roll, and through talks with him and Dr Whyte, they are both comfortable with you fulfilling the position. Now for the exact nature of the research.' The professor stopped and looked at Loris questioningly.

'You finish it up,' said Loris after a brief silence, having read the professor's look.'

'Andy,' continued Professor Smyth with an air of solemn

excitement and pride, 'we'll be attempting to find the origin of origins!' He stopped and looked at Andrew to see his response.

'Okay,' said Andrew in a rather thoughtful manner, 'how do you expect to go about it?'

'Loris is convinced that it's possible,' said Professor Smyth, 'and I'm fully inclined to believe the feasibility of it too. With the help of advanced technology, we will try to research deeper into what makes kinesin tick, the way we have researched the cell. Lori believes that if we can get to the core of it, we would have struck the core of origins!'

'I'm not one to guess where it will lead to or the end result,' said Andrew, having first looked disbelievingly at the professor and then at Loris, 'but when it comes to pure lab research, I have a great love for it. Dr Whyte briefed me before I came here that my new assignment is to start this coming Monday. I'll be pleased to do so and look forward to working with you Loris. I can foresee major adjustments in the beginning and many changing parameters before a course gets clearly set. Nevertheless, that's what research is all about, and I'll be up to the challenge.'

'There you have it, Loris,' said Professor Smyth smugly. 'You have your man, and I wish the two of you the best. Just remember that I have to answer to the top brass so need to be kept up to date on proceedings. Unless you have anything further, Lori, and if Andy doesn't have any questions, I think we can allow him to head on his way.'

'Nothing presently from my side,' said Loris, and turned to Andrew, 'I'll keep you posted throughout the week and let you know if there's anything I need your assistance with before next week Monday, but I doubt it.'

'Nothing from my side,' affirmed Andrew, 'I just look

forward to the new challenge and what it may bring about.'

The three gentlemen stood up without further ado. Andrew promptly shook hands with Loris and Professor Smyth before taking leave.

'Your thoughts, Loris?' questioned Professor Smyth shortly after Andrew had left the office. 'You seem to be contemplating something.'

'He's a bright bean, it seems,' considered Loris, 'and I quite like him if first impressions are valid. There's something different about him though, which I cannot quite figure out.'

'If it will be of any comfort to you,' remarked Professor Smyth, 'I've known Andrew since his first year at this university, and I've keenly noted his work since graduation. He was selected to accompany an overseas research party for a year, and he did very well according to the reports. He's been assigned by my special request to his employer – you wait and see.'

'I don't doubt your choice,' responded Loris, 'not by any means. Andrew seems positive about the research but in a way that's different to your or my perception. His response to you mentioning our intent to discover the origin of origins struck me, as though while our research will yield solid results, the source behind the discoveries is likely to be ethereal not material. Anyway,' added Loris quickly, 'let me not dwell too much at this point in time on it, lest I start finding things that aren't there. Sarah's in need of my immediate help, I'm terribly tired and have only one week before we plough full force into this task.'

'Don't make it sound like it's only going to be hard work, Loris,' said the professor encouragingly, patting the younger man gently on his shoulder. 'Next week you'll be up and rearing to go. I know you!'

Loris gave the professor a brief closed-lip smile before he

began to make his way towards the office door with the professor at his heels.

'Oh, yes!' said Loris, quickly wheeling round just as he reached the door. 'You enquired earlier from Andrew about Timothy and July. Are Andy and Tim perhaps best friends?' 'Tim's beautiful wife, July,' answered Professor Smyth, 'is the twin sister of June, Andrew's wife! Furthermore, Andrew Renshaw and Timothy Nicholls aren't only best friends but cousins!'

'Why do I get the odd feeling that there's going to be a catch somewhere down the line!' said Loris light-heartedly but with enlightened surprise. 'You haven't set me up in a trap or something, have you?'

'Fat chance of me attempting that!' exclaimed Professor Smyth, giving Loris a mocking look in jest. 'I've more pressing affairs to attend to and need your every energy and effort of genius and help. If I set you up in a trap, I'm likely to have my hide caught in it too!'

'Anything else I need to be aware of before I leave?' asked Loris.

'Not that I can think of,' replied the professor.

After shaking hands, Loris promptly exited.

'Oh, Loris!' called Professor Smyth swiftly, causing Loris to swivel round on his heel before he was a dozen paces from the office. 'Just one thing. Andrew is a Creationist and a Christian.'

'What's that you say!' exclaimed Loris, retracing his steps. 'You aren't being serious! If you knew that, why then did you select him for this task?'

'He's the best and most loyal assistant you'll get!' defended Professor Smyth adamantly. 'I'm not only fond of him but know that he can be relied upon. I have confidence in his abilities –

irrespective of his fanciful and phoney beliefs. Besides, it actually never came to mind until this very moment.'

'Never mind,' said Loris resolvedly, 'I'm more interested in the task at hand, not his concocted religious viewpoint. It irks me though that there are still biologists who believe in God and the Bible. I pity him for it. I'll have to just take on the added task of enlightening the blinded wretch, and I can promise you one thing – by the time I'm finished with my research so will his religion be finished! No-one will be able to believe in God then!'

'Seeking the origin of origins is a great task in itself,' responded Professor Smyth emphatically, 'but what you additionally seek to do will truly be a noble task! No small feat, I assure you, and I wish you every success!'

Chapter 3

Pepe

'**N**O way, Jose!' exclaimed Loris as he stepped out of the mantrap security door and into the newly-created lab that was to be home to his research, the tone of his voice clearly expressing his surprise. 'This is a far cry from what Professor Smyth told me!'

'It seems you've been the recipient of some form of trick?' responded Dr Llewellyn Whyte, he and Andrew amused at Loris' amazement and disbelief at what he saw.

Dr Llewellyn Whyte was not only a senior microbiologist at Microlab Industries but also the managing director. He was a short, chubby man but neat and precise in his presentation, a trait that was a trademark in his work as well. His thick hands looked clumsy and unsuited to lab work with fine instruments, but he had a skilful touch that never mishandled a thing. He had a little annoying cough when he laughed, but it troubled him more than others. He was a generally quiet man, often reserved, but when his position of authority was needed, he exercised his voice purposefully and powerfully, being clear with his expressions and intent to resolve whatever issues were at stake, without partiality or prejudice to any party concerned, no matter what. For this he was well-liked and well-respected, both within and without the company.

'Indeed!' replied Loris. 'Professor Smyth told me that unfortunately the lab was a small pokey and dingy place. He said that it was all you could offer but felt that it would suffice and actually be beneficial in that no-one would believe that anything decent went on there, thus removing all suspicion as to high-level secret operations. Blighter! He provoked every form of patriotism in me, loyalty to my profession and sacrifice on behalf of mankind in order not to hold back on pursuing this task despite the grim conditions. I should've smelled a rat there somewhere!'

'If it's any consolation,' commented Dr Whyte with a gentle laugh before coughing softly, 'we were none the wiser to Smyth's little practical joke. We were only asked not to mention anything to you, but in all kindness meant, I would have gone along with it and do so again, if I thought you would respond the same way! Your facial expression told a thousand words and more – priceless! Credit to the naughty prankster!'

Loris, who had a fairly good sense of humour, chuckled and let out a heavy sigh of relief. He could not hold back a broad smile as he stood surveying his surrounds.

'To say that I'm relieved is an understatement,' confessed Loris confidently, 'and all fears of failure relieved upon first sight. I'm sure we'll do well here!'

'I'm glad to hear the optimism,' said Dr Whyte encouragingly, putting his hand briefly on Andrew's shoulder. 'We're confident of good things from you and Andy.'

'You've done a stinking good job here,' complimented Loris cheerfully, still surveying the area, 'it looks to be a great skunkworks. I can already see, even before we properly look around!'

'Much obliged to you for the compliment,' responded Dr Whyte cordially, 'but the real person to thank is the Frenchman, Monsieur Giuseppe Le Peaux. He's a genius when it comes to labs, and we've used his services on a number of occasions in the past. He outshone himself this time. We had a few difficulties in creating a separate laboratory, as it impacted on other areas of operation, but he did a remarkable job in getting things straightened out for us. He took our every consideration into account and came up with sensible options and, I feel, optimal functionality within this laboratory, including with respect to the other laboratory areas affected.'

The new lab was spotlessly clean and bright. The tiled floor was an off-white colour, which removed excess glare from the large fluorescent lights above, while the walls and ceiling were a brilliant white. The two large windows looked out towards the sea, for the room was on the second floor of the building. When opened, they allowed a fresh, revitalising air to infiltrate and enliven the laboratory. White hanging blinds on the windows shut out the world when needed. Areas were clearly demarcated and partitioned, in a way that maintained openness between work stations and accessibility to the apparatus and equipment. There were only two distinctly isolated sections for specific work, which were behind the general work stations and completely out of sight of anyone. There were two open areas on the floor, but they were purposefully demarcated for equipment that would be needed further down the line of investigation. All the equipment was brand new and almost sparkled under the white lights shining approvingly upon them from above. The lab's clinical feel could not be denied and was purposely created that way, but its layout provided an aesthetical appearance that was nonetheless inviting and soft. Loris' and Andrew's cream-coloured, melamine desks were also neatly laid out, with computers, stationery, whiteboards and all necessary accessories provided in order to make their lives comfortable and functional. Soft, cream-coloured vinyl, adjustable high-back office chairs were also valued items in the mix.

The shelves and cupboards on the wall were clearly marked, with all supplies readily available. Glassware such as test tubes, conical flasks, volumetric flasks, graduated cylinders, pipettes, burettes and petri dishes were some of the commonly known apparatus carefully shielded and packed so that they were not unduly vulnerable to breakage. Sterilization equipment such as a hot air oven, drying oven and autoclave were neatly grouped in one area. A microbiological incubator and BOD low temperature incubator were ready for action, as were two thermal cyclers. A refrigerator, deep-freeze, electronic analytical balance, small distilled water plant, not to mention a number of microscopes of various shapes and sizes, and digital monitors were all present and operational, ready to serve man and his country unstintingly, with pride and loyalty to the best of their ability and strength. A number of other sophisticated apparatus and equipment, too confusing for the layman's mind to fully comprehend, were placed at their various stations, with counter-tops and under-counter cupboards standing at each station for ease of operation. White lab coats, protective clothing, boxes of blue latex gloves, a number of different mask types and various goggles were either on a rack or hanging on hooks alongside a wash basin, with a shelf filled with washing agents standing neatly like an army drill squad at attention.

'Security is important,' affirmed Dr Whyte purposefully, 'so we've provided the mantrap security entrance, with myself and Andrew's father, George, being the only staff members apart from yourself and Andy who have access cards. There's a separate security system in place, which operates independently from the main system, and a power generator is on standby for the equipment, should there be a power failure. Handheld emergency lights are placed at all work stations.'

'I see,' said Loris, satisfied with what he was being told, 'I'm happy to know that all eventualities have been covered.'

'Anyway,' said Dr Whyte with a pleased look on his face, 'I'll go through all the aspects in detail as we go along. Shall we get started then?'

Dr Whyte promptly picked up his clipboard that had his notes attached. After scanning them, he began to walk, with Loris and Andrew in tow, and went systematically through the whole laboratory identifying all the equipment, checking off items on his sheet and discussing different aspects with Loris. Except for a few comments and answers to a couple of questions asked, Andrew followed quietly, allowing Loris and Dr Whyte to confer and discuss as they saw fit. A foundational platform of operation was quickly established, and the current status of equipment still needed was extensively discussed. This process took the good part of the morning, and all three gentlemen were pleased at its completion to be able to head out to the staffroom for a cup of coffee and some biscuits.

'Oh, yes!' said Dr Whyte quite casually, almost as an afterthought while enjoying a piece of chocolate-covered shortbread. 'We've named the lab, and tomorrow the name plate arrives. There will be a short christening after the plate has been hung.

'What is the name given to the lab?' asked Loris with interest, clutching his mug of coffee in both hands and leaning forward with his elbows on his knees.

'Andy,' said Dr Whyte, trying not to laugh, 'seeing that you'll be working there too, would you like the honour of telling Dr Lang?'

'I'm sure you'll be pleased to know, Lori,' said Andrew as he turned to him, unable to stifle a big grin, with Dr Whyte's manner being contagious, 'that our "skunkworks" has affectionately been named Pepe!'

'And we're expecting the lab to be made famous,' laughed Dr Whyte, with intermittent coughs, 'and leave its mark not just on the world of biology but further afield as well!'

Loris howled with laughter, enjoying the light-hearted moment and ease with which he had settled in at Microlab Industries but little aware that what would eventually come from the very bowels of Pepe would kick up such a stink!

Chapter 4

A sorrowful blow

'**T**O heck with the lot of you!' cried Loris exasperatingly, his usual composed manner being overcome with utter frustration. 'You're a sorrowful sight, all of you!'

Andrew stood there quite taken aback by this outburst.

'If you speak to them like that,' spoke up Andrew eventually, 'they may just creep away under a cloud of scandalous embarrassment and shame!'

'Indeed!' responded Loris with a soft chuckle, seeing Andrew's comment come to life in his mind's eye. 'If there's anyone to blame, it's certainly not them, the poor fellows! Just doing their job the way they have been commanded by us wretched biologist rogues!'

Andrew could not help laughing at Loris' pragmatic sense of humour in the face of yet another disappointment, the bank of test tubes seeming to present a row of rebellious school kids in Loris' eyes, who scolded them with disapproval and scorn.

'Sorrowful, sorrowful,' moaned Loris as he carefully studied the results and examined the test tubes once again. 'What a wretched blow! Just simply awful. I thought we had it this time around!'

'So did I,' agreed Andrew, trying to encourage Loris. 'I felt that there should at least have been some form of clarity and positive response!'

'A sorrowful and pitiful sight you make,' bemoaned Loris once again. 'You should all be blindfolded, lined up against the wall and shattered – the lot of you!'

Andrew chuckled to himself at the play on words, much like his sister-in-law, July, would do. He quickly turned and busied himself as fast as he could with the petri dishes that were next in the line of fire, trying hard not to laugh out loud again at Loris' amusing sense of humour in the face of disappointment. He knew though that before the morning was over, they would have sat together once again on their high-back office chairs, putting their heads together in an attempt to figure out where they went wrong and the road ahead. It was this tenacity about Loris and his general calm, even with the odd amusing outburst, that kept sanity and motivation in the face of seeming failure and insurmountable odds. Andrew too had this disposition, and the two colleagues were able to keep one another motivated and moving through the challenging valleys that seemed to arrive at their feet more often than had been hoped.

It was now early Monday morning, the week of Thanksgiving, and for the past five months, the effort of the two microbiologists, along with the occasional help and input from George, Dr Whyte and Professor Smyth, had yielded no positive results. Results they had obtained, yes, but it all amounted to aspects they could just cross off the list as not being worthy to attempt again. They had set their initial goal at first testing some parameters and criteria before delving directly into their investigation of what was termed "The origin of origins". Loris felt that this would set a foundational basis from which to work, but it had been hard going. Andrew never said a word in opposition, he just continued to provide support and encouragement, contributing as positively as he could towards the research effort.

However, their initial optimism and hope for early success had followed the pattern of the weather. The hot, sun-drenched glory days of summer had been dry and very lean, trying and tiring the hard-pressed labourer with neither oasis nor promise of one. They had pressed courageously on with determination and grit, but one day had become two, two had become four, four had become sixteen, until they were now figuratively standing ankle deep in the late autumn snow that steadily fell upon the land, gently smothering house-tops, cars, roads and everything for miles around with a cold blanket of soft, wet, white velvet. Winter had already knocked at the door with the early snow falls, and the red, orange, purple and yellow leaves that had not yet fallen, were frostbitten and white with the liquid cold. The damp days only had dreary nights to look forward to and was a continual drab, melancholy damper that acted much like a soft pedal on a piano, quietening the joyous melody that usually overflowed from its core reaching far and wide. It left a feeling that soon even the bones of the stones and rocks would cry out in agony of soul from the cold, dank conditions if there was no reprieve before winter finally settled in and cast forth its heartless spell of bondage upon the land until the sun eventually lifted the burden and set everything free.

Loris and Andrew could feel the downcast spirit amongst their fellow colleagues, who were left in the dark as to what was being researched but who had hoped for some form of immediate success, even if unrealistically expected. The high level of optimism had been countered by a low level of results, and this had placed pressure on the two young men, but they brushed it aside as best they could. Dr Whyte soon cleared this up amongst the colleagues, and with encouragements from him, George Renshaw and Professor Smyth, who acted as a buffer between them and questions from the university, they continued steadfastly committed to the systematic route they had plotted.

'Andy,' called Loris from his desk, 'give me a minute, will you?' 'On my way in a second,' replied Andrew directly. 'I just need to finish marking the observations from the fluorescence microscope.'

Andrew finished in a minute and promptly made his way to Loris after quickly rinsing his hands at the wash basin and drying them under the hot air blower.

'I've been thinking,' said Loris with a look of serious contemplation about him as Andrew walked up to him. 'During my term at Bridgetown, there were occasions when I worked alongside an independent microbiological researcher, who over a number of months conducted some tests on both DNA and Kinesin. I had the opportunity to inspect his results, and they were very fascinating, but at the time it had no bearing on what I was busy with so never thought of it further. The research conducted was not directly in line with what we are currently doing. Nevertheless, there may be some value in obtaining those results and seeing if there's anything we can glean from them. What do you think?'

'It's worth a shot,' answered Andrew cautiously, 'but will you not be questioned as to the reason for wanting them?'

'I'm sure I'll be asked,' affirmed Loris confidently, 'but Jerry Neaps is an amenable guy who will not likely press me if I say that I'm working on something confidential, unless of course he's already handed over the results to another university or pharmacological conglomerate – that would be a blow!' Loris seemed to allow such a prospect to negatively impact his thoughts, and his countenance changed immediately.

'Give it try then,' encouraged Andrew, seeing Loris' downcast and sorrowful look. 'We really don't have anything to lose, do we? If you can obtain the results, I'll happily sit with my father and go through them with him. He may just have some perspective or insight into them that will be useful to us.'

'I'll give him a call before the tea break,' said Loris, receptive to Andrew's suggestion, his spirits never lagging in the Slough of Despond very long with Andrew around. 'I'm happy to have your father's input. I think we could use all the help we can get! I'm not totally unhappy with the work that we've done thus far, but I'd really appreciate a little more confidence and positive results as we now start more intensive work in the area of fluorescence microscopy.'

'Just a little bump upper,' agreed Andrew. 'I could do with that too!' Andrew headed back to the work station where he wanted to start his next set of tests and investigations.

After making a number of notes, Loris looked at his watch and then picked up the portable phone on his desk. He began pressing the buttons and soon he heard in the earpiece the long-distance call connect and begin ringing.

Loris got through to Dr Jerry Neaps immediately, and after ten minutes of conversation, in which Loris had smiled, looked serious, leaned forward over his desk, pressed back in his chair, waved his hands in gesture and written down a few notes, he said good-bye to his old associate and disconnected the call.

'Done!' exclaimed Loris excitedly, startling Andrew who, in

total concentration, had his eyes fixed to the eyepiece of one of the small fluorescence microscopes.

'Done?' queried Andrew, looking up at Loris. 'Are you referring to the research papers we talked about?'

'Yes, indeed!' answered Loris with a smug look. 'I got through to Dr Neaps immediately, and he had no objection to providing me with the results. He informed me that there were one or two issues that he had to sort out before releasing them, but that he did not foresee any problem whatsoever. Jerry said that he would send a message to my phone, just after lunchtime if he could, to confirm his agreement. He was interested in what I needed the research results for, but just like I said he would, he never pressed the issue and happily accepted my explanation. I additionally mentioned to him that when I was in a position to tell, I'd brief him. I cannot help but feel that this is an upshot, and that there may just be something in those results that will give us a clue or assist us with our research.'

'I never like to count chickens before they hatch,' said Andrew with a degree of liveliness, a broad smile quickly forming, 'but that's positive news at least! Let's see what the man comes up with this afternoon. Let's hope it's all good news!'

With an added spring in his step, Loris headed for the wash basin where he washed and prepped himself, putting on a lab coat, gloves and goggles so that he could conduct some tests in the Laminar flow cabinet before lunchtime.

The two hours until lunchtime passed quickly for both Loris and Andrew, who busied themselves diligently in their respective research tasks. Having got to a place where they could stop for a while, they both washed up and exited Pepe via the mantrap security door. Without delay, Andrew and Loris were soon in the staffroom along with their associates, excited and hungry.

Lunch was soon over, and they were back in the lab, with whole-wheat bread sandwiches filled generously with cold-meats, cheese and tomato having been enjoyed by both, along with fresh herbal tea or coffee depending on choice. With renewed energy, Andrew continued with his fluorescence microscopy work. Loris, on the other hand, first checked to see what messages had come in, his thoughts clearly aligned upon obtaining a reply from Dr Jerry Neaps. As Loris scanned through the email messages that had come in, he received a message on his phone, which instantly drew his attention.

'Oh, no!' cried Loris painfully, deep distress written all over his face as he slumped back in his chair, looking in disbelief at the message just received on his smartphone. 'This is truly a sorrowful blow!'

Chapter 5

Absolute disbelief

'ANDY, have you read this?' asked Loris distressfully, his eyes darting up anxiously to locate Andrew. 'It's almost hard for me to believe!'

'Read what?' enquired Andrew urgently, having heard Loris' agonizing cry and come quickly from his work station. 'What's the matter?'

'A message has just been posted on the university's bulletin page,' replied Loris painfully, his heart beating profusely from shock, 'informing of the untimely passing of Professor DeRoach this past weekend! Do you have the university's bulletin app?'

'I do have it on my phone,' informed Andrew, turning to look at his own desk, 'but my phone's lying on my desk, so I wouldn't have seen it until later. I'm truly sorry to hear that about Professor DeRoach,' he added, a tone of remorse clearly evident in his voice. 'It's always sad to hear such news! This will be a loss for the engineering department, I'm sure.' 'Not just a loss,' said Loris, still sitting slumped in his high-back chair in disbelief, 'but a setback indeed! He was instrumental in a number of projects, one of which was directly involved in facilitating co-operation with an ad-hoc group over at Bramford.'

'It wasn't related to our work though, was it?' queried Andrew. 'I've not been aware of any such association.'

'To be sure, no,' replied Loris purposefully. 'Nonetheless, it had significant influence on the relationship that the two universities have had – not to mention the success they were jointly sharing in the advancement of structural materials and design parameters. I'm sure this news must be a setback for them! It's unbelievable!'

'What happened?' asked Andrew, sitting down on the edge of Loris' desk, having picked up his own phone after receiving a message from Tim, who also informed him of the professor's sad fate.

'It says that Professor DeRoach took ill on Friday,' began Loris somewhat shakily, scanning the short notice, 'was admitted to hospital on Saturday morning after he took a turn for the worse and that was basically it! He seemed to have contracted some lethal virus or other. They aren't one hundred percent sure yet what it was.' Loris could not hold back noticeable distress. He was flushed, and his deep-set eyes watered at the comprehension of it all. 'On Saturday afternoon he was put under induced coma,' continued Loris after a brief pause, 'and on Sunday morning slipped away from society!'

'That's horrible,' declared Andrew sympathetically, himself a little peaky at the terrible news while also feeling for Loris. 'His family must be terribly distraught!'

'All just so sudden,' whined Loris distressfully, 'so quick and unexpected! It's almost hard to believe, but then we know what lethal viruses can do to mankind when they want to. It sickens me!'

Andrew briefly put his hand on Loris' shoulder, almost as a gesture of consolation. He knew who the professor was but did not know the man personally. Words at this point he knew would only be idle, and although he felt for the man's family and was saddened by what had happened, he felt that his words would also be insincere, knowing the professor's beliefs. Andrew quietly stood up and began to make his way back to his work station.

'Did you know him?' asked Loris emotionally as Andrew walked away.

'Not on a personal level,' replied Andrew, turning round to face Loris. 'Tim knew him though, having studied under his tutorship. Tim's actually just sent me a message informing me of the sad event.'

'I had association with him through Professor Smyth,' informed Loris, briefly recalling. 'There will be a memorial service on Wednesday afternoon before the Thanksgiving holidays begin. Sad, just so sad! I'll have to attend, even if it means a temporary setback in our research – work will just have to be put on hold! I'm not even sure that I can work at the moment, I feel so distraught.'

'I understand,' said Andrew sympathetically. 'Do what you can manage and what you feel you need to do. I'll carry the fort as best I can, and if there are things that have to wait, they just have to wait.'

Wednesday came round quickly, with the upcoming Thanksgiving holiday preparations creating more activity than usual for everyone. Ailensbury University was holding two memorial services in the lecture hall where the now deceased professor used to teach. One service was for students, the other was for the university staff members and fellow associates. The university wanted the memorial services over and done with before the holidays, so as not to have it drag over to the following week when it would be highly disruptive to their programs and student studies. Loris requested Tim to attend the memorial service with him, to which he agreed.

Timothy Nicholls, Andrew Renshaw's cousin, was 27-years old, of medium height, quite well built and athletic in appearance. He had somewhat Italian features, taking after his father, with deep, dark-brown eyes and hair to match. He was a structural engineer, having graduated from Ailensbury University and was working for Seven Spires Construction Company.

Tim entered the Structural Engineering's S1 lecture theatre through the top entrance he had customarily used when attending classes there as a student. Loris followed closely behind, his black suit matching his mournful heart's heaviness, clearly observable by his miserable look. It was a sad and sorrowful picture upon his usually colourful and bright features, but then the occasion did not warrant anything different, and his sunken eyes seemed all the more withdrawn into their sockets.

Tim, who was wearing formal black clothing rather than a suit, stood and briefly looked about. A degree of nostalgia overcame him as he considered the times spent there and in particular, his response to Professor DeRoach's defiant challenge to those believing in Creation and an Intelligent Designer. He could not stop emotion welling up inside as he considered the latter occurrence and the now deceased tall, heavy-set professor with his thick, wiry black hair.

The man's words would echo around the hall in memory but not in sound. All that he was, had done and had stood for, had now reached its summit or valley, whichever form it best represented. In the professor's deceased eyes, every task had been completed, every deed finalised and every purpose concluded, for there was nothing more that he would or could do. There was no withdrawing anything or reversing what had happened; no going back, no undoing the past, no retracting thoughts or words or deeds – it was final.

In light of what the man had stood for, Tim felt this weigh heavily upon his heart as Solomon's words in conclusion to the matter of life and recorded in the book of Ecclesiastes hung like a bold banner across the full spectrum of his thoughts, "Fear God and keep His commandments, for this is the whole duty of man. For God will bring every deed into judgement, including every hidden thing, whether it is good or evil." [1] A sadness sought to overtake him, but he swiftly suppressed it.

With Loris having indicated that there was no particular place that he wanted to sit, Tim quickly saw amongst the throng of professors, associates and invitees busy seating themselves that the seats where he usually had sat as a student were unoccupied so made his way calmly and quietly, with Loris in tow, down the steps at the side of the theatre to just short of half way down, where they both slipped into one of the rows and were soon seated. Within a few minutes the flow of people entering had become a trickle, and the seating was more than 90% occupied.

Promptly on time, Professor Jack Mertin, dean of Ailensbury University, stood up and approached the lectern. He spoke for a moment, then took his seat again, allowing a colleague who was one of Professor DeRoach's fellow departmental lecturers to take the floor. When he had concluded, another former associate spoke at length after which the dean once again took his position at the lectern.

The dean was an elderly man of average height but thickset. His grey hair and grey beard were neatly trimmed. Although he wore a large pair of glasses, his countenance clearly portrayed confidence, so too his gait.

The dean promptly began to speak, while looking from one side of the lecture hall to the other. For about 15 minutes he spoke briefly on a number of different aspects related to the deceased, without wavering or hesitation. He then paused and let out a sigh.

'It's hard for us to believe,' said the dean as he concluded his speech, 'but this was just one of those unavoidable circumstances; one which no-one cares to be the recipient of, but which evolution dishes out from time to time in its sometimes effervescent, many times melancholic climb to improve its chance of existence. Who can control it, who can avoid it? Man must be strong and take the blow on the chin like a man, when it beats upon us. Today we stand in disbelief, sorrowful and empty in heart at the blow on the chin we've all received as a result of Professor DeRoach's passing, not to mention the fatal and cruel blow evolution has dealt him upon the jaw – let us not forget it.'

The dean spoke solemnly but still seemed to hold an air of pride.

'However,' continued Professor Mertin, 'I'm convinced that if his ashes, which were scattered earlier this morning, could cry out, Professor DeRoach would have it no other way. He would encourage us to be strong, to continue the fight for the survival of the species, to hold to the tenets of evolutionary principle in the face of vast, almost insurmountable opposition from gods and devils, religion and tradition, the universe and life itself, as it groans and moans to exist in an endless mass of time and space. The man was a fighter to the bitter end, and although it's normal to shed tears of heartache at such a tragedy, we can toast with glasses lifted high – and his legacy will drink with us too – to a good man who lived much, influenced much and accomplished much. Should life have somehow been afforded an afterlife, which Professor DeRoach disbelieved in and rightly so, you can be sure that he would have sat upon a throne amongst rulers and wined and dined amongst princes and kings in eternal bliss. A charitable man, a man of good deeds and one who would have been worthy of being exalted in a life hereafter, should there have been one.'

Tim sat silently, but his heart cried out in anguish at such words.

'The void our dear colleague has left,' said the dean, 'will surely make us stagger for a while, but his resolve in life will only strengthen our hearts to move on. Our sincerest sympathies to his kinsfolk during this time of mourning, for their loss is greater than ours, yet may our gratitude for his service to us and to the cause of man lift their spirits and give them hope of a soon inner mending. I say with an unpleasant lump in my throat that although he no longer lives, his memory will live forever in our hearts. In pain he left this life, but in peace he is secure forever. Rest in peace, dear friend.' Professor Mertin then thanked everyone for attending and ended the memorial service.

The attendees, including Tim and Loris, did not waste any time in rising, and the lecture hall was deserted within minutes, leaving it to be just one big empty hollow, devoid of life, sound or movement.

Loris cast a solemn demeanour once out in the open and away from the main throng of people. The strong, chilling breeze blew his hair over to one side as he walked slowly and silently away from the lecture theatre and back to his car. Tim could see that he was in thought so remained just to the side of him but a few paces back.

Professor Jack Mertin's words had yet to fade in Loris' ears, and they rang strongly as though still in the process of being spoken. As his mind replayed the audio tape, Loris could not help feeling that although he shared the same sentiments and would have spoken the same words, something was missing. Something seemed empty in the speech, as though its foundation was floating on a void of dark matter, an eternal abyss of lifelessness. In his heart, it was almost as though the dead were speaking to the dead, yet in his mind, he supported every word as though it were true life itself.

Loris could not fathom this, and a state of conflict seemed to tear at his very soul until his body almost ached and bones burned with confusion. Was this emotion fighting pragmatism? Logic against sensationalism? Loris dared not try to answer that question just at that moment, for he felt too heartsore to try and discern. Yet, one thing he felt sure of and resolved to hold fast – there was no God, and there was no afterlife!

Even in his state of unrest, Loris' mind could still rationalise this however, and it left him with a disagreeable conclusion: it left him with no hope – and this left *him* with an unavoidable emptiness like he had never felt before! Loris stopped and stood motionless. He was not only in shock and trying to get to grips with Professor DeRoach's passing, but he had never before considered himself without hope, an unscalable, merciless and thankless prospect.

Oblivious to time or man as this consideration revolved around his mind's conscious universe, he continued to stand motionless. Tim eventually touched Loris gently on his arm, and he snapped out of it instantly, leaving behind his contemplation in the world of oblivion. Nonetheless, he knew that something he had never considered before had significantly troubled him and had left him standing in absolute disbelief.

Chapter 6

Misgivings at Thanksgiving

'NO, it's to the right!' shouted Loris rather energetically, causing Sarah to swing her car's steering wheel from one side to the other in an attempt to follow her husband's instructions while the two girls in the back screamed hysterically, more from the excitement than from fear. 'Blast, who gave you these directions – the blind beggar from Blantyre? I had misgivings about them right from the start!'

Sarah had been driving slowly enough to have been aware of her surroundings and still make the right turn without issue or danger.

'I wrote them down,' objected Sarah as they drove slowly along, 'in accordance with what June told me over the phone – and I'm no blind beggar, thank you very much! I had no uncertainty about what she was telling me; her instructions were clear as day!'

'I couldn't tell if I was reading it upside down or not,' complained Loris sarcastically, in an attempt to justify his poor remark rather than apologise for it, 'and what's this supposed to indicate? You could have made it a little clearer so that—'

'An intellectual like yourself could understand it!' cut in Sarah quickly, catching Loris off guard with her sharp humour. 'I should have listened to my great grandma's misgivings about *you* when I agreed to marry you!'

'You didn't have a great grandma when we got engaged!' snapped Loris, turning to Sarah.

'No,' retorted Sarah, the two girls looking silently on with big eyes from the back seat, 'but if she had been around, she would've had misgivings, I'm certain of it!'

'I see,' observed Loris, realising that Sarah was more jesting with him than angry, 'but look what you've done now, you've frightened the girls!'

'You nitwit!' scolded Sarah, laughing lightly as she grabbed the piece of paper with the directions on it out of Loris' hand, having stopped the car on the side of the road in a safe place. 'There are things to love about you, Loris Lang, and things to not! Don't make excuses and blame others!'

Sarah Lang, Loris' wife, could have passed off as being his younger sister. At 32-years of age, she was three years younger than him, had a plumpish figure and a round, bright and animated face that was always full of lively colour. Her bushy, shoulder-length, curly black hair complimented her tubbiness, and her big, dark eyes complimented her typically happy expression. She usually had a quiet and observant disposition. Their two girls, Mika and Abigail, were nine and eight years old respectively. Both were very much like their mother – observant and bright.

Sarah promptly turned and put her hand affectionately on each of the girls' heads before looking at the instructions purposefully.

'Now,' said Sarah, having finished surveying her handiwork, 'this is the right way up, and it's just like I explained to you at home. There's no mistaking it!'

Sarah put Loris right as far as the instructions were concerned and said no more about it, his sheepish look at having got so simple a thing all wrong was embarrassing enough for him. He did not need his wife to further rub salt into his wounds.

Sarah checked that the coast was clear and promptly pulled away again to the cheer and delight of the two observant onlookers in the back. They continued on their way to George and Kelly Renshaw's house, eager not to be late for the Thanksgiving dinner to which they were glad to have been invited, as neither of them had extended family in town.

There was a cold mist in the air, thick and penetrating to the marrow of anyone's bones who was not properly shielded from it.

'Brrrr,' mumbled Sarah as she got out of the car, rubbing her hands together. 'I could do with a hot cup of coffee and some warm hospitality in such weather!'

'You're likely to be provided with both,' remarked Loris, slamming the vehicle's passenger door shut without hesitation after assisting his two daughters out, along with their bags in preparation for a late night, 'just don't go about calling anyone a nitwit!'

'Are you giving me an instruction or some direction?' joked Sarah. 'You needn't worry, I'll do *right* by you!'

The four guests quickly made their way up the garden path and onto the porch, the flowers and plants on either side of the pathway fresh and clean after an earlier rain shower and glinting under the lights as a result of the small, clear droplets they were still bravely bearing the burden of.

'Silly *nitwit!*' said Loris, kissing Sarah's cheek and giving her a one-armed squeeze around her shoulder while ringing the doorbell with his free hand. 'I know you don't hate me. You love me as much as I love you, and I love you all the more for it!'

Sarah just warmed at her husband's embrace and could not help smiling, with the two girls on either side of them clutching tightly. They were soon inside, the Renshaw's alert and eager to get all parties arriving out of the wintery hazard and into the warmth of their home.

'Greetings, greetings,' said Andrew cheerfully, coming out into the hallway. 'I'm glad you could make it, Lori. It just wouldn't be right if we didn't see each other for more than half a day, now would it?'

'Probably wouldn't,' agreed Loris as they all chuckled, the adults fully aware of the long hours that he and Andrew had spent together in conference, running experiments, conducting research and pouring over data.

Andrew first took the Lang family upstairs to his old bedroom so that they could put the girls' things down where the little lassies could play and rest after dinner, then out onto the enclosed veranda where the rest of the family and guests were gathered.

Andrew's wife, June, was there, along with Tim and July and all their in-laws. Cordial greetings were plentiful, with light laughter intermittently dispersed, as comments and light jest flashed between the gathering, all pleased to see one another and eager to find out how the others were.

Coffee, tea and soft-drinks were readily provided to all according to their desire after which they all took their places, which were marked with name tags, at the table in preparation for a pleasant and enjoyable Thanksgiving dinner and time of fellowship.

Although the weather was cold and penetrating, the veranda was more than adequately shielded from its effects. The retracting roof had been extended, with the roll-up canvas sides having been let down and zipped closed. Two large gas heaters kept the ambient temperature regulated, making for a cosy environment where winter jackets could be relegated to the coatrack at the front door.

George and Kelly, along with Andrew and June's help, had prepared the place beautifully. The dark-green coloured cast iron table was covered with an exquisite tablecloth that had autumn leaves imprinted all over it. Matching placemats and serviettes were also present, with yellow, orange, red and purple decorations neatly and strategically placed all around. A few small wooden signs with various short messages such as *Happy Thanksgiving*, *Joy*, *Peace*, and *Praise the Lord* were hanging here and there, with small wooden bowls of sweets adding to the colour and attractiveness of the setting. Against the main wall of the house was a long, narrow serving table, along with a bain-marie. There were cold salads, steaming hot vegetables that matched the outside world's leaves in colour, delicious gravies and as the crowning show-piece, under a hood stood the oven-baked turkey just waiting to be carved and consumed by the hungry gatherers.

After a short while of general chit-chat, George stood up and gave a prayer of thanks and gratitude to the LORD for his mercy, kindness, faithfulness and provision. Loris just looked on sceptically.

George Renshaw, Kelly's husband, was in his early fifties. He was a tall man, and it was easy to see that he was Andrew's father, although he was not as athletic looking as Andrew. He was two years older than Kelly and equalled her gregarious nature. He was a microbiologist and as has already been mentioned, worked as a senior researcher at Microlab Industries.

They all then got up from the table and, amongst discussion about the mouth-watering and abundant food provided, dished up for themselves, Loris and Sarah assisting their two girls.

It was a pleasant and hearty meal, with equal enjoyment of conversation between them.

The gastronomical provision fully satisfying hungry tummies and taste buds alike. A light rain began to fall about half way through proceedings and tapped gently on the extended roof above the party as they ate, talked and laughed together, but it was no botheration.

There was a break before dessert became a prominent topic, and it was quickly followed up with the delectable provision of a choice of pumpkin pie, apple pie and carrot cake. Generous servings were had by all, Kelly's portioning hand purposefully not knowing what the words "Not so big!" meant each time she cut a slice. In the end, plenty was left over but plenty had also been consumed, to the satisfaction and thanks of all.

Sarah escorted Mika and Abigail upstairs to settle down in Andrew's old room while the others assisted Kelly in clearing up. After all was done, the three older Renshaw, Harris and Sparletti couples retired to the sunken living room, while the three younger couples of Andrew and June, Tim and July, and Loris and Sarah, were happy to remain on the veranda and chat.

Conversation was free and flowing amongst them, whose zest for life and array of activities they enjoyed kept their exchange fresh and interesting. Inevitably, however, towards the end of the evening, the conversation turned towards the sad passing of Professor DeRoach and how his family could not have enjoyed this Thanksgiving following so closely on the heels of their grief.

'I cannot help thinking about Professor DeRoach,' commented Loris sadly, just as George appeared with a fresh pot of coffee for them. 'I'm sure that if there was an afterlife, heaven's gates would open wide and welcome him in; he was a good man!'

Loris looked up, seeing George stop and noting his facial expression, realising that he had stepped on the toes of their religion. He instantly regretted having spoken without reservation or consideration, even though it was what he believed. A horrible feeling permeated his being to the core that what he was about to be told would undoubtedly leave him with misgivings that he would have to deal with!

Chapter 7

Too true

'I HAVE to confess,' responded George, looking directly at Loris, 'that I cannot agree with what you perceive to be true. Without trying to be confrontational, sadly, that's a misconception about God and man of great consequence and peril to those who believe it!'

'As I believe truth to be relevant,' countered Loris quickly, 'particularly with respect to religion, please explain yourself?'

Deadly silence instantaneously froze all conversation as tension barbarically hacked off the head of carefree commune. Andrew, with an air of apprehension, looked at his father knowing that he would not hold back at such an invitation and would spell out the biblical teaching. His concern did not emanate from a supposed fear of inadequacy on George's part but from a deep concern for Loris, for once he had heard the truth and reality of the matter, he would not stand guiltless before the Supreme Judge should he not take heed.

Andrew quietly lifted up a prayer to God and, unbeknown to himself, so did June, Tim and July, asking the Lord not only to help George answer concisely but also to open the eyes of Loris, one who was blind to the truth of the Gospel, and to soften his heart of stone that resisted so strongly Christ's salvation and embrace.

'Let me just fetch my Bible,' said George as he went to put the coffee pot down on the serving counter. 'June, would you mind pouring the coffee while it's still hot?'

'Certainly,' affirmed June, pleased to be able to assist, 'no hassle.'

'I'll get your Bible, Dad,' offered Andrew, quickly getting up along with June.

'It's in my study on the first shelf behind my chair,' informed George as Andrew nippily headed into the house.

'I mean,' said Loris while Andrew was absent, 'there's a right way and a wrong way, for some things.'

'True,' agreed George, leaning back against the serving counter.

'And,' added Loris, 'there are some things that are judged upon relevancy to an individual and his circumstances.'

'Indeed,' affirmed George. 'True too, but not with respect to God! The Bible tells us that God is a God of truth,[2] and that it's impossible for Him to lie.[3] Therefore, that which contradicts or doesn't line up with what the Bible says, cannot be truth.'

Andrew's footsteps were heard coming quickly towards them, and he soon appeared through the open sliding doors and onto the veranda.

'Andy,' asked George, looking at him holding out the Bible, 'would you please read for us Luke 16:15,19–31.'

'Will do,' replied Andrew, quickly sitting down before flipping the pages of his father's Bible to the mentioned passage. 'Luke 16:15,19–31, "He (Jesus) said to them, 'You are the ones who justify yourselves in the eyes of men, but God knows your hearts. What is highly valued among men is detestable in God's sight. There was a rich man who was dressed in purple and fine linen and lived in luxury every day. At his gate was laid a beggar named Lazarus, covered with sores and longing to eat what fell from the rich man's table. Even the dogs came and licked his sores. The time came when the beggar died and the angels carried him to Abraham's side. The rich man also died and was buried. In hell, where he was in torment, he looked up and saw Abraham far away, with Lazarus by his side. So he called him, "Father Abraham, have pity on me and send Lazarus to dip the tip of his finger in water and cool my tongue, because I am in agony in this fire." But Abraham replied, "Son, remember that in your lifetime you received your good things, while Lazarus received bad things, but now he is comforted here and you are in agony. And besides all this, between us and you a great chasm has been fixed, so that those who want to go from here to you cannot, nor can anyone cross over from there to us." He answered, "Then I beg you, father, send Lazarus to my father's house, for I have five brothers. Let him warn them, so that they will not also come to this place of torment." Abraham replied, "They have Moses and the Prophets; let them listen to them." "No, father Abraham," he said, "but if someone from the dead goes to them, they will repent." He said to him, "If they do not listen to Moses and the Prophets, they will not be convinced even if someone rises from the dead."'" Andrew stopped and looked up.

'Thanks, Andy,' said George, who promptly turned to look at Loris. 'You see, Loris, the Bible gives us a very unpleasant story of one who had it all but didn't repent and turn to God. We know this for he sought that his five brothers would repent. The rich man, therefore, knew what was required of him, but he was now in a place where he couldn't change his circumstance. If he could have repented then, he would have. Heaven's gates don't just open wide and welcome people because they are good. This is a misconception sadly putting multitudes of people in the same predicament as the rich man.'

Loris just looked at George, a feeling of resentment having quickly risen within him.

'What is of equal relevance to the story,' continued George, 'is that it was given by Jesus himself, not by someone else. He's the only one who had a true knowledge and understanding of the afterlife, for He came from heaven, and He clearly portrays a sobering reality that few want to comprehend. Jesus is also the one who said, "I will show you whom you should fear: Fear Him who, after the killing of the body, has power to throw you into hell. Yes, I tell you, fear Him." [4]

'That's all good and well,' responded Loris, maintaining courtesy but nonetheless irritated, 'if you believe Jesus. I do not! Besides, in my opinion that's hate speech on his part!'

'Is it hate speech,' asked George with a distinct questioning tone, 'or is it that you hate what Jesus said or what I say? In today's society, people have merged the two – hate speech and what they hate to hear – not because it's rightfully done but because of convenience and conscience, irrespective of whether it's true and beneficial or not. They more than often don't like what's been said, for it either doesn't suit their lifestyles or their belief, and many times it's both! They seek to have it silenced on the basis of it being hate speech, and oftentimes, it's the Bible or Christian principle at the heart of the matter. Instead of being manly enough to face up to their responsibility and consequences in defying Scripture – should it be true of course in their opinion – they seek to shut its mouth. A rather cowardly act, in my opinion. Particularly when it comes to the Bible, if it was nothing but total rubbish, why bother making such a protest against it? The reason is that it's not just rubbish, but as it self-declares, "For the word of God is living and active. Sharper than any double-edged sword, it penetrates even to dividing soul and spirit, joints and marrow; it judges the thoughts and attitudes of the heart." [5] Mankind never sits easy with a pricking conscience, and who would desire to feed such an annoyance? However, to the person who would heed the Word of God, it provides a way to freedom from bondage and brings about a liberty and life that only a truly repentant heart can understand. Christ's words weren't hate speech but sobering words spoken in love, for it is life – for there's life in love and love in truth, when spoken to alert man to the danger of the edge of the precipice he unknowingly totters on.'

Loris sat quietly listening out of politeness, but he was seething and ready to spit fire. The cup of coffee that June had placed before him remained untouched, his arms firmly folded against his chest. George was aware of it but knew that he had to give the message irrespective.

There was tension, and Sarah sat particularly anxious, alert to Loris' every twitch and movement. Her apprehension showed, her face being ashen-white, and she sat as stiff as a statue, for she too was challenged and convicted by what George was saying. She was unable to deny the truth of it for she did not have the answers, but deep down a smouldering wick seemed to be reigniting, with the small remnants of past Christian involvement testifying against her current position and fighting hard to smash down the wall of resistance she had created so long ago within her own heart.

'On the subject of hate speech,' said Tim, sitting up and clutching his hands together as he leaned his arms on the table, 'Plato has been accredited as saying, "No-one is more hated than he who speaks the truth." Many years back in my part-time work for Real Results Research Company while I was still a student, I worked on a research project for a world-renown brand. One aspect related to that project was that all reports for the brand's own stores had to be double checked before submitting to the client. At the time, this wasn't just to ensure that all data in the reports was correct but to ensure that each report was a positive one, for the client wouldn't accept or believe that any of their staff members would do anything wrong or not represent the brand in a good light. If the report was negative, a re-evaluation had to take place! So, in effect, the client was not prepared to receive the truth in respect to their own situation but was prepared to accept it in respect to competitors they were evaluating. The reality and truth wasn't of relevance to them regarding themselves, only a perception of what they felt reality should be. Accepting that which may have required them to search out and deal with issues in their own internal state wasn't convenient, even if it was of paramount importance to their company. Is this not like ourselves?'

The gentle rain that had been precipitating down until then suddenly began to fall much harder and banged aggressively upon the retractable roofing above, the weather forecast holding true to its claim.

'That which is inconvenient isn't something we want to hear,' continued Tim, speaking a little louder so as to overcome the thundering onslaught above, 'even if it's a truth that impacts our lives. If this is true for our physical lives, how much more in respect to our spiritual lives! We hate doctors who tell us frankly that our physical conduct and dissipation will be to our own destruction, and we hate all the more ministers who tell us about hell and eternal damnation. To reject either, will it ultimately be to our benefit, even if it's to our own convenience to do so? We can deny reality and truth, but does this remove its existence or the consequences if defied? The one great convenience of adopting such a position, is that we can say to ourselves that all is well; but, isn't the knowledge and acceptance of reality and truth to our benefit? Does it not place us in a position to do something about it before there's trouble? Is this not to our advantage? Businesses spend billions of dollars each year to learn the truth about markets and their products in order to gain an advantage and not bear the consequences of ignoring reality. Yet, when it comes to personal application, we seem to feel that what we believe to be true or feel suits us, is in fact reality and truth, but in the long run, will it not be to our own detriment for not seeking out the truth and heeding the warnings?'

Tim briefly looked at one of the enclosure's clear-plastic windows as the rain ran in streams down it but continued on without disruption.

'Today, it seems that what society wants is an appeased conscience and a convenient "truth", which amounts to a temporary reprieve that if we search deep down, know doesn't hold a lasting promise, much like the flimsy "nonaggression pact" paper that Prime Minister Chamberlain waved before the eyes of Britain only a few months prior to Hitler's complete annexation of Czechoslovakia and invasion of Poland in 1939. The majority of people do not want to recognise the truth and reality, particularly spiritually, for it means that something must be done about it that may upset their comfort. When men with insight – like Churchill, physicians and ministers – speak out, they're shunned and their words scorned, not because what they say isn't truth but because it's inconvenient truth. If we're rude and ugly, we hate them to their faces; if we're polite and decent, we hate them behind their backs. Is ignorance of such matters, particularly spiritual salvation, a wisdom or a folly? And where ignorance is not absent, is inaction not a greater foolishness? Do we end up waiting until it's too late? In the end, who do we harm, if not ourselves?'

Loris silently stared at Tim, his face aglow with annoyance, and his eyes speaking a thousand words.

'That's a very sobering reality,' confirmed George, breaking the few seconds of tense silence, 'and what's further sobering is that God has said, "By Myself I have sworn, My mouth has uttered in all integrity a word that will not be revoked: Before Me every knee will bow; by Me every tongue will swear." [6] The apostle Paul affirms this when he says in respect to Jesus having humbled Himself and been obedient even to death on a cross, that God exalted Him to the highest place and gave Him the name that is above every name, that at the name of Jesus every knee should bow, in heaven and on earth and under the earth, and every tongue confess that Jesus Christ is Lord, to the glory of God the Father.' [7]

'So there's a connection,' concluded Loris, clearly not loving all that was being said, 'but I'm not a believer!'

'We understand that,' responded George calmly, knowing that his words to Loris were like lemon on the man's tongue, 'but herein lies another sobering reality: The Lord is the Sovereign God, and He knows it. There will not be one unbeliever in hell! Scripture tells us that just as through one man sin came to all men and death through sin, so too has life come to all through the one, Jesus Christ. [8] Therefore, Christ's work was a work effective from eternity to eternity. Every person will have to bear witness to it and bow the knee. There's none more penitent than he who sits in prison, nor he who can bear testimony to judgement than he who bears the sentence. All will eventually acknowledge Christ as Lord, irrespective of where they are in eternity. It's better therefore that man bows the knee willingly while he can, than do so when his doomed fate is sealed without reverse!'

'Too true' retorted Loris rather disdainfully, 'if it's indeed true!'

Chapter 8

Wrath and an unquenchable fire

'**W**ELL, thanks for that, Georgie,' said Loris a little disrespectfully. 'I didn't mean to stand on your religious toes with my original comment. I was basically just speaking my thoughts that's all!'

'I understand,' responded George coolly, the others looking on in silent apprehension, aware of Loris' wrathful countenance. 'There's a proverb in Scripture that says, "There is a way that seems right to a man, but in the end it leads to death." [9] I didn't respond as a result of being offended by your comment but was rather intent on providing you with an aspect you may never have considered before – an aspect that according to Scripture, which I believe to be inspired by God, is a very real danger to the soul of man.'

Loris just looked at George, then at Tim.

'Are you not going to finish your coffee, Loris?' queried Sarah, looking at him and gently taking hold of his arm. His demeanour troubled her greatly, and she did not want him to insult the gracious hospitality that they had been afforded.

'No!' answered Loris a little too abruptly for Sarah's liking, having turned to her. 'I've had more than enough of everything!'

The rest of the gatherers just looked at Loris, not sure if he was using a play on words or not, his usually composed manner not holding fort just then.

'George,' said Loris a little more calmly as he stood up, 'we need to be going. It's pouring with rain, and we still have to get the girls into their own beds. Besides which, we have a lot planned for tomorrow's holiday, and I don't want to stay out longer than is necessary.'

'Fully understandable,' responded George amiably, 'it was a pleasure to have you, Sarah and the kids over for Thanksgiving.'

Sarah also quickly got up, braving a smile to everyone as she thanked them but a pained look of distress nevertheless clearly evident.

Andrew kindly assisted Loris in fetching the girls, while Sarah was left for the main part to provide cordial good-byes to the older folks still sitting in the living room. Loris gave a fleeting good-night greeting on his way past, also thanking Kelly for her provision and hospitality, and was out the door in a flash.

Hunched over and holding in his arms one of his precious daughters carefully wrapped in a blanket, he cautiously made his way down the drenched pathway to their car and placed her inside. Andrew assisted in the same way with the other daughter, the men's jackets being soaked in the process from the unabating rain. Sarah quickly but cautiously followed, having been given an umbrella to use by June.

The Lang family soon backed out of the Renshaw's driveway and were on their way home.

The earlier mist had been driven down and washed into the drains by the driving and relentless rain that had set in for the night. The night was dark, and the thickset clouds were close and ominous, almost eerie. They seemed to press upon a man's soul and laugh with mockery and contempt at his inability to restrain their power and influence.

Loris could feel this impact as he sat staring out the vehicle's passenger window, the glass directly in front of his mouth misting up as he breathed heavily. Although it irked him no end, the penetrating wet from the intense pluvial downpour could not penetrate his soul and dampen the unquenchable fire that raged within the depths of his being, which continued to be fed from a source of conflict within his brain.

Loris burned with anger at the impudence, as he perceived it to be, of George presenting him with a passage of Scripture so demeaning to any intellectual who was at the forefront of biological research and on the cusp, so he hoped, of enlightening the world about the source of its origins that he clenched his fists in silent seething and wrathfulness.

Sarah could not only see his vehement disapproval, as it was plainly displayed in his countenance, but she could feel the intense tension and was almost too afraid to make comment to try to ease the situation, fearing that the lava which was bubbling and boiling in the throat of the great volcano would erupt and spew forth words of destruction that she would not be able to quench or escape. Sarah was wise enough to sit silently, trying to concentrate on getting the family safely home, even though she knew that Loris was pondering on the very same thing that she was. Internally, she was trembling, for she had never seen her husband so enraged, nor yet heard anyone speak the words that George and Tim had spoken just prior to their somewhat abrupt departure. For the present, however, that which was nearest to Sarah's eye concerned her the most as she cautiously glanced across at Loris periodically.

Sarah had no sooner pulled into their driveway and stopped the car when Loris climbed out purposefully and slammed the passenger door shut, waking the two girls. He walked with intent across the neatly paved area towards the front porch, not caring about the drenching rain.

The front door was unlocked and opened, and the girls quickly hurried inside and up the stairs to their bedrooms. Not wanting Loris' cauldron of anger to spill over and trouble the girls, Sarah promptly took charge of getting them into their pyjamas, their teeth brushed and into bed, leaving Loris free to head back downstairs.

Loris went back outside onto the front porch and just stood there looking out into the inky blackness, the heavy downpour creating a white motion picture of unending broken lines as it plummeted past the small Victorian garden lights and smashed into the ground, leaving large puddles of water everywhere.

He stood for about 20 minutes just brooding over the evening, completely bypassing the pleasantness of the Thanksgiving dinner and focusing solely on the conversation about man's eternal destiny.

Loris eventually stepped forward, exposing himself to the full force of the heavenly provision as it continued to saturate the earth beneath. He was drenched, with water dripping profusely from his thick black hair and running in small but powerful rivulets down his face and off his hands. He was thinking hard, but there was no dampener to the fire still raging in his soul. The wind had picked up and was now howling, harassing and tormenting the bushes and trees round about, but Loris stood unmoved, leaning against one of the square, wooden, overhanging roof support posts.

'Come inside,' called Sarah anxiously, having opened the front door and poked her head outside. 'You don't want to catch a cold!'

Loris just turned and looked at her, then turned back again to face the driving rain.

'Loris!' called Sarah once more.

'Don't badger me,' groused Loris, still looking out directly before him, although he could hardly see the disquieted and tumultuous black waters of the sea below. 'I'll come when I'm ready. I won't be more than a moment.'

Sarah saw that Loris was not to be pressed so said no more and quietly shut the door, leaving him to himself and his thoughts.

As the rain continued to beat upon his face, he could not help comparing Dean Jack Mertin's message given at Professor DeRoach's memorial service alongside the chapter of Luke that Andrew had read, including what George and Tim had said. As Loris analysed point for point, he was shocked at the complete opposite that each represented:

Dean: *"I'm convinced that if his ashes could cry out, Professor DeRoach would have it no other way and would encourage us to be strong, to continue the fight for the survival of the species, to hold to the tenets of evolutionary principle in the face of vast, almost insurmountable opposition from gods and devils, religion and tradition, the universe and life itself, as it groans and moans to exist in an endless mass of time and space."*

Scripture: *"I beg you, father, send Lazarus to my father's house, for I have five brothers. Let him warn them, so that they will not also come to this place of torment."*

Dean: *"we can toast with glasses lifted high – and his legacy will drink with us too – to a good man who lived much, influenced much and accomplished much."*

Scripture: *"Son, remember that in your lifetime you received your good things, while Lazarus received bad things, but now he is comforted here and you are in agony."*

Dean: *"Should life have somehow been afforded an afterlife, which Professor DeRoach disbelieved in and rightly so."*

Scripture: *"The time came when the beggar died and the angels carried him to Abraham's side. The rich man also died and was buried. In hell, where he was in torment, he looked up and saw Abraham far away, with Lazarus by his side."*

Dean: *"You can be sure that he would have sat upon a throne amongst rulers and wined and dined amongst princes and kings in eternal bliss."*

Scripture: *"Father Abraham, have pity on me and send Lazarus to dip the tip of his finger in water and cool my tongue, because I am in agony in this fire."*

Dean: *"A charitable man, a man of good deeds and one who would have been worthy of being exalted in a life hereafter, should there have been one."*

Scripture: *"Between us and you a great chasm has been fixed, so that those who want to go from here to you cannot, nor can anyone cross over from there to us."*

Dean: *"Who can control it, who can avoid it? Man must be strong and take the blow on the chin like a man, when it beats upon us."*

Scripture: *"I will show you whom you should fear: Fear Him who, after the killing of the body, has power to throw you into hell. Yes, I tell you, fear Him."*

Dean: *"The void our dear colleague has left will surely make us stagger for a while, but his resolve in life will only strengthen our hearts to move on."*

Scripture: *"Abraham replied, 'They have Moses and the Prophets; let them listen to them.' 'No, father Abraham,' he said, 'but if someone from the dead goes to them, they will repent.' He said to him, 'If they do not listen to Moses and the Prophets, they will not be convinced even if someone rises from the dead.'"*

Dean: *"In pain he left this life, but in peace he is secure forever. Rest in peace, dear friend."*

Scripture: *"In hell, he was in torment and agony."*

Dean: *"This was just one of those unavoidable circumstances; one which no-one cares to be the recipient of, but which evolution dishes out from time to time in its sometimes effervescent, many times melancholic climb to improve its chance of existence."*

Scripture: *"You are the ones who justify yourselves in the eyes of men, but God knows your hearts. What is highly valued among men is detestable in God's sight." "There is a way that seems right to a man, but in the end it leads to death."*

Loris suddenly became aware of the goosebumps that had formed all over his body. He began to tremble. Where then was Professor DeRoach? If the Bible was true and Scripture accurate, then the eternal status of Professor DeRoach was devastating and hopeless. He could not deny it! He mused. Where then would he himself be if this was all true? He was sure it was not true, but if it was, he knew that he could not deny that he would be in trouble – a thought that he did not want to contemplate – and that God's wrath and a raging, unquenchable fire awaited him! Loris' mind swirled at the thought, and he felt weak and empty, the recollection of his being aware of an emptiness and without a hope the day before, just after the memorial service, plaguing him as well. He turned to go back inside the house but stopped and returned to his spot, a determined look on his wet and dripping face.

'I have to make this discovery!' exclaimed Loris through clenched teeth. 'I have to prove the origin of origins and thus disprove God once and for all!'

Chapter 9

A loving June

LORIS returned to work on the Monday morning after the Thanksgiving weekend with more determination than ever to succeed in his research task, remembering too his confident promise to Professor McKenzie Smyth when he was informed by him that Andrew was a Creationist and a Christian, *"I'll have to just take on the added task of enlightening the blinded wretch, and I can promise you one thing – by the time I'm finished with my research so will his religion be finished! No-one will be able to believe in God then!".*

For a number of days following there was some uneasiness between Loris and Andrew but more particularly between Loris and George. Thankfully, Andrew was the one working directly with him, so tension for the most part could be avoided between the parties. However, progress continued to be lacking, and the stagnant waters were slowly becoming green and slimy. Although the two microbiologists worked diligently and conscientiously, it was becoming increasing toil and less pleasurable.

The bare winter wilderness had been traversed, with little taking place in the cold, grey natural world outside and even less in the climate-controlled lab affectionately named Pepe. Spring had come and gone, and they were now in the height and heat of summer. The first anniversary of the Origin of Origins research project had just been passed, but there had been no celebrations.

Within Pepe's borders the summer months had been dry and parched, but Loris and Andrew were hoping that the empty clouds that drifted irritatingly overhead would soon fill with an abundance of water and drop a heavenly cargo of results upon their work that they so desperately desired to receive. It was as if they were thirsty and hungry for a decent breakthrough. They felt as though their mouths were dry, their throats sore and hoarse and their tummies tender from the harsh reality of coming up empty-handed every time they dug a hole in search of water or cast a net in hope of a catch. Days were long, nights were short, and the enticing sea which lay within walking distance from the lab could have been a thousand miles away, it would have made no difference to them in their relentless pursuit to obtain a result.

They had to press hard, for despite Loris' desperate personal reasons in seeking success, which he had never communicated to anyone, the lack of substantial results demanded it of them. Questions were now being asked as to the feasibility of the research, whether it should be continued or not, if Loris was competent enough in the task and capable of managing. Andrew, too, was not without scrutiny from the outside sponsors and interested parties unduly questioning his worth in the endeavours. It was hard going for them, and despite the continued support and effort from Dr Whyte, George and Professor Smyth, they felt not only the ground but also themselves trembling from the strain and stress. It was either breaking time or breakthrough time, and despite a continued outward show of hopefulness, no-one dared raise the stakes in favour of success.

Thankfully for Andrew and Loris, they maintained maturity and a professional approach. Tension between them was minimal, the five main persons involved having discussed the likely prospect of its increase and resultant volatility if vigilance to keep it at bay was not part of their armoury ready at the forefront of the battle. It was tough though, and when in private chambers, the true internal struggle and feeling of despondency was sometimes expressed.

'Hi June,' greeted Andrew, shutting the front door of his small semi-detached house, having just arrived home from work.

The sun was just slipping behind the distant horizon, but the summer heat was still alive and vibrant, making its presence felt upon everyone.

'Evening, Andy,' greeted June as she came through from the kitchen, her bright face and bubbly manner clearly displaying her pleasure at seeing her husband. 'You look a little ragged?'

'I am,' replied Andrew after embracing June and giving her a kiss. 'It seems to be getting tougher, and I'm finding the going a little trying. I've been talking to God all day, hassling with Loris, fighting apparatus and rebellious, unyielding test samples. I'm on the brink of giving up! I'm so tired that I've almost had it!'

'Come,' said June, taking Andrew by the hand, 'I'll pour us each a glass of fresh lemonade, and we can sit at the table for a while.'

Andrew always warmed to his wife's loving touch. With them never having held hands before marriage, it always remained something special during their marriage, and June's support and interest in him was a pillar that he cherished most dearly.

Andrew wearily pulled out one of the oak chairs at the dining room table and sat down while June disappeared into the small but well-fitted-out kitchen.

June, Andrew's wife of the past three years, was the same age as him. She was of medium height and delicate build, with a healthy complexion and an animated expression. She had long, golden-brown locks and bright blue eyes. Although June had a bubbly character, she was not in any way brash, frivolous, forward or an attention seeker. She was a loving soul, had a wise head on her shoulders and a considerate manner. June was also the twin sister of July and the elder twin by 10 minutes, the two having been born across the midnight divide of the departing and dawning sixth and seventh months.

The small, semi-detached house that Andrew and June were living in had been their abode for the past three years. They felt happy there, with loving and contented memories right from the time they had moved in after their honeymoon. Although it was small, it was adequate and manageable for them both. They never felt claustrophobic or that they were treading on the other's toes. It was a double-story home, with the downstairs area being solely dedicated to operations when awake; the kitchen, laundry, guest bathroom, dining room and living areas were located there. Upstairs solely consisted of sleeping quarters and a bathroom. Furniture which had been sparse when they had first moved in had slowly been acquired with the help of June's father, Mr Harris, who was the branch manager of the Ottenger's Department Store's Ailensbury branch down on the foreshore. The semi-detached house had been made cosy and comfortable, with both Andrew and June having similar tastes. They also ensured that unnecessary things were not present, in order to keep the feel of the small place as open and airy as possible.

June was soon back with two glasses of fresh lemonade, little droplets of condensation having already formed on the outsides due to the excessive heat wave presently being experienced. She put the glasses down on coasters, pulled out a chair and promptly sat down opposite Andrew.

Andrew discussed some of the issues with her, details that he was permitted to share, and highlighted his concerns and struggles. Seeing that he was near to tears, June tenderly held his hand across the table, her own heart in as much pain as his as she shared his burden.

'I actually feel like Simon Peter and his associates,' confessed Andrew at the end, 'who had been fishing all night and caught nothing. I'm desperately hoping that sometime soon, really soon, the call of my Master's voice, "Cast your net on the other side of the boat" will be heard skimming over the top of the choppy water. I truly am desperate, June!'

'You'll get there,' encouraged June lovingly. 'God is faithful to all His servants, do not despair. You'll see.'

'I know He's faithful,' agreed Andrew with a sigh. 'I'm just taking heavy strain, and my body is feeling it too.'

'Come, up you get,' said June caringly, lifting Andrew's hand as she got up quickly, causing him to instinctively rise. 'You go and have a nice soak in the bathtub with two cups of Epsom salts in the water, and I'll prepare dinner. There's no need for you to help tonight, as I actually bought dinner on the way home from work. Take courage, and tomorrow you can try again when you're fresh.'

June gave Andrew a big hug and an affectionate kiss before they parted ways. Andrew was more than grateful, as his body ached all over just from the stress and tension, not to mention the long energy-sapping hours of concentration and focus that were currently being put in.

Half an hour later Andrew was back downstairs, feeling a lot better and looking forward to a delectable meal with his precious wife. The table had been set, with a bowl of Mediterranean salad already placed in the centre. June brought out a dish of roasted seasonal vegetables and a plate containing soft chicken breasts, which she had heated in the eye-level oven. The steaming food and appealing aromas aroused Andrew's senses even more. After they had each dished up and given thanks to God for His gracious provision, the happy couple enjoyingly satisfied a basic need of human survival, with each other's company and general light-hearted chit-chat adding vastly to the pleasantness.

Andrew and June sat and prayed together after the calm and unhurried dinner, lifting Andrew's difficulties before the LORD, seeking His help, intervention and guidance in what to do and how to go about it. The couple prayed about other issues upon their hearts and also lifted their hearts to the LORD in thankfulness and gratitude for His provision, faithfulness and mercy, as they did every evening. Andrew, although feeling better, still felt emotionally exhausted from the struggle but rested his concerns in the Lord his God.

The table was cleared and all dishes and utensils washed before they headed upstairs, Andrew in need of an early night and some good rest.

Andrew rose early the next morning, the smell of fresh percolating coffee and French toast having aided the cause. Normally the couple woke at the same time, but this morning June had risen earlier and busied herself in the kitchen so that Andrew would not have to attend to his own breakfast, which was normally a simple but healthy mix of cereals. Andrew was very grateful for June's care and effort, and he could not help loving her. He gave her a warm and loving embrace after they had finished sitting down to breakfast, and headed on his way to the lab and his work inside the heart of Pepe.

Chapter 10

A major breakthrough

'**I** WONDER?' thought Andrew as he drove along, the dawn of the day still yawning and stretching out its arms as the first rays of sunlight split the air with bright beams of light. 'Maybe there *is* something that we missed?'

From the moment Andrew had left his house, he had begun to consider their Origin of Origins research. As he dwelt upon what they were doing, Dr Jerry Neaps' research results that lurked in the back of his thoughts kept stepping forward and making their presence felt. Andrew weighed up the issues, and while stopped at one of the traffic lights, he quickly pulled a writing pad out of the vehicle's glove compartment and scribbled a few points that he wanted to look into at the lab.

When he turned into Microlab Industries' parking area, Andrew determined that the data that had been received the day before Thanksgiving would be worth looking at again, just in case. Andrew and his father had spent numerous hours going through these results before, analysing and checking various findings and looking at all the photos that had been provided. He was not sure that it would not be a waste of his time, but as the thought kept presenting itself, he felt that he should not ignore it.

Andrew headed straight to Pepe, not bothering to first go and make himself a cup of coffee. He entered through the mantrap security entrance and promptly sat down at his desk, switching on his computer. While the computer booted up, Andrew made a few notes, highlighting what he felt needed to be checked. He soon had Dr Jerry Neaps' files open and was pouring intently over his computer screen, checking meticulously each aspect referenced and each detail documented. Andrew opened a number of files in different windows so that he could switch easily between them for cross reference.

After about half an hour of scrutiny, he was suddenly taken by a foot note to a photo and information that he had previously looked at. Andrew was aware though that this had also cropped up somewhere else but in respect to a different aspect of information. He quickly began to search the data carefully with a single objective in mind – find that matching information.

Another half hour passed and Andrew was still systematically searching, methodically checking and keeping a note of where he had been and where he was going. Then again, there appeared another note, this time in the main body of a document, that was similar in nature to what he was looking for but not under the same classification and was referenced differently. Andrew noted this and copied the file to a separate folder just as Loris entered.

'Morning, Andy!' greeted Loris energetically with a show of enthusiasm, trying to keep moral up . 'You're in early this morning?'

'Good morning, Lori,' greeted Andrew, his intent look

startling Loris a little and causing him to stop. 'I wanted to get an early start.'

'What are you busy with?' questioned Loris, looking over Andrew's shoulder at his computer screen. 'You look as though you're deep in concentration!'

'I had a thought to go over Dr Neaps' research info again,' replied Andrew, not really wanting to stop and chat just then.

'Let me not interrupt you,' said Loris, moving on and sitting down at his desk. 'You look focused. I have a few tests I want to run again, but let me know if you find anything significant.'

'Sure, will do,' confirmed Andrew, his eyes already back at his screen, trying not to lose where he was in the proceedings.

Andrew continued to open files and check data specifically related to the foot note that had grabbed his attention. After another two hours of intense investigation, he had isolated 12 files and another 20 photos that he felt were relevant, although in the research they had not been related to each other. Andrew quickly scribbled a few notes on his writing pad and then once again checked each file in the folder that he had made. Once done, he carefully viewed each of the photos, firstly in relation to the original research information that had been provided and then in relation to the specific aspect that he was looking at. Andrew isolated specific areas on each of the photos, then enlarged those areas as best as possible. He leaned back in his high-back office chair, his heart racing with excitement as he carefully examined each of the enlarged isolated areas.

'Loris!' called out Andrew eagerly, now almost shaking with exhilaration. 'Come and look here!'

Loris, hearing the keenness in Andrew's voice, immediately stopped what he was doing and was at his side in seconds, pulling up his own office chair.

Andrew quickly ran through the information and then the photos, but Loris could not see what Andrew was looking at or the connection between the photos. Andrew then went carefully over the details from the beginning of what he had been alerted to. As he systematically explained, Loris' eyes grew larger. He then understood Andrew's processing and train of thought. The very hidden pattern and detail, almost like a web of secret code, that Andrew had unearthed and brought to the surface was being illuminated right before his very eyes.

Both microbiologists now sat with their eyes fixed to Andrew's computer screen, discussing various aspects about what Andrew had brought to light and life. Files were being brought up again and again, fingers were being pointed at the photos, notes were being jotted down, and a lively discussion was being had between them.

They eventually headed off to the largest fluorescence microscope they had, which ran digitally with a large TV monitor so that external observation could be provided to others as well.

Loris fetched a live cell, and as Andrew had made the observation, handed it to him to attempt the extraction of what he felt would be a decisive breakthrough and bring forth the forerunner to their ultimate goal of investigation.

Using highly advanced equipment, Andrew proceeded cautiously, with Loris keeping an eye on the large external TV monitor, watching his every move. After about 20 minutes however, the procedure failed, and Andrew had to stop. A red indent and sweat beads were on his brow from pressing hard against the apparatus' eyepiece, and his hands felt clammy from the level of concentration and tense apprehension.

Loris handed Andrew another live cell for a second attempt, but it too failed. The two men then decided to take lunch, their excitement not wanting to allow them a reprieve after so many months of leanness, but sensibility encouraged them to fill their tummies with nourishment as they may yet have a long and demanding task ahead of them. Loris suggested that they remain silent about what had been discovered and their current attempts, even to those closely involved, just so that they could first see where their efforts were leading. With so much despondency having been experienced up until then, he did not want to explain another let down, not just yet.

Andrew and Loris only took enough time as was necessary to eat their food, and even then, it was consumed more hastily than normal. Desire and interest in the morning's efforts prevented their being detained by any diversion, small or great, and they were back in the heart of Pepe without delay.

After conferring with each other, Andrew had another attempt and after an hour's intense effort had managed to successfully extract 12 kinesin and store them safely. Loris gave Andrew a high-five and a fist pump, well pleased with his associate's work, having once again watched the entire proceeding on the TV monitor, providing counsel as he saw fit.

Celebrations were kept short though, for what they had done was no great accomplishment. What they were really seeking had yet to be attempted. The 12 kinesin were affectionately named Tobe 1–12 (pronounced Toby), after the notion, "*To be*, or not *to be*" the answer to their efforts.

Loris prepared himself for stage two of the procedure, with Andrew now having a break and playing the observer. He took Tobe 1, the first extracted kinesin and carefully placed it where he needed it to be to begin a new extraction. Andrew sat glued to the TV monitor, filled with excitement and nervousness at the same time, praying and watching Loris' every move.

Loris worked carefully but came up short in his efforts. He repeated the exercise with Tobe 2, but again he failed. Two more attempts frustratingly ended in failure, at which point Loris switched places with Andrew so that he could rest a little and ease his strained eyes.

Andrew first went back to his computer and carefully studied the photos he had earlier selected. It was now late in the afternoon when he began his first attempt at dissecting Tobe 5 and with great caution, slowly began the process. Andrew was skilful at the touch, his delicate accuracy and patience enabling him to make steady progress. Yet he too failed, and poor Tobe 5 fell victim at Andrew's hands. Tobe 6 was called upon for the cause but was also a sacrifice; the cause of mankind's strive for knowledge and understanding none the better and mankind none the wiser.

Andrew took a quick breather and went to look out one of their large windows, just to allow his eyes to adjust again to distance. It was nearly dusk and seemed smoggy as the late sun reflected off the stagnant, low-lying cloud cover hanging idly around in the expanse above. There was not a breath of wind anywhere, and the still, calm sea trickled up and onto the beach with a sluggishness that would have embarrassed a sloth. It was still hot and muggy, and Andrew could see it reflected in how the people down below his second story location moved about. He and Loris were now not only isolated in the bowels of Pepe but also alone in the building, with all the staff members having already clocked out. Andrew did not linger long however and before starting again, quickly studied the photos on his computer once more.

This time he decided to tackle the extraction from another angle, and soon Tobe 7 was under his watchful eye. As before, he started cautiously, his skilful touch not deserting him although fatigue had started to take its toll after an already long day. He knew, however, that patience and delicate accuracy had to be maintained, so he applied himself with greater effort and concentration to try and overcome his body's need for rest.

Loris too remained patient, silently observing and only commenting when he felt it was absolutely necessary thus affording Andrew every opportunity of success. Andrew's progress was slow but steady, almost like a high-level marathon operation. As he neared the end of the extraction procedure, the two men held their breath in anticipation, hoping desperately that Tobe 7 would yield what they were looking for. Finally, Andrew managed to extract this "nano-particle", which they now had to scrutinise to see if it really was what they had expected. After another high-five and fist pump, Loris promptly took over the reins.

As darkness began to cover the world outside, light began to shine in the heart of Pepe. Loris carefully checked and shaking with excitement, turned and hugged Andrew before giving him a pat on the back. Andrew stood speechless, only able to quietly laugh. Where the day before tears of despair had nearly been shed, today tears of pure joy were welled up and ready to burst the banks of their ducts. There was no expressing how the two microbiologists felt at that time. Once they had settled down after what had been achieved, they quickly secured what they needed to, documented what was required and left Pepe to rest peacefully and contentedly for the night.

'June!' exclaimed Andrew, having phoned her just after driving out of Microlab Industries' parking lot, not willing to wait the few minutes it would take him to get home. 'You won't believe it or maybe you will – we had a great breakthrough today!'

'That's awesome, Andy!' responded June, her delight clearly evident at her husband's success. 'What did I tell you last night! Praise the Lord! But believe it or not yourself, those are the same words that I wanted to tell you!'

'What do you mean, June?' asked Andrew somewhat bewildered, his tiredness and swirling emotions not helping him just then.

'I'll tell you when you get home,' said June, realising that Andrew must be exhausted and was not far away anyway.

'Could you at least give me a hint?' pressed Andrew, his interest having been aroused.

'I received a phone call from Sarah Lang early this evening,' replied June in a more serious manner. 'She was weeping bitterly on the phone, but there's been a major breakthrough!'

Chapter 11

Sarah's revelation

AFTER Andrew had ended his call to June, he raced home. He was eager to tell his own story and hear what June had to say. He soon pulled into his driveway and parked his car in the garage. June opened the front door and with a bright and lively smile, welcomed him in with open arms. Andrew could not contain his affection and gave June an energetic embrace and lively kiss, squeezing her tightly and lifting her onto tippy-toes. He held her face gently in his hands, she automatically putting her hands on his, their faces brimming with delight, and laughing briefly like two adolescent youth as they looked at each other.

'June!' exclaimed Andrew overjoyed. 'I love you so, so much! You're the best in the world and the best that God could have ever given me, you know that? I thank God for you every day!'

June cast her eyes down slightly, her humbleness expressing itself coyly. Andrew kissed her multiple times before hugging her once more, joy filling her being to the core and livening her attractive features as his words and affection penetrated her heart. June knew they were genuine and sincere, as they always were, and she never tired of hearing his spontaneous outbursts of deep love and affection for her. To Andrew, June's lips were like honey, sweet to the taste. Her kisses were like a tonic, livening his very being and lifting his spirits.

The couple eventually went inside and headed for the kitchen. June took two glasses from the overhanging cupboard while Andrew fetched ginger ale from the fridge. They were soon sitting at the dining room table enjoying the cool refreshment, Andrew eager to tell his story.

'So,' said June excitedly as she reached over and took hold of Andrew's hand, 'let me hear it!'

'We were able to isolate and extract a Miganguinem nacellulam,' announced Andrew energetically, his eagerness and enthusiasm nearly overflowing.

'What's that?' asked June, her countenance still bright and bubbly with excitement.

'A micro nano-cell,' answered Andrew, beaming brightly. 'To explain it, what a nano-cell is to a normal cell, a micro nano-cell is to a nano-cell. We affectionately dubbed it "Midge" for short.'

'That's wonderful, Andy!' exclaimed June, tears of joy welling up in her eyes as she quickly reached in her pocket for a tissue paper, the night before coming to mind and God's gracious mercy bestowed in answer.

'To give you some idea,' elaborated Andrew, happy to educate June about his work, 'there are approximately 5-million red blood cells in a drop of blood the size of a pinhead. We've estimated that there are approximately 5-million micro nano-cells in a micro-nano pinhead drop of kinesin blood!'

'Wow!' exclaimed June. 'That's amazing. So the proportion remains the same, it just gets more intricate as it gets smaller?'

'That's what I feel is the case,' replied Andrew thoughtfully.

'Although blood cells don't have a nucleus, Loris is sure that a nucleus must exist within Midge – a simple core-like structure that just functions like a star or distant planet or like the core of the earth. I cannot go along with that possibility though, because God is infinite!'

Andrew promptly told June the whole story, of how Dr Jerry Neaps' research papers had come to mind on the way to work, his investigation and cross referencing of the data, his discovery and the long, demanding work by himself and Loris in finally isolating and extracting Midge. June sat and listened intently, her heart swelling with pride, gratitude and satisfaction at the achievement of her husband and the kindness of the LORD their God.

When Andrew had finished, they both just laughed with joy. The struggles, tension, heart-felt pain, stress and emotional turmoil that had been experienced at various times over the past year were released in happy celebration.

As it was already very late by the time Andrew finished narrating his day's happenings to June, they decided to go and prepare dinner while June told Andrew what took place with Sarah.

'Okay,' said Andrew while washing his hands at the sink, 'what was the issue with Sarah? I'm all ears!'

'Firstly,' began June, drying her hands on a towel after having already washed them, 'she phoned me just after I arrived home. She was sobbing uncontrollably and could hardly talk through her tears.'

'Oh, dear,' commented Andrew, turning to June, a concerned look on his face. 'It already doesn't sound very good!'

'Wait, my precious Andy!' said June. 'You haven't heard the half of it yet!'

'Sorry,' apologised Andrew, flicking water from his hands at June, causing her to pull a face and instinctively move out of the way.

'As I could hardly understand her,' continued June after gathering herself quickly, 'she asked if I would mind if she came round for a while to talk. I said that it would be fine, so within a few minutes she arrived, bearing all the marks of her tears.'

June promptly removed the ready prepared food from the shopping bags, having slipping into town to a local Ailensbury delicatessen after Sarah had left. She had realised that there would not be enough time to prepare food before Andrew arrived home so had utilised the service that the delicatessen provided, the equal of their home cooking but just more expensive.

'I made Sarah a cup of tea,' related June as she and Andrew dished up their dinner, 'and sat her down at the table. She explained that she had been having a battle with her conscience for months after Thanksgiving. She was troubled in her heart; that was the reason why she had avoided us.'

'So that was the reason!' exclaimed Andrew, emptying the tossed salad into a bowl.

'Indeed,' concurred June, 'I was also surprised. I had thought it was more to do with us than with her! It was the issues that had been discussed at Thanksgiving – that which your father and Tim had mentioned. It had pierced her heart like an arrow, and she was troubled by it. She couldn't get away from it. Sarah told me that she had been brought up in a nominal Christian home, where they went to church on occasion, had attended Sunday school as youngsters, but there was nothing more to it than that. She said that she followed Christianity more out of practise than anything but that when she met and married Loris, it petered out completely.'

'That's understandable,' interjected Andrew, now busy with the crockery and cutlery they were intending to use. 'If she didn't have a solid foundation, there was no reason for it to remain. Loris certainly wouldn't have encouraged her in the ways of the Lord!'

'Indeed,' agreed June. 'Sarah told me that Loris' grandmother was a strong Christian and would talk about Christian issues. Loris was always polite and accommodating, but her words were like arrows against a stone wall. Sarah said that she heard his grandmother but never took much notice, as Loris' influence was strong, and his adamant resolve kept her from bothering with God and investigating Christian involvement further. Yet, she could see something bright and lively in the eyes of his grandmother's old, haggard face. She also didn't want confrontation, for in their house any form of religious conversation is generally a topic of great conflict!'

'What brought Sarah to phone you?' questioned Andrew with interest.

'Loris' grandmother,' answered June, busy dishing Andrew a large helping of juicy vegetable bake, 'sent her one of Charles Spurgeon's *Morning and Evening* daily devotional messages – March 6, Evening, if I correctly recall her saying – and she actually read it, the scripture verse used catching her attention.

'What was it?' enquired Andrew, taking side plates from the overhanging cupboard as June had yet to take them out.

'John 3:7,' replied June, '"Ye must be born again". She read it to me at the table. She still has it on her smartphone. I remember the gist of the reading but cannot remember it clearly. I'll fetch my *Morning and Evening* book and read it to you.'

June quickly wiped her hands on a cloth and made her way upstairs to their bedroom. She was soon back in the kitchen, paging through the book of daily devotions while Andrew still continued with dinner preparations.

'Here it is,' announced June. 'I was correct, it's March 6, Evening, and the scripture is John 3:7, "Ye must be born again."'

June leaned back against the counter, resting her arms on her sides as she held the book in open palms before her.

'"Regeneration is a subject which lies at the very basis of salvation,"' read June clearly, her sweet soprano voice gliding fluently over every word, '"and we should be very diligent to take heed that we really are "born again," for there are many who fancy they are, who are not. Be assured that the name of a Christian is not the nature of a Christian; and that being born in a Christian land, and being recognized as professing the Christian religion is of no avail whatever, unless there be something more added to it—the being "born again" is a matter so *mysterious*, that human words cannot describe it. 'The wind bloweth where it listeth, and thou hearest the sound thereof, but canst not tell whence it cometh, and whither it goeth: so is every one that is born of the Spirit.' Nevertheless, it is a change which is *known and felt*: known by works of holiness, and felt by a gracious experience. This great work is *supernatural*. It is not an operation which a man performs for himself: a new principle is infused, which works in the heart, renews the soul, and affects the entire man. It is not a change of my name, but a renewal of my nature, so that I am not the man I used to be, but a new man in Christ Jesus. To wash and dress a corpse is a far different thing from making it alive: man can do the one, God alone can do the other. If you have then, been "born again," your acknowledgment will be, 'O Lord Jesus, the everlasting Father, Thou art my spiritual Parent; unless Thy Spirit had breathed into me the breath of a new, holy, and spiritual life, I had been to this day "dead in trespasses and sins." My heavenly life is wholly derived from Thee, to Thee I ascribe it. "My life is hid with Christ in God." It is no longer I who live, but Christ who liveth in me.' May the Lord enable us to be well assured on this vital point, for to be unregenerate is to be unsaved, unpardoned, without God, and without hope."'

'He had such a way with words,' commented Andrew, always appreciating Charles Spurgeon's writings, 'and such a profound insight. There's no possible misunderstanding there!'

'Sarah had read this,' said June, continuing the story, 'and realised that she was without hope. She knew that she had never made such a commitment although as a youth she had considered herself to be a "Christian". She was distraught and knew that she had to get her life right with God. She understood that God was speaking to her, calling her to repent and turn to Him, so she called on the name of Jesus to save her. She repented before God for her sins and neglect of Him, for never actually committing her life to Him and for turning away completely when Loris came into her life. She recognised that she had cast out one, God, in order to receive another, Loris, even though she knew that she had never actually made a commitment to the Lord in the first place. Sarah said that her faith was just that – religiosity and nothing more, no personal relationship with God, through Jesus Christ.'

Andrew stood still now, just listening as June spoke.

'It was after that that Sarah phoned me,' continued June, 'a feeling of peace within her spirit but also a feeling of being overwhelmed by what she had been and had not been! She knew she had been forgiven, but waves of remorse kept washing over her. She has a tender and sensitive heart.'

'That's amazing,' said Andrew, 'quite something. I pray that

God will hold her firmly, grow her carefully and establish her commitment like a deep-rooted tree. I'm not sure that it's going to be plain sailing with Loris though. Wow! I wonder what he would have to say about all this? A turn up for the books, but praise God, for His mercy endures forever.'

'Indeed,' affirmed June, sharing Andrew's sentiments and hoping and praying in the depth of her heart that the Lord would do even more. 'God is faithful though, so we can pray for her and help her were needed, but it's the LORD who needs to do the work and on whom we rely. It's God who convicts the hearts of men and women by the power of His Holy Spirit, and it's God who saves, by the power of Christ's blood and the work accomplished on the Cross of Calvary.'

'Absolutely!' agreed Andrew wholeheartedly. 'Though let us always be a true testimony of His grace and mercy in the way we live our lives, and let us always present His Word and salvation not through words lacking in power because our lives lack evidence of His power at work in us. There are so many so-called "Christians" today who profess Christ, but He may as well be a million miles away from them; they would never know it, for their lives lack the fruit of repentance. That's very much what Charles Spurgeon is saying and as he said, "salvation is known by works of holiness." The Scripture tells us that without holiness, no-one will see God.[10] This is declared in the New Testament, so no-one can claim that they are under grace and that it doesn't apply, and that they have freedom to do as they wish so long as they have accepted Jesus as their saviour.'

'True, my precious Andy,' agreed June, giving him a look of approval, always happy to receive a little Bible teaching from him. 'We need to be producing godly fruit in our lives, and it isn't achieved through "works of men" but through submitting to God and through the Holy Spirit working in us.'

It was now Andrew's turn to appreciate June, her walk with the Lord always bringing joy to his heart.

'Getting back to Loris,' said June after a pause of consideration by the couple. 'Sarah said that she didn't know what will happen when she tells him, but she was not concerned about it. Her decision was between her and God, and she had to ask herself who she should fear, man or God, for who has the power to cast into hell? This was one of the scriptures that your father had quoted at the Thanksgiving dinner, and it had stuck with her. She said that she'll have to face Loris but knew that no matter what, her Redeemer lives, and in light of His mercy all these years that she was opposed to Him, His grace to her now has been overwhelming, considering that her breath could have been snuffed out at the blinking of an eye, and her soul lost for all eternity.'

'Brave girl,' said Andrew, 'we can only pray for her.'

'Periodically, she wept quite a lot,' mentioned June, still leaning against the counter, 'All I could do was fetch her a box of tissues and sit quietly. In the end, I prayed with her, then she left.'

Andrew lifted up a short prayer specifically for Sarah after which he and June finished the final touches to their dinner. They exited the kitchen, set the table and sat down to their hearty meal of colourful, fresh tossed salad, delectable vegetable bake, crisp roast potatoes and delicately seasoned steamed fish.

'Oh, yes!' exclaimed June, just shortly after they had begun eating. 'I don't know how I forgot. At the door when Sarah was leaving, she hugged and thanked me but also revealed that she's expecting their third in early March!'

Chapter 12

Breaking news

THE next morning, Microlab Industries was abuzz, with Loris and Andrew breaking the news about their discovery. They had asked Professor Smyth to come round to join Dr Whyte and George and in the heart of Pepe, had revealed to them the whole of the previous day's effort. The three men were ecstatic, and amongst words of congratulations, there were handshakes, hugs and pats on the back. Andrew could sense, however, that despite this there was a small degree of withdrawal in Loris. He assumed the likely prospect to be that Sarah had informed him of what had taken place in her life the day before. Nevertheless, there was much to be done and much to be said, with a press release hurriedly set for lunchtime. As Ailensbury University had a small Public Relations department, which included a press release room, it was selected to be the venue for announcement, as there was nothing that really needed to be set up there. As the leader of the research activities, Loris prepared a press release statement. Andrew was to be in attendance in order to answer a few questions. Professor Smyth returned to the University in order to arrange proceedings and get the PR department to contact the media, requesting their attendance. No sooner had Loris and Andrew finished what they were doing than they had to head off to the University. The press release went off without hitch, although restraint was maintained when it came to sensitive information and details of the planned road ahead. They were not prepared to reveal anything that would jeopardise their efforts, and photos were not provided. Within a couple of hours thereafter the airwaves were running the story around the world. Social media sites, news agencies and scientific journals were all having their part to play in its transfer across the globe.

'I don't know about you,' remarked Loris, 'but I'm expecting that the University and Microlab receive a lot of emails and phone calls.'

'I never really gave it much thought to be honest,' responded Andrew, having turned to look at Loris as they walked up the stairs to the second floor where Pepe was located, 'but now that you mention it, it wouldn't surprise me one bit if what you say turns out to be true.'

The two men made their way through the mantrap security door and were soon sitting at their desks deep inside the heart of Pepe.

'See, what did I tell you!' exclaimed Loris, a degree of irritability in the tone of his voice as he looked at the emails that had been forwarded to him from Microlab Industries' contact centre. 'Scavenges, ferrets, vermin, the lot! They're all looking for an inside scoop about something that we didn't reveal or for photos. Just as well that nobody has my telephone number. It would be ringing—'

Loris stopped in mid-sentence, his mobile phone alerting him that someone was trying to get through to him.

'Ah!' said Loris, a smug look on his face as he looked at the screen of his phone. 'Breaking news travels fast. It's professor Dudley Kensington, a former doctoral student at Ailensbury University and fellow colleague of mine at Bridgetown University during my term there. Duke' exclaimed Loris, having got up from his desk and begun walking around inside Pepe, 'how are you? What gives me the pleasure of your call?' Loris laughed quietly to himself, knowing very well the reason.

'Typical joker!' scorned Duke light-heartedly as he began to chuckle. 'Don't try running me round the bush, Lang! You and I both know the reason for my call – and it's not to wish you a Merry Christmas!'

'Indeed!' responded Loris, pleased to hear the voice of his friend but sceptical nonetheless. 'You met Midge?'

'I wish I had met Midge!' exclaimed Duke loudly. 'You seem to have hogged the lot for yourself. What gives, what troubles, Lori? Could Bridgetown University not have been a support and help? Are you running the second phase of your investigations on your own too? As you have recently completed a 5-year stint at Bridgetown, my superiors are wanting me to see if we can come to some co-operative agreement with you for stage two. They have already contacted Ailensbury University and Microlab Industries. They really would like to get involved, so they're putting a little pressure on me, knowing that we're close friends, to get you to talk to your partners and seniors. They're wanting that Bridgetown will be seriously considered for joining in. Come, Lang, consider it?'

'Sorry, Duke,' said Loris, feeling that there was more to Bridgetown University just wanting to be part of the research, and he was not going to buckle or be manipulated like this. 'We already have all the partners we need in place. As much as I'd like to be obliging, I cannot agree to the request.'

'Okay, Lori,' said Duke. 'Maybe I'll have to send some nocturnal parasites to visit you one night in order to get you to consider us!' Duke began to guffaw in his arrogant manner. 'Anyway,' said Duke after settling down, 'I think it's a fantastic breakthrough, and it certainly was breaking news worth reporting! Credit to you, Lori! I'll inform my superiors of what you said, but I'm bound to be the recipient of disapproval.'

Duke and Loris shared a few more words before the phone call was ended.

'Andrew,' said Loris, walking up to him after ending his call from Professor Dudley Kensington, 'we have a head start and great advantage at this point in time, but I guarantee you that before long there'll be more players seeking to find what we're looking for. The one advantage that we've given them is that although they haven't seen Midge yet, they know what they first have to look for! We've got a job on our hands – and we cannot delay pressing forward with our research efforts!'

'One problematic issue that we have though,' observed Andrew, remaining practical and not worrying himself about others, 'is our ability to observe the currently unobservable. In order to extract Midge, we were operating at the extent of our magnifying capabilities. That was one of the reasons we failed a few times – we just couldn't see properly.'

'I know,' groaned Loris frustratingly, pulling a face. 'I don't really know what to do about that. We've been waiting months for the new machine to arrive, but because we weren't doing very well ourselves, we couldn't exactly shout and scream and belly-ache about it, could we?'

'It would certainly be convenient to do so now!' said Andrew. 'A little hypocritical and arrogant, granted, but it's the one machine that we're desperately needing. How else are we going to be able to investigate Midge's internals? That machine couldn't be received at a better time!'

'I'll give Professor Smyth a call this evening,' said Loris thoughtfully. 'I know that he had a lot on his plate this afternoon, so I'll see if he has some time later on to discuss this. Maybe he can do something for us? I know he's exceptionally keen for us to get that new fluorescence microscope too!'

Andrew and Loris then went through all their data, ensuring that their findings and related information had been properly crosschecked and accurately referenced. Having carefully completed their task by early afternoon, they spent a bit of time glancing at the different media reports on the breakthrough. All the news posts were short, with personal public comments taking precedence. Andrew was annoyed with a number of the reports, particularly one of note from the *Scientific Daily* online journal that read as follows:

A breakthrough in the advancement of biological research has just taken place at Microlab Industries located in the town of Ailensbury. They are working in co-operation with Ailensbury University and sources say, with some unnamed partners as well. A Miganguinem nacellulam, which is a micro nano-cell, dubbed "Midge", has been extracted from a kinesin. The microbiologist who succeeded in extracting "Midge", Andrew Renshaw, said that he thanked the LORD God for the success. This statement seems ironic when scientists are hailing the discovery as another of man's glories, expecting it to lead to a quantum leap in microbiological discovery and possibly the biggest since the discovery of the human cell. They are claiming that it is another nail in the coffin of religion, that has duped the world for millennia, and believe it likely to lead to the ultimate demise of the notion of the existence of God altogether, thus setting mankind free. There were no photos provided at this stage, just the statement of what had been achieved.

Andrew and Loris were able to leave Pepe before standard closing time. Loris, however, still had a few things to attend to back at the University as a result of the press release before he could head home.

'Loris,' called Professor Smyth as he walked down the corridor, seeing Loris about to walk into one of the PR rooms, 'I heard that you were here again so was just on my way to find you! Please accompany me to my office for a moment, will you?'

'Certainly,' replied Loris, having swivelled round and made his way towards the professor. 'Is there a problem of sorts?' Loris had immediately wondered if it had anything to do with Professor Kensington.

'I think not at this stage,' replied Professor Smyth with a smile as the two men walked side by side. 'I'll brief you in my office.'

A couple of minutes later the two learned men entered the professor's office.

'Take a seat, Lori,' said the professor politely as he made his way round his table to his chair. 'I'll get right down to business.'

The professor waited for Loris to seat himself before proceeding.

'I assume,' began Professor Smyth purposefully, 'that you've already heard that your former employer has tried to stick their fingers in the pie?'

'Indeed, I have,' replied Loris, eager to hear what the professor had to say. 'I received a call from Duke earlier today.'

'Well, don't worry about it,' said the professor. 'We've politely shut the door on their involvement on this research. Dean Mertin informed them that we're running a number of collaborate research projects with them so felt that it was necessary to assign another university to this project.'

'I'm glad to hear it,' responded Loris, quite relieved.

'Anyway,' continued Professor Smyth, a serious but bright look about him, as though he had something up his sleeve, 'this was not the reason why I brought you in here. I have some breaking news for *you*!'

'Ah!' said Loris, seeing the professor's pleased look. 'Ours was not enough for one day.'

'I received a call this afternoon,' said Professor Smyth, 'from Professor Stanley Burg.'

'The head of design at Bramford University?' queried Loris.

'The very same,' confirmed the professor. 'He told me that – call it what you will, providence, luck, chance – they finished the BEAFT microscope two days ago. BEAFT is an acronym for Bald Eagle Assisted Fluorescence Technology.'

'Sounds interesting,' commented Loris, well-pleased with what he was hearing.

'Don't ask me what the bald eagle has to do with it,' remarked Professor Smyth with a light-hearted show of ridicule, 'that man uses all sorts of animal structures in the development of his creations. You'll have to ask him about it! He told me they've been testing nonstop for the past 48 hours to ensure that all was working correctly. He heard the news today about Midge so was well-pleased that they are right on time with you. He's absolutely excited about it and wanted you to fly over right away to Bramford so that he could brief you on the workings of the machine. They could have it shipped out in a week!'

'That's incredible!' exclaimed Loris, almost disbelieving what he heard. 'This is breaking news! But how am I going to get to them so soon?'

'Not just you,' said Professor Smyth with a pleased look, 'you and Andrew – it's all done!'

'Done?' said Loris with a querying look. 'What's done?'

'Everything!' replied the professor with a smile as he pushed a large envelope across his table towards Loris. 'Here are your and Andrew's special visas, which the university was able to obtain at short notice for work purposes, your air tickets and hotel reservation. You'll only be there for two days, so it's no holiday sightseeing tour!'

'Incredible,' said Loris softly, peering inside the envelope. 'When do we go?'

'That's the catch,' replied the professor. 'You leave tonight!'

'Tonight!' protested Loris, looking up quickly. 'How—'

'There's no time to waste,' interjected Professor Smyth. 'Besides, it was the only flights still available on such short notice. It's Thursday evening already, so it means you'll be there for Friday and Saturday and back home in the early hours of Sunday morning. I'll see you at the lab first thing on Monday morning for a report back.'

'But,' gulped Loris, a little taken aback, 'we—'

'You have exactly 6-hours to get to the airport and get checked in,' said the professor, interrupting once again, 'so I advise that you don't delay! You still need to inform Andrew, so I suggest you get to it. The airfare and hotel accommodation has already been paid for; use your credit card for the rest. All expenses will be reimbursed, I assure you. I received the green light – we all want this to happen!'

Loris burst out laughing, seeing the answer to what he and

Andrew had been talking about that very afternoon and the professor's eagerness to get the new fluorescence microscope all mingling into one big ball. Without further ado, Loris shook Professor Smyth's hand, who gave him a reassuring pat on the arm, and headed for the door.

'Oh, Loris,' called the professor before he exited, causing Loris to turn around. 'One bonus you and Andrew get by Hobson's choice is that for your flights you have business class seats. By Hobson's choice or maybe that of mine, I couldn't really tell, you also have 5-star accommodation! Enjoy your trip.'

Loris gave the professor a brief smile of appreciation and promptly exited his office. With such a task before them, he and Andrew had no time to delay!

Chapter 13

Off to Bramford

'**H**URRY, Andrew!' shouted Loris, running along the conveyer belt between terminals. 'That was the third and final boarding call they'll make for us.'

'How can I run any faster?' responded Andrew slightly breathy, as he was quietly laughing at Loris at the same time, being right on Loris' heels. 'You're holding me up!'

The two had been held up in traffic due to late-night roadworks taking place and only managed to get to the airport in the nick of time. The usual one-and-a-half hour's drive to Central City International Airport had taken them more than two-and-a-half hours this time. Thankfully they had packed lightly, with carry-on bags only and no need to have luggage checked in. On the way to the airport, Andrew had phoned the airways and explained the situation, so the check-in for their flight had been kindly extended. They had run past the automated express check-in machine and swiftly managed to clear customs. All they now had to do was get to the boarding gate before it was shut.

'It's there in front of us,' called Loris, still running, seeing in the distance the bright white illuminated number 17. 'Hop to it, Andy!'

'I'm right here,' replied Andrew, nearly tripping from his amusement at Loris' manner, knowing that he could outrun Loris by a country mile. 'You just keep going!'

The wheels on their travel bags were whizzing profusely as they worked to the maximum, the bags being dragged behind the two late travellers. Half a minute later they met the neatly dressed boarding gate staff.

'Terribly sorry,' apologised Loris, breathing heavily, his chest heaving desperately in anguish, lungs burning and pain squirting through his side in objection to being overworked every time he inhaled. 'There were traffic delays, but my colleague did phone in to report it.'

The two attractive airways personnel just looked at Loris and Andrew and smiled with sympathetic expressions, Loris' sorrowful state and penitent demeanour due to his difficulty in getting there impacting upon their good natures.

'It's okay, sirs,' replied the one as she quickly checked the boarding passes, 'we were actually informed. Please just hurry down the ramp; the captain is waiting for you but is eager to get his bird in the air. Hope you have a pleasant flight.'

'Thank you, kindly,' managed Loris as he and Andrew hastily took their gate passes from the lady and rushed off, intent not to delay the flight or hassle the captain any further.

They clanged noisily down the movable connecting bridge and in seconds were presenting their tickets to one of the stewards.

There were cheers and claps from some of the passengers when the captain announced that the two missing passengers had now boarded, and the plane would be pushed back in the next minute or two, having obtained immediate departure clearance from the control tower.

Loris and Andrew quickly secured their travel bags in the overhanging storage compartments.

'That was close,' mumbled Andrew, flopping down in his comfortable seat, he and Loris seated side by side in the middle isle. 'Not something I'd like to do every day that's for sure!'

'Indeed!' agreed Loris, still out of breath. 'At least we can settle down now. The plane can do all the rushing!'

They had no sooner seated themselves in the blue seats with cream and light-green prints than the plane began its push back from the apron parking, the door having been closed and locked the moment the two had entered. The cabin crew immediately commenced demonstrating the safety procedures.

Even though Loris and Andrew were so late, one of the flight attendants had still kindly provided them each with a moist and refreshing towel to wipe their hands and faces, but that was all that could be offered to them until the plane was airborne.

After buckling up, Andrew leaned his head back against the headrest and closed his eyes, just trying to settle himself as quickly as possible.

The large wide-bodied plane rolled gently along the taxiway, the engines purring sweetly. It eventually turned onto the runway, and without hesitation, the engines began to whine as the captain pushed the throttles forward. The two extra-large engines roared to life with great purpose. The plane shuddered gently as it awoke from its slumber and began to move graciously down the runway. It lumbered at first like a limousine as it gained momentum, but the big hulk was soon thundering down the tarmac as it bored its way through the stiff headwind. The landing lights to the side began to flash past ever faster, with the buildings quickly disappearing behind the plane. Moments later there was calm beneath the plane's belly as its nose proudly rose, and the wide-bodied plane gracefully soared into the air like a giant eagle.

Andrew and Loris sat quietly resting, their bodies almost limp as they relaxed in their comfortable business class seats while the plane climbed and climbed into the black midnight sky.

They soon crossed the shoreline, with the spotted lights far below giving way to the eerie blackness as far as the eye could see. A ping was heard throughout the cabin as the seatbelt lights went out, followed by a mountain of clicking metal buckles from passengers disconnecting their seatbelts. Andrew loosened his seatbelt but still kept it fastened in case unexpected turbulence should rock the floating fortress. The plane dipped its left wing and arched out over the sea before slowly levelling out and setting its course for its intended destination, which lay six hours away on the other side of the Atlantic ocean.

'What book have you got there, Lori?' asked Andrew, the cabin having come alive as the airhostesses quickly went about their business of supplying midnight snacks and drinks before everyone was to settle down to slumber or sleep until breakfast five hours later.

'It's called *Beginnings*,' answered Loris, holding up the book and showing it to Andrew. 'It's by Donald Browning. I read it quite some time ago, but after yesterday's discovery, I thought that I'd read it again on the plane.'

'Oh,' responded Andrew with curiosity, 'is there some connection or just an interest?'

'A very close connection!' informed Loris enthusiastically, having first received his tray of eats and drinks from the well-groomed airhostess. 'It's only a fictional novel and there's no mistaking that, but it raises my interest exceptionally. It's about a scientist who is about to make the world's greatest discovery, which will disprove the existence of God. It shows how that when religion is challenged by such a prospect it crumbles. The reality of such a discovery finishes it off.'

'That is interesting,' said Andrew, trying to maintain composure. 'I agree on the part that if a true discovery were found that disproved God it would finish religion off. However, that could only be achieved on the assumption that God is not really real, but the reality is that He is! Furthermore, religion can be disproved for much of it is manmade. However, Christianity is not based on religion but on relationship with God through repentance and the acceptance of Jesus Christ as Lord and Saviour. It's a supernatural occurrence that's not accomplished by the hands of men, only by God. Additionally, as the true LORD God exists and is alive, such a "discovery" is impossible, only the reverse thereof can be achieved – the discovery of the Almighty God Himself!'

'Believe it the way you want to,' said Loris abruptly, having just looked at Andrew for a few seconds, 'but I'm going to be that man! I'm going to prove, through discovery, that God does not exist!'

Loris rested his head back against the seat's headrest and promptly began reading his book, not intent on starting another confrontation the same as what transpired at Thanksgiving. Andrew, not being argumentative by nature, similarly returned to settling himself in to enjoy his midnight snacks while lifting a prayer to the Lord for Loris.

The business class cabin was cosy and spacious, with the seats being generously set apart and providing plenty of comfort and room for even large passengers. The cream-coloured interior with shades of blue and green gave a feel of nature to it with heavenly influence, and the discreet lighting provided a softness to the overall ambience, creating tranquillity and inviting rest.

As it was a night flight, the cabin lights were dimmed substantially within half an hour after departure, thus affording passengers enough time to enjoy their snacks before settling in to gain some much needed sleep before arriving at their destination.

Loris switched on the reading lamp next to the side of his seat and promptly continued to engross himself in the pages of his book, intent on another hour's reading before closing his eyes. Andrew fully reclined his seat and grateful for the soft pillow, sleep mask and blanket, was soon breathing deeply and restfully.

All too soon, Andrew found himself being gently woken up by the soft touch on his shoulder from one of the airhostesses, alerting him to the imminent serving of breakfast as they were now only 45 minutes to touchdown. The flight had been pleasantly smooth, enabling him to sleep without disturbance. Loris was next to receive the airhostess's gentle touch while Andrew promptly headed for the restroom. By the time he came back, his seat had been adjusted for him, the pillow and blanket removed, and in its stead a tray with a steaming cup of coffee and a hot, damp towel awaited him.

'Certainly welcome, isn't it?' mentioned Loris, wiping his face with the hot towel that he had received.

'Particularly when you've only had a few hours' sleep,' noted Andrew as he sat down and looked at his watch. 'It's just past 5 a.m.!'

'Indeed, if you're back home in Ailensbury,' informed Loris as he put his towel down. 'It's just past 8 a.m. where you are now!

Time zones, Andy. Time zones! Look out the window, it's bright already!'

Andrew quickly peered through one of the oval side windows. He beheld the beauty of the early morning sun radiating up through the sky and brightening the blotches of soft, puffy clouds dotted everywhere while also glistening off the jewel-studded ocean below. The plane had flown into the rising of the dawn and was floating softly on the wings of the wind, waiting patiently for its time to descend to its destination that was soon to be in visible sight.

'I had forgotten that!' exclaimed Andrew, having returned to his seat. 'I should have remembered from the time I went on the expedition.'

No sooner had he freshened up with the hot towel and drunk his sweet-aromatic coffee, than breakfast was served to the business class passengers. Fresh orange juice, different cuts of fruit, a warm croissant with soft mozzarella cheese, scrambled eggs, small beef sausages and a slice of brown bread toast with a choice of jams was neatly arrange on each of the trays that were carefully placed before Loris and Andrew. They tucked in heartily, enjoying every bit of the delicious meal before them.

As they blissfully ate, the plane neared the coast, and the pilot dropped the plane to an altitude just above the scattered clouds. On the horizon the clouds seemed more dense, almost like travelling from the rural outlands into the heart of a city.

The plane eventually began a gradual descent. It approached the bank of low-level, clustered clouds jostling for position. They pushed up in tall columns at places, with many shades of grey clearly revealing their temperament. Loris and Andrew had finished their breakfast just in time, for a continuous turbulence set in as they crossed the coastline.

The plane plunged head first into the clouds, gliding swiftly through the mass of condensed watery vapour. Minutes later it broke out below the water mass, continuing its path of descent. The turbulence became more intense, but the huge hulk moved effortlessly along, the two engines singing clearly on pitch. The ground came ever closer, and once over a number of hillocks, the wide-bodied plane banked to the right and made its final approach. Seats were all in the upright position, seatbelt lights burning brightly, all passengers seated and fastened in, with cabin crew also having taken their places.

The plane dropped gracefully down over the runway, and the majestic giant settled back on terra firma with ease. Reverse thrusters were immediately applied, the plane shivered slightly, and the rough sound of rushing air dominating momentarily, as the pilot brought the plane to a calm crawl. It turned off the runway and onto the taxiway, heading for the assigned apron parking at Sir Henry Rowe International Airport's international arrivals terminal, intent on safely delivering its precious cargo of passengers.

Chapter 14

Bramford

IT was just past 9 a.m. when Loris and Andrew disembarked from the plane. Although they were both a little tired from their hair-raising time catching the flight and shortened sleep, the sights, sounds and even different climate ignited their senses and, coupled with the coffee they had drunk, raised their levels of alertness. They were both glad that the flight had at least been pleasant and uneventful and were hoping that there would be no untoward surprises instore further on.

The two microbiologists passed through customs with ease and were out into the open air on the other side of the international arrivals building shortly after Loris had hired a taxicab from one of the local operators located near the exit. Despite the airport being a hive of activity and a bustling period for flight operations, in no time at all, the two men were standing before a hoard of hackney carriages on the edge of the pavement, waiting for their taxicab to pick them up.

'Here it comes,' announced Andrew, seeing the bright metallic-green Jaguar come ambling up to them and confirming that it was for them by the registration plate on the front of the vehicle.

'We couldn't very well travel in anything else,' commented Loris with sarcastic animation, seeing Andrew's smile and questioning look, 'it would just not do after business class seats!'

'Of course not!' said Andrew jestingly as he put out his hand and hailed the driver.

'Besides,' said Loris with a tone of defence, 'you know as well as I do that all the smaller vehicles were already out or booked. It was only a few bucks more than the smaller ones, and I was not going to shop around! I'll happily pay in the difference if it's questioned.'

'And I'll share that difference with you,' mentioned Andrew supportively, 'if there's any argument, but I don't foresee that.'

The taxi pulled up next to Loris and Andrew and the driver was soon greeting them warmly. He placed their two pieces of luggage in the trunk of the car, and after they had climbed in, with Loris in front and Andrew at the back, they departed for Bramford.

At Loris' request, the driver bypassed the main highway and journeyed through the outer areas and countryside so that Andrew could get some sightseeing in, despite their short visit and important task ahead. The beautiful Jaguar meandered through the narrow country lanes, the endless rock walls that channelled the roads menacingly close and ever threatening to rip off the side-mirror should the driver have a lapse in concentration.

The land was green as far as the eye could see, and the rolling hills with their lush pastures were tranquil and calm. Small, old farmhouses dotted the landscape, adding colour but blending in as though the picturesque scene would be spoiled without them.

The rock walls and wooden gates separating properties and pasturelands broke the flow of green slightly, but their natural splendour drew the eye and pleased the heart. The bright sun warmed the backs of the grazing livestock that from time to time sent deep-throated bellows hurdling the partitions and disturbing the serenity.

Andrew had his window down, the slow speed of travel facilitating it, and enjoyed the fresh air and new sights while the driver provided commentary on the surrounds, general farm life and activity in the areas.

All too soon the countryside arrived at Bramford, a quaint town flanked by small villages. There were only a handful of hotels, which in stature to large urban city hotels, were tiny by comparison. Off the main road and hub, small lodges and Bed and Breakfasts dominated, catering particularly for tourists. Small side roads branched off the main thoroughfare, like veins from an artery.

The Jaguar slowed and pulled up outside the 3-story Bramford Regality, its sign outside small but bold. The cabdriver quickly removed the luggage from the trunk and cordially bid Loris and Andrew a pleasant stay and safe travels, leaving them to the attendance of the hotel's concierge before departing.

'It's not quite what I'm used to,' remarked Andrew as he looked at the old Victorian-style hotel, it almost giving him the feeling that he might not have an en-suite room with running hot water available.

'Never fear,' assured Loris, observing Andrew's facial expression, 'these towns and villages may be happy to live in the past, but you can be sure that what makes you comfortable makes them comfortable too!'

After checking in at reception, Andrew made a small video

recording of the reception area and entrance, having already taken photos of the front from the outside. They climbed the extra-wide walnut stairs to the second floor, with its thick handrail, chunky balustrades and soft velvety carpeting not being anything like the staircase Andrew was used to back home at his parents' house, which he had tormented on a daily basis for years. This magnificent creation uttered not a sound at the weight of the two men stepping upon its ribs. Its robustness was evident, and it stood almost proud, wanting to show off its strength to many a coming generation.

Andrew made another short video as he ascended, marvelling at the craftsmanship and on the second floor landing, turned and videoed the stairway from the top. He did the same with his bedroom, videoing a panorama of its interior and the bathroom, which he was relieved to find was very pleasant, before walking to the lone, large window and videoing the basic view from there. Before settling down, he forwarded the recordings and photos to his family, who were eager to hear how he was doing and share in his experience.

Andrew was quite taken with the décor – colourful wallpaper, the four-poster bed, heavy velvet curtains and drapery, wooden lampstands with frilly shades and dark mahogany furniture. It was a pleasant change of scenery. In the bathroom, the freestanding bathtub and unusual faucets caught his interest.

'Coming, Andy?' called Loris, having knocked on his bedroom door. 'Are you ready for some crumpets and tea?' It was now 11 a.m., and they had one and a half hours spare before being fetched and taken to Bramford University.

'I'm on my way,' called Andrew as he zipped his travel bag closed. He shoved it into the mahogany cupboard and closed its heavy door before joining Loris.

'I'm eager to look around this place,' said Andrew as he and Loris made their way quickly down the stairs. 'It's another world from what June and I are used to.'

'I'll show you around a little,' responded Loris. 'We have enough time, provided we get a move on. I'm no tour guide that's for sure, but during our 5-year stay in this country we visited a number of places, this being one of them. Crumpets and tea can wait until last.'

It was not long before the two visitors had walked two blocks along the main road and turned up one of the side roads that branched off into alleys a little further along.

Loris weaved his way through the maze, guiding Andrew along back lanes and past colourful, poky shops. Each shop specialised in only one area of trade, with the shop owners personally knowing most of the townsfolk due to their being a close-knit community. The cobbled streets, quaint homes atop the shops, colourful flowering pots on balconies and slow movement of people made the place seem contentedly trapped in the past. For Andrew, it made for interesting viewing, and he happily took a number of photos.

They entered a few of the shops which solicited great interest, and Andrew eventually bought June one box of specially handcrafted caramel chocolates and one box of mint chocolates from a chocolatier whose creations were irresistible.

Their final stop was back near the Bramford Regality hotel at a small family-run café, whose home stood atop their business. Delicious crumpets with homemade butter and strawberry jam along with a large pot of English tea were placed before Loris and Andrew by the amicable husband and wife duo. The two visitors sat quietly and enjoyed the tasty tradition after which they returned to the hotel to await their lift to the university.

Having first been to their rooms to quickly freshen up and get what they wanted to take with them to the university, Loris and Andrew entered the Bramford Regality's lobby promptly at 12:30, the time for their rendezvous with their escort. They were immediately approached by a tall, thin young man who had been sitting on one of the soft sofas to the side. He introduced himself, showing his university ID card and provided some details that he was instructed by his superiors to give.

Loris and Andrew followed the young man to his car and were soon whisked away to Bramford University, located just on the outer edge of the town. After only a few minutes' drive, the university came into view, and it was clear as they approached that it was only the grand old entrance that distinguished the town from the university. The centuries-old oaks stretched their arms over the entrance, their grey-brown bark wrinkled and coarse from old age, their stature strong and sturdy and leaves evergreen as in the prime of life. The car zipped underneath without respect and made its way onward with purpose.

Andrew and Loris were soon ushered down the echoing corridors of the university and brought to the office of Professor Stanley Burg, their interest having risen and suspense livened, with every step taken, as to what now lay before them.

Chapter 15

A great surprise at Bramford University

'Aʜ, my dear fellows!' greeted Professor Burg warmly upon seeing Loris and Andrew enter his office, his English accent strong and clear. 'It's nice to see you both. Awfully good of you chaps to come.'

Loris and Andrew, drawn by the likeable man, cordially introduced themselves and felt well at ease in his presence.

'Did you have an agreeable flight?' enquired the professor, looking from one to the other questioningly. 'Can I offer you lunch before we get started or perhaps some tea?'

'We had a pleasant flight, thanks,' replied Loris on behalf of them both. 'Just prior to departing the hotel we enjoyed crumpets and tea at a charming family-run café, so we're okay for now.'

'Splendid, my dear fellows,' responded Professor Burg with a smug look. 'There are not many things more pleasing and satisfying to the palette than crumpets and tea, I'll grant you that! Anyhow,' he added, gesturing with outstretched arm and open palm, 'we'll have some tea and biscuits later, but in the meantime, would you fellows kindly accompany me to the design room. I'd like to get started right away but will be pleased to first show you the BEAFT drawings. You may not be mechanical as such, but I'm sure you will find it all interesting nonetheless.'

Loris and Andrew promptly exited the office, followed by the professor, who gently shut the door and led the way down the echoing corridor and out along the courtyard portico.

Professor Stanley Burg was a short man with small frame, in his early sixties. His short cropped hair was straight and smooth, light-grey with streaks of dark coming through on top. He was clean shaven, and his pleasant and friendly-looking features complimented his quiet, humble nature that was warm and drawing. He had a PhD in Biomimetics Engineering and was head of Department of Mechanical Engineering. He also led the Design Engineering Research and Development Group. He had a great mind when it came to solving problems and a special love for incorporating the "already created" into new technology and advanced mechanical structures.

As they went along, Andrew marvelled at the masonry and elaborate detail that the old building contained. The tall columns of the portico were sturdy and strong, having bravely born for centuries the archways upon their shoulders in quiet, loyal duty. Although the building was there to serve academia and man's insatiable desire for knowledge and development, it was nonetheless a work of art that remained as attractive to the eye as the day it had been constructed.

'Here we are,' said Professor Burg, opening a large wooden door, having left the portico and entered another echoing corridor, 'this is our design room.'

Loris and Andrew both looked at each other when they entered, taken by surprise by what they saw. The walk down the echoing corridors and along the old portico had slowly indoctrinated them into a feeling of antiquity, causing them to momentarily forget the advanced operations of the university and the modern technology deployed in its effort to remain at the forefront of development. It was like going from darkness to light, and the array of computers and digital equipment neatly arranged around the room was impressive. Large printers, 3D printers, oversized digital screens, countless highly advanced computers and various other high-tech equipment were in operation, with a number of students and personnel engrossed in various undertakings.

The professor led them to a small conference area that was partitioned off with glass.

'Take a seat, my dear fellows,' said Professor Burg as he switched on the laptop lying on the oval conference table, causing the large wall-mounted monitor to spring to life and reveal a beautiful 3D rendered lifelike drawing. 'This is Bald Eagle Assisted Fluorescence Technology – BEAFT for short.'

'That's impressive!' commented Andrew, eyeing the rendered drawing with great interest as the professor rotated it on the screen so that it could be viewed from all angles.

The whole unit was encased with a Perspex covering, with the eyepiece, various computer pads and tubes protruding at strategic places. There was a mass of sophisticated tooling with wires neatly fastened inside the Perspex housing. A number of different magnifying lenses were affixed to a rotary head just above the observation table, which was adjustable to accommodate tiny robotic arms used during investigations.

Professor Burg then opened a file on the computer and showed Loris and Andrew all the different working mechanisms, the mass of different lines more confusing than educating. The professor isolated different sections so that the two microbiologists were able to comprehend it and appreciate not only what they were being shown but what had gone into this innovative apparatus.

'Please tell me,' asked Loris, having been silent up until then while he observed what the professor had been showing them, 'what does the bald eagle have to do with it? Professor Smyth said that he had no clue whatsoever.'

'Ah, the bald eagle!' sang out Professor Burg with animation and a tone of pleasure. 'The very life of the apparatus. You would never know it by mere external observation, but it represents the core of what you see – or will see, I should rather say! You see, my dear fellows, the structure and functionality of the bald eagle's eyes were modelled and used to create the new observation lenses.'

'That *is* interesting,' responded Andrew, turning his focus from the large monitor to the professor.

'It is,' agreed Professor Burg, 'particularly when you know what is involved. Eagle eyesight is renowned, being 4–5 times stronger than our own. It can be likened to seeing an ant crawling on the ground from the roof of a 10-storey building.'

'That's quite amazing,' interrupted Loris, 'but not surprising when you consider the way they operate and have to scout for prey.'

'The bald eagle's eye is very large compared to the head size,' continued the professor, 'roughly the same ratio as our own, providing a large imaging area on the retina. Each eye has two foveae, whereas humans only have one. The fovea is responsible for sharp central vision, which is what we need for specific identification. It contains the type of photoreceptors known as cone cells, which are responsible for colour vision.'

'And you've managed to incorporate this into BEAFT?' queried Loris, looking intently at the drawings.

'Yes, we have,' replied Professor Burg with a pleased look. 'It was tough going, but we finally managed it. Out of interest, one of the eagle's foveae is directed forwards, the other to the side. This enables very precise distance perception. The eagle's foveae also have five times the density of cells than those of humans, and its vision extends into the ultraviolet spectrum of light, which as you know, is invisible to humans. Fascinatingly, adult bald eagles can also correct for refraction when catching fish – but I don't quite think that that is your intention with this apparatus!'

The professor smiled, amused at his own joke. Both Loris and Andrew were drawn by the elderly man's pleasant manner.

'Hats off to you and your team, Professor Burg!' said Andrew energetically. 'I'm looking forward to seeing the real thing!'

'Yes,' agreed Loris, 'from what we've seen and heard thus far, hats off to you! It's quite extraordinary how these birds have evolved,' added Loris, looking at a picture lying on the desk of a bald eagle catching a fish from calm waters, 'but then they've had millions of years to improve upon their requirements and hone it to what it is today. Impressive, greatly impressive to say the least! Incidentally, it's my intention to use this apparatus to try and discover the origin of origins and thus disprove God. I expect to find a core-like structure giving nuclear-type energy, which is self-replenishing. I feel that we're one step away from that now.'

'Ah, my dear fellow,' responded Professor Burg looking at Loris purposefully, 'that is where you and I differ sharply. Be my guest to search for the origin of origins, I bid you well and wish you all the best in your endeavour, but I must tell you that as a Christian, I feel that should you discover it, the results will not yield what you think they will.'

This took Loris by surprise, and he almost took a step backwards.

'Furthermore,' said the professor, to Loris' annoyance, 'the eagle's eye is certainly impressive, but it was "honed" in just one day; it did not take millions of years to develop it! When you do your research, know that the design principle for the lenses of this advanced fluorescent microscope was based on the bald eagle's eye, in order to assist with the magnification and clarity and minimise distortion on micro-nano objects. So, when you discover whatever you discover, you need to remember that the bald eagle's eye, designed by a Sovereign Designer, has played a significant part.'

Loris nearly choked when he heard this but did not have time to respond before the professor continued.

'Believe it or not,' added the professor, 'accept it or not, how else could such a sophisticated eye have been created? Our intelligence could not have comprehended its structure and complexity, how then is something without intelligence going to do so?'

'Each to his own,' countered Loris, not wanting to be quarrelsome.

'Indeed,' said Professor Burg, 'but I must tell you that as a Creationist and biomimetric engineer, I stand daily in awe of the complexity of what has been created. Even more so, I stand in awe of a God who has infinite power to do so in one day by immeasurable wisdom and the sovereign authority of His word. From my perspective, it is more difficult, or should be, for engineers who spend so much time considering "designed" objects to embrace Darwinian evolution than it is for biologists. There are two reasons: firstly, since the design by human beings is not limited by the step-by-step change that evolution is limited by, human engineers should produce designs which are far more sophisticated than those found in nature. Yet the opposite is true. Nature has by far the most sophisticated designs. For instance, the design of the peacock feathers is so precise that engineers cannot replicate it. I'm always reminded of the scripture in Psalm 100:3b, "Know that the LORD is God. It is He who made us, and not we ourselves".

'A second reason is that engineers know that you cannot design by making random mistakes. If you randomly change a single parameter in a car engine it will always result in a retrograde step. Design improvements always require careful planning and careful changing of many parameters at the same time. An example of this is the Envisat satellite, which had hundreds of thousands of components and several million separate pieces of design information, like dimensions and material properties. It would only have taken one or two errors in the design information and the whole mission would have failed. This kind of project illustrates how difficult design is and how design does not happen by chance.' [11]

Professor Burg's words were a pleasant surprise to Andrew and sweet music to his ears, causing his heart to leap with joy and spirit to be lifted.

'Well, I—' fumbled Loris.

'You are not alone, my dear fellow,' interjected the professor, seeing Loris' expression. 'My views are not widely approved of by the fraternity, but the faculty staff here at the university know the work that I do and the achievements that my team and I have made. Deep down they know too that a belief in evolution is inconsequential to the practical work and that such a belief would not have helped one bit, so I keep my job.'

Andrew was standing silently looking on, wondering what was next as he could see Loris' attempts to conceal his disapproval failing miserably.

'I see,' managed Loris, trying to force a smile.

'Anyhow, my dear fellows,' said Professor Burg, turning off the laptop, 'we still have a lot to do, so let's press on. I'll take you now to see BEAFT; it's in the test room next door to us.'

A minute later the three men had entered the test room. It was immaculate, clinical and professionally laid out.

'There, my dear fellows,' announced Professor Burg, pointing to the fluorescent microscope quietly resting on one of the spotlessly clean work benches. 'That is BEAFT. Go and take a look.'

Loris and Andrew promptly poured over the new fluorescent microscope, with Professor Burg pointing out all the different aspects that he had highlighted to them on the drawings. Loris soon settled again, the prior tension created through different beliefs giving way to the real object that sat before his eyes, captivating his curiosity.

'I'll give you a demonstration of it now,' said Professor Burg after the briefing, 'but first, I have a great surprise for you!' The grey-haired man possessed a youthful look.

'What is it?' asked Loris, first looking round.

Without saying a word, Professor Burg pointed to the new fluorescent microscope.

'But we know about this!' exclaimed Loris, trying to understand the professor's purpose and smug expression.

'Take a look,' said Professor Burg, beaming a bright smile.

'But we've already looked at it!' reasoned Loris, a little confused and wondering if there was some trick at play. Andrew was also not sure of what the professor was up to.

'My dear fellow,' said Professor Burg with amusement, 'take the cover off the eyepiece, switch the machine on and have a look.'

Both Loris and Andrew looked at the eyepiece and realised that they had not yet looked into it. Loris switched on the microscope, bringing it immediately to life. He carefully removed the eyepiece, putting it on the workbench and promptly placed his eyes on the soft rubber eye support. Loris adjusted it to fit comfortably and then looked intently, his eyes brightening instantly!

Chapter 16

The invitation

'**W**OW!' exclaimed Loris, fixing his eyes on the tiny object that lay before his observation. 'You caught me by surprise there. Interesting design; what's it for?'

'It's nano-tweezers,' replied Professor Burg, chuckling to himself as he realised that Loris had not quite perceived what he was looking at.

'I can see that,' responded Loris, his eyes still fixed to the microscope's eyepiece. 'We already have nano-tweezers. We used them along with soft laser and a sucker tube for extracting Tobe 7.'

'I believe you did,' said the professor in acknowledgement. 'Our dear fellow, Professor Smyth, described to me what you had done.'

'Andrew,' called Loris, before lifting his face from the newly created apparatus, 'come take a look.'

With eagerness Andrew took a look through the eyepiece.

'What do we want those for?' enquired Loris, addressing Professor Burg.

'Loris!' interjected Andrew before the professor could answer. 'There's something here.'

Andrew lifted his head away from the eyepiece, quickly fixing his gaze upon the digital data pad, causing Loris to turn his attention to him in puzzlement.

'Take a look at the magnification settings,' remarked Andrew with amazement. 'You've judged that item on the settings we use back at Pepe, but this is much higher!'

'I was waiting for one of you to be alert to it,' said Professor Burg, a pleased look in his countenance. 'Welcome to BEAFT – and the eagle eye!'

Loris quickly took a second look through the microscope's eyepiece, having politely moved Andrew out of the way. He withdrew and glanced at the magnification settings again and then went back to the eyepiece.

'I don't believe it!' exclaimed Loris, his tone of voice expressing his astonishment beautifully.

'If I'm reading you correctly, my dear fellow,' said Professor Burg, 'yes, you are looking at supernano-tweezers, not just nano-tweezers. What you have there before you clip into and operate via the ones that you already have at your lab. These are for extracting even smaller items or bodies of matter.'

'I don't believe it!' exclaimed Loris again, lifting away from the fluorescent microscope and looking with bewilderment at the professor. 'That's amazing! How come we never heard about this?'

'My dear fellow,' responded Professor Burg, quite pleased with Loris' bafflement, 'I kept it a secret. Even Professor Smyth never got wind of it, poor fellow. You will be able to break the news to him. I wanted it to be a surprise for you, and besides, we were not one hundred percent sure that it would be ready in time for your visit. I felt that such a tool may be required to assist you in your research, so I'm glad we managed to complete it.'

'Along with BEAFT,' exclaimed Loris eagerly, 'I'd love the opportunity to try it!'

'Your desire will be granted, my dear fellow,' responded the professor pleasantly. 'Although BEAFT was the chief reason for inviting the two of you over here, the supernano-tweezers were always part of the agenda, if we could get them finished in time. It's available for you both to try. It can be shipped along with BEAFT – you won't be able to work those tweezers without BEAFT! Anyhow,' added the professor, looking at his watch, 'I do not want to make a meal of it. If we do not buckle to and get on now with your training we'll miss tea, which is not something I enjoy doing if it can be helped!'

Professor Burg first showed Loris and Andrew the apparatus' ability to toggle between conventional microscope use and fluorescence microscopy, then its ability to use a mixture of both by digitally fixing points to targeted objects, thus allowing the machine to track them specifically. He was thorough, continually referring to the manual on the laptop that had all the necessary information already documented. The information was substantial and the demonstration intense, with the professor working carefully and methodically but not letting up in his pursuit to cover all areas before tea. He finished a few minutes past 15:30, pleased with his efforts and the responses that he received from both Loris and Andrew.

Tea was taken, and the threesome headed off to the staffroom to enjoy a good, strong cuppa and some freshly-baked ginger nut and shortbread biscuits.

Loris and Andrew were introduced to other staff members who had worked on the BEAFT project, and a pleasant and enjoyable time was had chatting about various aspects surrounding the newly developed apparatus. Professor Burg maintained watch however and had the two microbiologist "students" back at the grindstone at the stroke of 4 p.m.

Each feature of the new apparatus was gone over again, with Loris and Andrew taking turns to operate the unit and see that they had every aspect – from manual settings to digital pre-settings for various applications – clearly understood and correctly programmed. The hybrid facility was also operated, with the two men taking turns once again. They did not find it so easy to manage the digitally operated arms but with larger items eventually began to get a feel of the apparatus' functionality, Loris expressing multiple times his determination to get it right.

'Well, my dear fellows,' announced Professor Burg, looking at his watch and then from one tired face to another, 'it's now just past 7 p.m., and I think it's been a very long day for some. You've both progressed marvellously well, but enough until tomorrow.'

'Indeed,' affirmed Loris, 'I think we've both had a long and taxing day. Rest will be welcome.'

'It's light till quite late in this neck of the woods,' mentioned the professor, 'but I don't suggest that you make a night of it. Tomorrow will be a hard day, with high levels of concentration required.'

'I don't think we could make a night of it,' said Loris, looking at Andrew's weary eyes. 'It looks like the only thing Andrew is going to make is his bed!'

'It will be dinner and bed for me,' acknowledged Andrew, chuckling lightly at his own state. 'For sure, I'm now exhausted!'

'No worries, my good fellow,' said Professor Burg with a smile, 'you get some needed rest. Tomorrow I'm going to put you through your paces with supernano items! Today you had it easy, but let me not worry you unnecessarily now.'

Loris and Andrew could only laugh, the professor making them feel no better in their tired, worn-out states. He was correct, the thought of being put through their paces in only a few hours' time was not something they wanted to hassle their weary brains over just then.

'On the subject of dinner,' continued Professor Burg, 'we have not planned anything formal for the express reason that we knew you would be busy till late and thought that due to your travelling, you may want to just make your own way and sort yourselves out. We're more than willing to attend to this for you, with a number of the staff members on standby to take you both to dinner. It's up to you two fellows?'

'Thank you kindly, Professor Burg,' spoke up Loris, 'you and your team are more than considerate. However, looking at Andy here and knowing how I feel, it would be wise for us to just make our own way. We'll dine at one of the small family-run restaurants we passed in town this morning and thereafter promptly retire for the night.'

'Good then,' said the professor, beginning to switch off plugs and shut down the test room for the night, 'I'll have you driven back to your hotel and picked up again tomorrow morning at 8 a.m. sharp. We need an early start, for there is much to get through, including a special lunch with other staff members that has been arranged in our dining hall.'

Loris and Andrew happily agreed to this and were then escorted by Professor Burg to the university's reception area, where transport back to their hotel was arranged for them.

With Bramford University being only a few minutes from the town's hub, it was not long before Loris and Andrew were back in their hotel rooms freshening up for dinner.

The sun was still burning brightly outside when they exited the hotel just before 8 p.m., with a warm breeze blowing gently through the town that added to the evening heat. The town was quite abuzz, with people milling around, some still doing last minute shopping at the few stores remaining open, while others were dining.

Andrew and Loris headed straight for the corner bistro that had taken their fancy earlier that morning. It was a medium-sized enterprise with homely hospitality a standard on the menu. The tired, hungry men were soon seated at a table next to an open window that looked out across the town's main street, giving them an interesting view of the evening activities.

Within minutes of having received the menu, a waitress was summoned by Loris, who did not want to wait longer than was necessary, the delectable smells coming from the plates on nearby tables and the kitchen eating at his unfilled stomach and troubling his wearied state. Drinks and the meals were ordered at the same time, Loris opting for a pint of local ale, while Andrew stuck to his customary request for a glass of cola.

There was some general chit-chat between them, but it was short-lived as Loris' Lancashire hotpot, consisting of lamb and onion topped with sliced potatoes was soon placed before him, and Andrew's bangers and mash with onion gravy was placed before him. A small bowl of hot vegetables – peas, carrots and green beans – was a complimentary dish kindly provided to the out-of-town visitors by the owners. The two men promptly began eating and enjoyed the tasty provisions, both later managing to consume some Hollygog pudding as well.

They were out of the restaurant as the sun was setting, a beautiful red and deep-blue sky as backdrop for their walk back to the Bramford Regality hotel. They found their beds neatly turned down, inviting them to climb in, for which they needed no second invitation.

Andrew phoned June and spoke to her for a while before turning in, her pleasant conversation always a joy to his heart, causing many a difficulty and care to fade during such times. Upon nightfall, both men were tucked in under their covers and sound asleep, the morning tasks only to be sooner reached by dream.

They were up at the crack of sparrows and after checking out of the hotel, were whisked away to the university once again in exactly the same fashion as the day before. Professor Burg was already there, and the test room operational.

No time was wasted, and Loris and Andrew got stuck right in to their training. The professor held to his word, and the supernano-tweezers were part of training, which the two microbiologists found extremely difficult to operate. It took every ounce of their concentration, working on pre-made nano-items that Professor Burg had created based solely on information that he had heard from Professor Smyth during their conversations.

Under the guidance of the professor and another of the project team members, the two men worked hard. They worked right up until it was time to attend the special lunch in the dining hall with the other staff members who had been involved in the project. Afterwards, they were back in the test room, Professor Burg and his colleague once again overseeing proceedings. Afternoon tea was skipped, and they trained right up until 6 p.m., Loris having copied all the operational files and related program information onto his laptop while Andrew took the last turn training.

'Well, my dear fellows,' said Professor Burg happily, having first looked at his colleague, 'we both agree that you've done extremely well, although you may not think so.'

'We made a lot of mistakes,' admitted Loris, 'that's one thing I know.'

'Ah, yes, my dear fellow,' confirmed the professor, 'but none so many as you might have. Progress was made nonetheless, and I have a good report to give to Professor Smyth, not to worry. I'm confident in placing BEAFT in the hands of you chaps and am sure that it will not be long before you will have honed the skill of operating it along with the supernano tweezers.'

'Thank you, Professor Burg,' said Loris, pleased with what the professor had said, which he felt were words genuinely spoken, 'it is much appreciated.'

'I will suggest, however,' said the professor with a smile, 'that you somehow stock up on a few more Tobes, poor fellows!'

'Indeed!' exclaimed Andrew, he and Loris laughing heartily. 'That goes without saying!'

'That's it then,' said Professor Burg. 'Unless there's anything we can assist you fellows with, other than what has been arranged, I'll escort you to the reception area to ensure that your transport to the airport is waiting. Please feel free to freshen up before you leave.'

'Everything's fine,' answered Loris, 'thank you. We have business class seats, so we'll freshen up at the airline's business lounge and grab dinner there too.'

'Splendid, my dear fellows,' responded the professor with a pleased look, 'no time to waste then.'

Loris and Andrew promptly thanked Professor Burg's colleague, fetched their travel bags and walked with the professor down the echoing corridors, along the portico and back down another echoing corridor to the reception area.

'As a matter of interest,' said Professor Burg as Loris and Andrew were about to leave, the cabdriver having already placed their luggage in the trunk of his car, 'I'll be a guest speaker this evening at one of the churches in Plumberry. The topic of the talk will be *Inspiration from Nature*. It will be live streamed from 20:30, so can I kindly invite you two fellows to connect to it? I would love to have you listen in, and I'm sure you will find it interesting, if not challenging!'

Chapter 17

Loris' determination – part 1

'Aʜ, I—,' replied Loris hesitantly, determining that he did not really want to listen to the professor after what the man had declared the day before about his beliefs. 'I'll see—'

'I'd love to connect and listen in,' replied Andrew butting in, to Loris' annoyance, when he saw Loris' hesitancy but not wanting to miss such an opportunity. 'We'll have free WIFI connection in the business lounge and by 20:30, should have freshened up and even grabbed some dinner. We have a late flight, so there will be plenty of time to listen.'

'Yes, indeed,' managed Loris, wanting to give Andrew a disapproving look but not prepared to do so in front of the professor. 'Andrew's correct, we'll tune in – you can count on Andrew to ensure that we do!'

Loris now managed to give Andrew a quick glance to show his displeasure while the professor scrolled through his phone to obtain the link details, but Andrew was looking at the professor and did not take notice of him.

'I'll be pleased to know that you are watching,' said Professor

Burg with a smile, having located the information, 'and rest assured that I'll not be divulging any information about BEAFT! It has been a pleasure assisting you two fellows. Hope you have a pleasant flight and safe trip back home. Please feel free to contact me directly regarding what we have gone through in the past two days, should you need to. I'll be happy to assist.'

Andrew gave the professor his phone number so that the live stream link details could be forwarded to him. They all greeted warmly after which Loris and Andrew climbed in the taxicab and headed off to Sir Henry Rowe International Airport.

They checked in via the automated express check-in machine, not having luggage that needed to be stowed in the cargo hold and promptly made their way to the airline's business lounge.

The two men from Ailensbury showed their business class tickets at the reception counter and entered, making straight for the restroom to freshen up. The pristine restroom was a breath of fresh air in itself, with its brightness, clean smell and top-quality facilities making for a pleasant visit. With colour in their faces from the cold water, hair dampened and in place and the smell of deodorant penetrating out from their shirts, they entered the main lounge.

Blue Pacific Airline had a large business lounge that was divided into different areas for general sitting and relaxation and for the restaurant area. It was neatly arranged, with the blue hue throughout in keeping with the airline's main colour but done in a way that maintained a poshness while providing a calm and relaxing ambience. They provided both an a-la-carte menu and a buffet, with a vast spread of eats available for different tastes. Desserts were in abundance too, from basic sweet muffins to decadent cakes and elaborate pastries.

Loris and Andrew strolled through the lounge, passing by the buffet and reading the a-la-carte menu on their way to find a table. They picked one out of the way, in the far corner of the dining area next to the observation window, where they could watch the movement on the tarmac below and the planes landing and taking off. The lounge was surprisingly quiet, with less than two dozen people present, so Andrew knew that they could happily connect the laptop to the live stream without it being bothersome to fellow passengers if it stayed that way.

Having placed their belongings at the table they had selected, Loris and Andrew obtained some liquid refreshment and just sat quietly watching the planes after their intense day of training. It had been a gruelling two days at the hands of Professor Burg, who was constantly polite and patience personified, but who had worked them over having maintained an intensity and purpose that raised the need for extended concentration, requiring them to apply themselves as diligently as possible. The gnawing at their stomachs, however, soon had them both at the buffet.

'I'm determined to master BEAFT, Andy,' said Loris firmly as he picked up a serving of spinach lasagne with a spatula, 'and particularly those supernano-tweezers. I must master it, I just must! Everything's hinging on us being able to use that apparatus to its potential, and I'm determined that we do!'

'You're right there, Lori,' agreed Andrew, selecting two beef sausages with a pair of tongs. 'The advancement in our research requires that we're able to use this technology to its fullest. It's amazing that we have it, so it wouldn't be wise not to use it. Even though Professor Burg was way better than us at using the apparatus, it was clear that even he was not using it to its potential. In my opinion, they've created a masterpiece in BEAFT!'

'Indeed,' confirmed Loris, now picking at some mixed vegetables, 'we have a great opportunity at our fingertips – literally! I'm determined to maximise that!'

'I'm with you on that one,' said Andrew, looking at Loris, 'but at the moment the only thing I'm determined to do is enjoy a quiet dinner. I'm so tired and hungry that I cannot think beyond the now!'

'Okay,' said Loris with a smile, realising that his own zeal was driving his adrenalin levels up, 'I understand. Nothing further until Monday morning, I promise.'

They promptly helped themselves to bits and pieces from the various dishes the buffet offered and returned to their table, each with a decent-sized plate of food ranging in colour and shape. They ate slowly and enjoyed the meal, with Andrew also keeping a check on the time so as not to miss connecting to Professor Burg's talk on time.

Loris and Andrew finished dinner with enough time to comfortably move to the main lounge area to set up and connect Loris' laptop to the live stream. They fetched themselves a cup of coffee and each helped themselves to two of the scrumptious-looking desserts before settling down in the plush seating. Within a few minutes the broadcast came through.

Although Loris was not very eager to listen, he obliged Andrew and Professor Burg, to whom he had said he would tune in. He did not want to break his word of honour.

The size of the church where the professor was speaking could not be accurately determined as the cameras focused on him, the projector screen and the stage and not directly on the audience. From the few angles available, it seemed to be a simple, mid-sized building, with the usual musical instruments and basic lectern present.

An introduction was made and a few comments given at which time the Professor calmly and confidently began his talk. He spoke in general about design and its applications, referring to engineering processes, but as the topic of his talk was *Inspiration from Nature*, this aspect was kept at the forefront, with Professor Burg able to speak in depth about projects that he had personally worked on, providing insight into his experience and vast knowledge.

Although Loris was tremendously apprehensive at first, he quite enjoyed listening to the professor. However, the talk began to take a turn to his disliking.

'There are hundreds of examples in nature,' said Professor Burg, 'where engineers are being inspired by nature and copying nature. The reason is that bio-inspiration improves performance. Evolution predicts bad design in nature because evolution is blind and clumsy. On the other side, biblical creation predicts supreme design in nature because the Creator is perfect in knowledge. Bio-inspiration shows what is found in nature, and it is wonderfully complex. A leading evolutionist made this admission, "The evolutionary process faces constraints far more severe than anything impeding human designers."' [12]

'I knew this was coming,' moaned Loris softly, sitting up and gesturing with his hand at the screen, determined not to be indoctrinated. 'What are we going to get now?'

Chapter 18

Loris' determination – part 2

'**Y**OU see,' continued Professor Burg, speaking calmly and fluently, 'evolution is limited by what is needed for survival, and this is a huge limitation. It cannot add beauty or added functionality. The following has been quoted, "Evolution does its job as well as it needs to, and no more." [13] Creation has supreme design for God has no limitations. He is not limited to step-by-step change nor by what is needed for survival. I'm often reminded of the scripture in Job 37:14–16, "Listen to this, Job; stop and consider God's wonders. Do you know how God controls the clouds and makes His lightning flash? Do you know how the clouds hang poised, those wonders of Him who is perfect in knowledge?" God is perfect in knowledge, and we need to stop and consider His wonders. It's only in the last twenty years or so that engineers have been able to understand how certain insects fly, with such intelligence only now being discovered.'

Professor Burg then elaborated in greater detail certain points in line with his statement and provided pictorial and video explanation.

'Engineers are being taxed to the maximum,' continued the professor after his elaboration, 'to try and copy the unbelievable design and functionality in nature such as the dragonfly. How an insect is supposedly going to create itself with such sophistication is mind boggling!'

'Listen to this stuff!' exclaimed Loris quietly, scooping a chunk of his blueberry cheesecake and shoving it in his mouth. 'Ramblings, pure ramblings!'

'I often ask biologists,' said Professor Burg, unaware of Loris' distant objections, 'how they know that something like aerodynamic braking in birds could evolve by chance? They sometimes say to me that they do not understand aerodynamic breaking. My response then is that if they do not understand the mechanics and aerodynamics, how do they know it could evolve by chance? They sometimes say that they have faith that it could evolve by chance. They often say the same about insect flight, that they do not understand it but have faith that it evolved. I find this hard to comprehend. From my studies, creation is true and evolution is not. I give glory to God the Creator!'

'I want McKenzie to hear this nonsense,' said Loris angrily, picking up his phone as he stood up. 'Please send me the link to this live stream, Andy.'

Andrew promptly did so, and Loris walked away for a few moments to type a message to Professor Smyth while Professor Burg continued his talk. Loris fetched himself another cup of coffee before he returned.

'Professor Smyth isn't available at present,' commented Loris as he sat down, his usually composed manner once again on strike. 'Let me hear the rest of this rubbish!'

'You've missed quite a bit,' commented Andrew. 'The professor is drawing near the end of his talk.'

'I cannot say that I'm not relieved,' quipped Loris mockingly with a wry smile. 'It hasn't been exactly *inspiring* to me, to put it bluntly – excuse the pun!'

'To me,' said Professor Burg, drawing near to his conclusion, 'the lessons are clear when you get close to studying bio-mechanical designs and designs in nature: a) the natural world contains supreme design, not bad design. It's proved by the fact that engineers are copying nature; and b) bio-inspiration confirms biblical creation. I must make a note here that death and disease are due to the Fall – Adam and Eve sinning in the Garden of Eden. Bad joints are not due to bad design but due to the curse upon man as a result of the Fall. I believe that the Creator is the God of the Bible.'

Loris let out another groan and mumbled under his breath.

'Bio-inspiration,' continued the professor, 'is based on observational science or what some would term operational or experimental science. It's real science, whereas evolutionary theories are based purely on speculation. Science has not proved evolution, it remains a theory based on speculation. To me it's better to believe observational science, and bio-inspiration shows the truth of design in nature. Nature contains irreducible designs.'

'Just wait, my friend,' snorted Loris disapprovingly, 'until we've finished with our work!'

'I draw two big conclusions,' said Professor Burg, the WIFI connection to the laptop keeping his talking coming through consistent and clear. 'Firstly, God loves mechanical engineering for it's everywhere in nature. Secondly, there is a Creator because there are mechanisms such as the 4-bar mechanism, which are prevalent in design in nature that cannot evolve as all four parts are needed simultaneously. The best way that evolution could explain this is by claiming that there were several unusual "breakthroughs". In simple terms, such an explanation actually says that man has no idea how such an irreducibly complex mechanism could have evolved, with comment being made that in such instances, evolutionary history is occasionally punctuated by major transitions in engineering design! [14] Once again, the admission is that what we seem to be looking at is an amazing design.'

Andrew was well pleased with what Professor Burg had to say, but Loris had a very sour look about his countenance.

'There are those who have much to say about design,' said Professor Burg in conclusion, 'even calling the human body poorly designed and its internals a shambles. They are wrong, and what is worse, the most vocal in this regard have never studied design nor designed anything. They speak as expert authorities, but it's from a platform that does not exist, for they are not qualified in the science of design. There is a battle of origins between creation and evolution.'

'And evolution will win!' exclaimed Loris emphatically.

'It's a battle of worldviews,' continued the professor, 'not faith versus science. It's one worldview against another worldview – a biblical worldview where science includes God against an atheistic worldview where science excludes God. Based on my knowledge, observation and work, I have to ask the question, why should modern science rule out special creation? There's no reason to rule out a creator. Modern science and evolution rules out God without any justification whatsoever. The message that I get from bio-inspiration is that there is a Creator and that people are without excuse not to believe in a creator, as Romans 1:20 tells us, "For since the creation of the world God's invisible qualities—His eternal power and divine nature—have been clearly seen, being understood from what has been made, so that men are without any excuse." Creation contains things we may never be able to find out and wonders without number, as Job 9:10 tells us, "He (God) performs wonders that cannot be fathomed, miracles that cannot be numbered." Creation contains things that we cannot comprehend, as Job 37:5 tells us, "God's voice thunders in marvellous ways; He does great things beyond our understanding." God is perfect in knowledge, as Job 37:16 tells us, which was mentioned earlier in the talk, "Do you know how the clouds hang poised, those wonders of Him who is perfect in knowledge?" I declare that the Creator is the Lord Jesus Christ, who Himself came into this world to seek and to save sinners, the lost – all those who will come to Him in true faith and repentance. My hope is that people will not only come to believe in a creator, but come to know *the Creator* as their Lord and Saviour!' [15]

'That's enough,' groused Loris, quickly reaching forward and closing the website that was streaming the feed. 'Intellectual baboon! People like that should never be given grants!'

'Please just kindly remember,' spoke up Andrew, a little annoyed by Loris' response, 'that I fit into the same category as your "intellectual baboon"!'

'I look down on his words,' said Loris with a look of disrespect written all over his face. 'He deserves the criticism he gets – and so does anyone else who plays his lackey! It seems to me that there are three Creationists in the circles of science – you, your father and Burg – and for some reason I've had to work with all three of you at the same time! You should start a Mickey Mouse club called The Three Science Stooges!' Loris instantaneously realised that he had overstepped the mark but could not bring himself to apologise.

Andrew got up and went to help himself to a chocolate-chip muffin and another cup of coffee, deciding that an argument with Loris would only prove pointless; it was best left in the hands of God.

Loris sat brooding over what the professor had said, his very words gnawing at his flesh and eating at his soul. Vehemence rose in his spirit and a determined, hard look was upon his face. He was determined to use the professor's own newly-developed apparatus to destroy his very belief, and no-one was going to stand against him! A determined pride rose in Loris' heart and an arrogance filled his being, similar to what had taken place the night of Thanksgiving when he had stood out on his porch during the heavy downpour. He ate the last of his blueberry cheesecake, savouring its sweet taste and pleasant texture, just like he felt he would savour the sweet, pleasant taste of victory against the Christian dogmatism he felt was like the Great Bubonic Plague. Loris pulled out his book, *Beginnings*, by Donald Browning and began reading just as Andrew returned.

The one thing, however, that seemed to puzzle him was that in recent time his usual calm manner and relative degree of tolerance seemed to be yielding to a hard-core stand when directly confronted with the gospel and creation. He was not sure why, almost as though he was subconsciously resisting, in the only way he knew how, that which he felt sought to convict him of what he felt sure was not real. Loris momentarily balked at the thought, but the instant he began reading his book, his intent returned full force.

The flight home was uneventful, with both Loris and Andrew being very tired and keeping much to themselves in quiet solitude. Andrew slept most of the way, having passed up the snacks, and only roused himself for the breakfast that was served a short while before landing. Loris had engrossed himself in his book, drawing inspiration from its pages in the hope of following suit and fulfilling in reality that which was confined to fantasy in the black print on cream pages. He eventually got some sleep after one of the airhostesses had championed its value, but his mind was set and his thoughts lingered long into the night on what he purposed to achieve.

The behemoth eventually caressed the Central City International Airport's runway with gentle affection, and the plane was safely brought to its allocated parking on the apron. The three hours that Loris and Andrew had lost due to the time zone change while crossing the Atlantic had instantaneously been returned to them upon their arrival.

The long drive back to Ailensbury was also a quiet affair, with very little traffic and both men a world apart in their thoughts. The low moon lit the sky, but it seemed sick, a pale yellow rather than its radiant silvery glow. It lit the soft clouds directly in its path but with no great strength, leaving the rest in relative darkness to mope about and find their own way. It almost seemed to be aching for the moment when it could retire and allow the sun to beam its light and bring life to that which it could not.

The first hope of Sunday morning's dawn began to appear upon the horizon when Loris dropped Andrew off at his home. One thing the two men were both grateful for was that they could sleep in, Sunday's buffer being a welcome reprieve before returning to work on the Monday. Loris, however, also harbouring what he had set his mind to do, in his determination to stand firm and prove himself correct and the professor wrong, likewise desiring the dawn of Monday's workday!

Chapter 19

Loris pursues his purpose

'**W**ELL, my dear fellows,' said Professor Smyth, making jest of Professor Burg's way of addressing them, 'it seems that you've done quite well, and I'm sure Llewellyn will agree?'

'Indeed I do!' confirmed Dr Llewellyn Whyte wholeheartedly, causing both Loris and Andrew to smile. 'I think that Loris and Andrew have done a great job thus far, despite the difficulties encountered. The briefing just provided about BEAFT and trip to Bramford University over the weekend are greatly encouraging.'

'In the report from Professor Burg,' said Professor Smyth cheerfully, 'sent to me yesterday afternoon, he confirmed your effort and progress. He only had high praise for the two of you. I think he's assisted us all very well – despite what you may think of him, Loris!' Professor Smyth gave Loris a lofty look with raised eyebrows, to which Loris did not respond. 'Additionally,' said Professor Smyth getting back to business, 'the professor informed me that the new equipment would be airfreighted to us this afternoon, so we should have it by Friday.'

'I really want to get stuck into using it!' said Loris eagerly. 'There's still much to learn, but my purpose is that the work progresses, now that we've had a breakthrough. I'd like to avoid a lack of progress at all costs!'

'We know how you feel,' said Dr Whyte, having had firsthand experience of the frustrations up until the time Midge was extracted but not aware of Loris' additional desire, 'however, there's nothing we can do until it arrives.'

'There's still other lab work to be done,' interjected Andrew, 'so not all time will be lost until the apparatus arrives.'

'Yes, that's true,' agreed Dr Whyte with a pleased look, 'but at present it can wait a week.'

'Wait a week?' queried Loris, a little surprised. 'Whatever for?'

'Till your holiday is over,' remarked Professor Smyth with a smile.

'My holiday!' sang out Loris in disbelief. 'I haven't put in for leave!'

'Nor have I,' affirmed Andrew, also not sure of what Professor Smyth meant.

'Relax, gentlemen,' said Dr Whyte calmly. 'Professor Smyth is toying with you a little by not coming out with it. As a result of your extensive effort, the breakthrough last week and the tiring load placed upon you with the added trip abroad, we've decided to give you both this week off as a reward. It doesn't come out of your annual leave, it's a bonus. Wednesday is a public holiday, and we're filling in the rest of the week for you. BEAFT will not be here until the end of the week nor operational before the start of next week, so the rest of the work can also be carried over.'

'From when are we on holiday?' asked Andrew, quite delighted with the prospect as he was still very tired from the weekend.

'With immediate effect,' replied Dr Whyte, chuckling at Andrew's overjoyed look. 'I'm glad you approve, Andrew.'

'Boy do I approve!' exclaimed Andrew. 'I cannot fully express my delight and gratitude.'

'If Loris doesn't have any objections,' said Dr Whyte, looking at him, 'the two of you can be off, and we'll see you both next Monday.'

'No objections,' confirmed Loris, his thoughts having already turned to a task that he wanted to do.

After the men shook hands and exchanged general greetings, Loris and Andrew exited Dr Whyte's office, leaving him and Professor Smyth to continue chatting.

'Andy,' said Loris as they walked down the corridor towards the reception, 'I'd like to visit your minister, if that's possible. What is his name, and do you have a contact number at hand?'

Andrew stopped walking, having been taken by surprise at the request, and looked at Loris, who stopped next to him.

'His name is Mark Marsh,' replied Andrew, still looking at Loris questioningly, 'and I have both his office and mobile phone numbers. Without seeming to be nosy, could I perhaps assist you though?'

'No!' replied Loris emphatically. 'I want to see him. I want to present to your minister the fact of our breakthrough and imminent discovery, just like the story in the book that I'm reading.'

'Are you referring to the book, *Beginnings*?' queried Andrew somewhat baffled at Loris' purpose.

'Yes,' replied Loris, 'and the religious men who were approached by the central character in the story were unable to stand against a discovery that would denounce their faith. They knew they would have to buckle under it, throw in the towel and basically close their doors. You and I have differing opinions, but I want to present this to your minister, for I'm sure that with us on the verge of a major discovery that will change the way the world thinks about humankind and God, he'll not respond any differently to those in the story – I'm sure of it!'

'That's up to you,' said Andrew beginning to walk on again, with Loris following suit. 'I'll give you his telephone numbers, and you can see if he's available to see you. If he is prepared to see you, I would just request one thing, that you maintain civility please.'

'I give you my word,' responded Loris, realising that Andrew was referring back to his responses during Professor Burg's talk. 'I'll be forthright, but I'll try to maintain good manners.'

'I must warn you beforehand of another aspect,' said Andrew seriously. 'Don't be surprised if your story gets buried face first in the dust. Fantasy may just trip over the rock of reality in an ungainly, undesirable manner! Mark's not a character from a storybook!'

'I hear you,' responded Loris defensively, 'but I'm representing reality, not fantasy. We've got to a place where we're truly on the verge of a great discovery! Your minister will not be able to treat it as though it were just a story, nor be able to respond any differently to what I feel is a truth wrapped up in the pages of a novel – and I want to prove that!'

Andrew did not reply to Loris' comment and scrolled through his phone's address book as he walked passed the reception and out into the parking lot. He promptly forwarded Mark's contact details to Loris, and the two men parted company, heading off on their respective ways.

Loris wasted no time in pursing his purpose, phoning the

Ailensbury Christian Fellowship office from his car while leaving Microlab Industries' parking lot. He was able to get through to Mark, who was in a position to put aside what he was doing in order to see Loris immediately. Loris jumped at the opportunity and made a beeline for the church, intent on following the storyline in *Beginnings* and proving the accuracy of what at that point could only be considered fantasy. He was sure that he would succeed; particularly should they be successful with their discovery, which he was confident of doing, it would leave Christianity's foundation badly buckled and just waiting to crumble under its own colossal weight of the man-made edifice. He did not expect to find Mark off his guard, just unable to counter a prospect of reality with the make-believe, or in other words, he did not expect him to be able to face off fact with faith. Loris was sure that this would ultimately leave modern-man completely liberated from the fantastic inventions of ancient men once and for all and consign the Bible, Christianity and other religions to museums of history.

His thoughts whirled through his mind as he drove along, the early morning sun beating down intensely all around, almost in anger. The air was still and the surrounds silent, with the wind holding its breath almost in anticipation of what was to come. The few off-white, bloated clouds present hung motionless, having stopped to view what was taking place below.

Loris eventually spotted the small, neat but recognisable signboard indicating the Ailensbury Christian Fellowship and, unmindful to everything but his purpose, pulled into the cobbled parking area belonging to the church. He made for one of the parking bays nearest the church building and pulled up against the sidewalk. He hopped out of his car with energy and locked it before looking about him.

'If you're looking for the church offices,' called the gardener, who was tending the flowerbeds along the sidewalk, 'you need to follow the pathway round to the side of the building. There's no missing it.'

'Much obliged,' called back Loris politely, feeling that he would have found it anyway.

Loris made his way past the gardener, who promptly greeted him with a smile, and rounded the corner of the modest church. He could see that the gardener took pride in his work, with the soil neatly tilled, the colourful flowers bright and lively and evidence of an abundance of liquid refreshment having recently been carefully distributed over them all. The grass too was immaculate, with its evenly trimmed deep-green coat thick and healthy.

The pathway led Loris straight to the office entrance, where he mounted the few steps, knocked on the thick wooden door and opened it. Mark's office assistant welcomed him in to the oval reception, its grey-brick walls, tan carpet and abundance of potted plants all around giving it a naturalistic feel. The sun streaming in through the arch-shaped bay windows added warmth to the ambience.

'Dr Lang,' greeted Mark as he came out of his office, having been expecting Loris and hearing him introduce himself to his assistant, 'I'm Mark Marsh – Mark for convenience. Please come into my office.'

Loris greeted Mark and shook his hand. He entered Mark's office, and Mark shut the door behind them, having first given his assistant an instruction that they were not to be disturbed.

Mark Marsh was in his late forties and married to an attractive and quiet lady named Annabelle. He himself was somewhat on the quiet side too, even when he preached, yet he always came across with authority and purpose and never seemed to bore. He was an athletic person, enjoying outdoor sports and exercise and had a good sense of humour that accompanied his composed demeanour.

Mark's office was of average size and minimalistic. A computer workstation stood at the side of his general purpose desk, a simple book case against the right wall and pot plants, some on stands and others about the arch-shaped bay window that looked out onto the garden and flowerbeds outside, making the office pleasant and peaceful.

'Please take a seat, Dr Lang,' said Mark as he made his way behind his desk to sit down, a little unsure of what he would be facing. 'How can I be of assistance to you this day?'

Chapter 20

Missing the mark

'LORIS, if you please,' said Loris. 'No need to call me Dr Lang. Mark, my words will be to the point. They may even be distressing. Frankly, I must tell you that I generally see Christians as fools, believing what they believe!'

'That's one way of starting off on a good footing,' said Mark, a little taken aback by the basic insult but not fussed with the general opinion of some.

'I'm not wanting to try and make friends,' informed Loris matter-of-factly. 'My ultimate purpose is to address an issue and ask some questions.'

'I understand,' said Mark coolly. 'I wasn't expecting anything different nor had high expectations of your regard. I'm not sure though what you expect to gain from a "fool", other than perceived ammunition to further whatever your cause may be.'

'I'm not actually seeking ammunition for a cause,' responded Loris, 'but seeking to present you with a case that in the very near future will tear at the heart of your religion. Christianity is marked!'

'I see,' said Mark, leaning back in his chair, 'and what is this case based on?'

'Through Andrew,' answered Loris, 'you're likely aware of some of what we are doing at the lab.'

'Only what has been announced through the press,' responded Mark. 'Andrew doesn't disclose details, but I do know that you're working on trying to uncover something monumental in the area of biological investigations, if I'm correct?'

'You're correct at that,' said Loris, 'and that is the case. In all confidentiality, we're on the brink of discovering the source of life – the very core of existence. When we do, and mark my words, we will, it will prove evolution and disprove God! This is what I want to present to you, that our discovery will shake religious circles forever and leave Christianity staggering in its age-old traditions of intellectual ignorance. How will you deal with that, how will you be able to continue? Men will no longer tolerate religious shackles around their necks.'

Mark let out a heavy sigh, making Loris almost feel triumphant already.

'Loris,' said Mark sympathetically, 'you've missed the mark.'

'What!' exclaimed Loris huffily, his eyes alight. 'What do you mean by that remark?'

'You're automatically making the assumption,' answered Mark, 'that your discovery in relation to the origin of man excludes the existence of God, and thereby applying it solely in the realm of God as being man-made, a basic and crude figment of the imagination dating back to a supposedly primitive age when man could think and do no better.'

'I do believe that,' stated Loris.

'Therein lies two flaws,' said Mark. 'Firstly, you're taking your observational science and transferring it into the territory of unobserved theory as though it were interconnected, but it is not. You may have a view based upon your discovery, but then there may also be another view, and there is, based on that same discovery. In fact, you're faced with this very problem, for Andrew, your co-worker and equal in terms of the work being done to bring about the discovery, holds to that different view. If he had to answer your question, he would point you in the opposite direction – with regard to your observation, not your discovery. I see God having put him right there next to you so that you have a counterbalance to your claims. Psalm 4:2 tells us, "How long, O men, will you turn my glory into shame? How long will you love delusions and seek lies?" So, I see your application as missing the mark.'

Loris just looked at Mark, not pleased with what he had said but nonetheless in his office to hear what he had to say.

'Secondly,' said Mark, 'you're making the assumption that God is created in the image of man. By that I mean that man decides how God should be, whether it's in the form of self, animals or the heavens above, and that man decides how this God operates, whether in love, wrath, indifference and so on. There are two major problem to this: a) God is sovereign and not controlled by the commands of men; and b) His eternal presence is not influenced by temporal proclamations. God dictates the terms, not man!'

'With so many religions,' countered Loris, 'there has to be man-made gods fashioned from the figment of the imagination.'

'You're absolutely correct,' agreed Mark, 'but that doesn't disprove God. In speaking about Jesus, the apostle Peter through the anointing of the Holy Spirit said, "Salvation is found in no-one else, for there is no other name under heaven given to men by which we must be saved." [16] With 3000 plus religions in the world, most believing that all roads lead to God, this creates an issue, but the biggest problem that it creates for man is with himself – "no other name" means that I cannot save myself with my effort and my strength. There is only one Way and that is through Christ Jesus.'

'That's if you believe that you need to be saved!' snapped Loris.

'Ask yourself if you have ever told a lie,' said Mark, 'and if you have, where do you stand before an eternal, omnipotent, totally holy and completely righteous God?'

'If one existed,' answered Loris, 'He would know that I do what's right, and my good deeds would be enough.'

'Before an almighty, all-powerful, eternal God,' said Mark, 'your good deeds compare to an ant offering an elephant a leg up! As far as your self-righteousness goes, Scripture says that it is like filthy rags.[17] The apostle Paul also explains that the Jews missed the mark because they did not know the righteousness that comes from God and sought to establish their own, they didn't submit to God's righteousness. He continues to say that Christ is the end of the law so that there may be righteousness for everyone who believes.[18] True righteousness can only come through Christ, by faith.'[19a]

'You've already created a foundational flaw in your God,' stated Loris. 'One very good reason not to accept it at all!'

'And what is that?' questioned Mark.

'The character of your God!' answered Loris. 'You've just said that there's only one way to God, but I've heard it said that God wants us to *choose* Him, that's why we have a free will. So He gives me a choice and condemns me for making it – if it doesn't fit His choice or as you put it, His Way! What type of a God is that? What kind of a character does He possess! In itself, your

God has tied a knot that He cannot untie!'

'I don't see it that way at all,' responded Mark confidently, 'but it's nonetheless a very commonly raised objection. If it were true, it would most certainly be objectionable, but it isn't true, and the central point is on the word choice. I'll answer your question with respect to two aspects: a) with regards man, in other words, yourself and b) with regards God. In order to do so though, you need to answer me a few questions.'

'Fine,' agreed Loris, his speech a little clipped.

'You're a father,' queried Mark, considering his words as he spoke, 'with two daughters?'

'Yes,' affirmed Loris.

'As the father,' continued Mark, 'you love your "created beings"?'

'Yes,' confirmed Loris.

'You acknowledge your authority over them?' asked Mark.

'Yes,' replied Loris.

'You acknowledge your power to command,' questioned Mark further, 'and expectancy of obedience?'

'Yes,' answered Loris.

'You acknowledge your power of judgement to reward or discipline?' asked Mark lastly.

'Yes,' said Loris.

'On the basis of your affirmative to these questions,' said Mark, 'I'll present to you the following: you go to your two daughters, who are of similar age, and say, "I'm going out for a while. Do your homework and do not eat the cake because it is for tomorrow's celebrations. If you do as I say, when I get back I'll give you a chocolate, but if not, you'll be sent to your bedroom for the night!" One daughter obeys, but the other disobeys – not doing her homework because she sits eating the cake. As a result of this, you are pleased with the one and angry with the other – at the same time. At the same time you give a chocolate to the one who was obedient and send the one who was disobedient out from your presence! Were you right and justified in your judgement and conduct?'

Loris just looked at Mark, not answering.

'I would expect,' continued Mark, 'that you would agree that you were right and justified. So it's acceptable for man to conduct himself in this way but not for God? God's character is considered to have a foundational flaw based on what you would consider a righteous and just trait in your own? Rather a convenient and hypocritical accusation to lay at the door of Him who is a righteous and just God, don't you think?'

Loris continued to remain silent, a serious look about him.

'The issue is,' said Mark, 'that it's not a matter of a choice but a command. In the human example provided, you never gave your girls a choice but a command and a consequence. They exercised their freewill to obey or disobey, and they received accordingly, is this not so?'

'I cannot disagree,' responded Loris grudgingly after a brief silence.

'Now in respect to God,' said Mark, 'we must first note that He has declared that there are two kingdoms, and He views all things in this respect. There's the kingdom of light, which is of God, and the kingdom of darkness, which is of the devil. Because of Adam's sin, we are automatically born sinful. Man isn't naturally good as he supposes, God tells us that, and man too often proves Him correct. Those without Christ are considered by God as reprobates for when speaking to the church in Corinth, Pauls says, "Examine yourselves, whether ye be in the faith; prove your own selves. Know ye not your own selves, how that

Jesus Christ is in you, except ye be reprobates?" [19b] The meaning of the Greek word used here for reprobate is unapproved, in other words, rejected; by implication, worthless (literally or morally) — castaway, rejected, reprobate! Not a nice thought is it? But it is God's word, and it is His perspective when viewing the kingdom of light and the kingdom of darkness. It means that he who is without Jesus Christ is separated from God. For mankind, that is truly missing the mark!'

Chapter 21

Mark my words!

'NOW in respect to God and choice,' continued Mark, 'let me present it to you like this.'

Mark picked up his black leather-covered Bible from his desk and quickly paged to the scripture he wanted.

'Firstly, God to Adam: "And the LORD God commanded the man (Adam), 'You are free to eat from any tree in the garden; but you must not eat from the tree of the knowledge of good and evil, for when you eat of it you will surely die.'" [20] That is a command and a consequence, not a choice! Then there's God providing the Ten Commandments.[21] They are commandments, not choices. There are also the laws that followed directly after, which were not choices either but commands and consequences. When the Jews entered the Promised Land, God had them divide and stand on two mountains, Mount Ebal and Mount Gerizim. From Mount Ebal they were to declare the curses that God had pronounced for disobedience, and from Mount Gerizim they were to declare the blessings that He had pronounced for obedience. [22] Once again, they were commands and consequences, not choices. Then there's God to all men, where Paul says when talking to the Athenians about their many gods, "In the past God overlooked such ignorance, but now He commands all people everywhere to repent. For He has set a day when He will judge the world with justice by the man He has appointed (Jesus Christ)." [23] Again, no choice, just a command with a warning of judgement to come. Jesus says, "If you love me, you will obey what I command" [24] and "You are my friends if you do what I command." [25] There are no suggestions or requests, just commands. There's an authority over us, which we must obey! The word choice is a misleading term in the manner in which it is used. Do you follow?'

'Yes,' replied Loris abruptly.

'Let me go back to the example I used with you and your two girls,' said Mark. 'Would you not come home with a reward for both, having made provision for both of them to receive your blessing? You would desire that both have been obedient and thereby receive their reward. Even if you knew that the one was highly likely going to be disobedient, you would still bring home the promised reward for her because you're faithful to your word. Furthermore, you would desire both to be in your presence, sitting next to you on the sofa eating their chocolate. Is this not so?'

'I cannot disagree,' replied Loris, a little out of sorts.

'God is the same,' said Mark. 'He doesn't want mankind to be separated from Him. He doesn't want people to be classified in His sight as reprobates! He has provided the Gift; He desires all men to be saved and to come to a knowledge of the truth in Jesus Christ[26]; He desires that none should perish but everyone to come to repentance! [27] Scripture tells us that the wages of sin is death, but the gift of God is eternal life in Christ Jesus our Lord.[28] God isn't to be considered changeable, because He will carry out His justice. Christ's sacrifice is evidence that God will hold true to His word and carry out His judgement upon mankind. The choice that you have is to obey God or to disobey Him. The consequences are fixed, and it's now your choice!

'Listen to what the LORD said to the disobedient Israelites,' added Mark as he skilfully paged in his Bible, promptly finding the desired page in the book of Isaiah, ""Though your sins are like scarlet, they shall be as white as snow; though they are red as crimson, they shall be like wool. If you are willing and obedient, you will eat the best from the land; but if you resist and rebel, you will be devoured by the sword.' For the mouth of the LORD has spoken."" [29]

'That's all good and well,' countered Loris, 'but there's the reality that our discovery will destroy the gospel message and neutralise the effect of the Bible and religion on mankind, for it will reveal the true source of life! Mark my words, it will require that you have to at least change the view of the Bible and the message that you believe it conveys!'

'To use your scientific language,' countered Mark confidently, 'the Bible is irreducibly complex. You cannot remove portions of it without doing damage to the whole, and the functionality of it is also hindered when you alter the Gospel message. Therefore, we cannot allow "mutations" into the Word of God; they degrade it as all mutations do. As you know, mutations are never upward, they always degrade functions, they never enhance it. To deny God as the Creative source of the universe is to suppress the truth, and that cannot be done without consequence and damage to the society that does so. And to reject God as Creator is to deny the existence of absolute truth, leaving society to do what is right in their own eyes. Believing lies will always lead to rampant moral failure, which has been evidenced in the societies that have done so.' [30]

'Your outline,' responded Loris, 'is based on the belief that the Genesis account is true, but if we provide the answer for the origin of origins, the already strong consensus that Genesis is a book of myth will further oil your already steep and slippery path. What then?'

'I would dispute,' replied Mark, 'that there's a strong consensus that Genesis is a book of myth, for although there are many who believe it is myth, their "consensus" is irrelevant as they don't know God and are anyway opposed to His Word and authority over their lives. Even within "Christian" circles, there are those who believe what you claim, but I would question their level of Christian understanding, for there are two themes in the Bible, 1) what has gone wrong with our world, and 2) how can it be put right? The book of Genesis tells us exactly what has gone wrong, and the rest of the Bible tells us how it's going to be put right, or in better terms, how God Himself will put it right. Only God could solve a problem the size of our world, and He's going to do it by rescuing the human race from itself! Without the book of Genesis, the rest of the Bible would really not make a whole lot of sense. [31] Additionally, reference to God as Creator is throughout Scripture, both the Old and New Testaments, including God Himself referring to Himself being the Creator. Therefore, you cannot just remove the Genesis creation account and not have it impact upon the rest of Scripture!'

Mark picked up his Bible again and quickly paged.

'Regarding an "already steep and slippery path",' said Mark, having found what he wanted to read, 'Psalm 73:18 says regarding the wicked, "Surely you (God) place them on slippery ground; you cast them down to ruin. How suddenly are they destroyed, completely swept away by terrors! As a dream when one awakes, so when you arise, O Lord, you will despise them as fantasies."' Mark quickly turned the pages again. 'However,' he continued, 'Isaiah 26:4 says, "Trust in the LORD for ever, for the LORD, the LORD, is the Rock eternal." According to my understanding, it would seem that the shoe is on the other foot!'

'You fail to recognise one thing,' bit back Loris, unhappy with Mark's last comment, causing his politeness, that was already frail, to hang on a thread being rubbed against a knife blade. 'The Creation account is so simplistic, almost playschool in its account! How can you believe in it?'

'To quote Leonardo da Vinci,' responded Mark, '"Simplicity is the ultimate sophistication." God's incredible ability to present such a simple form about that which is so sophisticated must not overrule His genius or render it unscientific. Your alternative is evolution, which is based on secular reasoning. There's something to consider that limits the secular reasoning – testimonies versus speculation. The Bible is a testimony from the beginning, past, present and warning of the future. The theory of evolution is a speculation from the present, trying to answer the past, in anticipation of the future. Testimonies include witnesses, while speculations include non-observed hypothesis. The secular world is at a disadvantage because the Christian worldview trusts a witness – God himself – who created everyone and everything. The Christian worldview includes the evolutionists because God tells us that there will be those who trade Him for a lie. Reality plays out what God says, and this is where we have what you could term a trump card – prophecies! There are hundreds of prophecies throughout Scripture, many of which have already been fulfilled and many that are being fulfilled in our day. One of those prophecies is that in the last days, knowledge shall increase.'

Mark paged in his Bible once again.

'"But thou, O Daniel,"' read Mark, '"shut up the words, and seal the book, even to the time of the end: many shall run to and fro, and knowledge shall be increased."' [32] You, Loris, are a part of that increased knowledge. You are a player in fulfilling that prophecy whether you like it or not. Only an all-knowing, all-powerful God could know such things and see them accurately fulfilled. God clearly and firmly tells us this when He says, "I make known the end from the beginning, from ancient times, what is still to come. I say: My purpose will stand, and I will do all that I please."' [33]

Mark once again paged swiftly to a place in his Bible.

'The apostle Peter confirms the omnipotent, omniscient, omnipresent God behind the Bible and prophecies,' said Mark, 'when he says, "And we have the word of the prophets made more certain, and you will do well to pay attention to it, as to a light shining in a dark place, until the day dawns and the morning star rises in your hearts. Above all, you must understand that no prophecy of Scripture came about by the prophet's own interpretation. For prophecy never had its origin in the will of man, but men spoke from God as they were carried along by the Holy Spirit." [34] The whole of the Bible hinges on the first few chapters of Genesis, and if the prophecy throughout Scripture is accurate and stands as a faithful witness to God, why then should I doubt that which represents the foundation of it all? That would be foolish on my part. God is the beginning and the end, the first and the last. [35] He is from everlasting to everlasting. [36] He is the origin of origins and the true source of life!'

'That's not taking into consideration what we are likely to discover,' countered Loris, 'which when we present it to the world, will in itself likely turn people away from "the foundation of it all"! Men will seek to stamp out the Christian faith.'

'With your likely discovery,' responded Mark, 'you're not taking into consideration what I've just told you. The foundation doesn't have its roots set in the temporal but in the eternal. That which is eternal isn't dictated to by that which is temporal, nor can the flesh control that which is of the Spirit. In fact, men have tried in the past and continue to try in the present to destroy the Christian faith, but what took place nearly 2000 years ago holds true today. There was an attempt to crush the early church and stamp it out through persecution. However, the only thing that was achieved was its spread to all the corners of the then known world. We see this happening even today in many countries where the gospel is suppressed. You cannot kick against the goad, as Jesus said to the apostle Paul. God is eternal, and His purposes are eternal. What He has said will be, will be, and no man can undo that – no matter what man feels he has discovered or will discover, nothing can undermine it!

'You see, truth can never be destroyed, even if it's denounced, for God is truth and His word stands true forever. Truth conforms to reality, for truth is reality, and it connects to the spiritual. Psalm 119:160 tells us, "All your words are true; all your righteous laws are eternal" and as Numbers 23:19a says, "God is not a man, that He should lie, nor a son of man, that He should change His mind." A great danger lies in the fact that where lack of knowledge is bliss, it is foolishness to be wise. Your efforts are honourable in the practical work that you're doing but misdirected in your worldview application. I hope with all my heart that you succeed in your discovery, also because Andrew is involved, and I know his efforts and desire to succeed certainly equal yours. I have to tell you though that I do not fear it, for it will never unsteady the Rock of our salvation, Jesus Christ, nor the true church, which is founded through repentance and faith in Him. For although you may overthrow the faith of some, nevertheless, the solid foundation of God will stand [37] – mark my words!'

Chapter 22

Off to see The Ark

'WELL, that's that!' said Loris, recoiling a little at Mark's calm but emphatic confidence in the Word of God. 'It's your zealous opinion against my soon discovery. We'll see! You stick to the Ark, and I'll sail in a little added comfort on a more modern cruise ship.'

'The Titanic isn't a cruise ship I'd want to sail on,' remarked Mark quickly, 'and it's going full steam ahead while evolution plays host to its travellers! The ark, remember, landed its passengers safely on dry ground, with not one missing – and it would have done so with 2435 passengers too!'

'Yes, indeed!' responded Loris, 'I'm not one who subscribes to the account, but I understand that according to the legend, the Ark survived the ordeal. Answer me one further question,' requested Loris. 'Where did God come from? How can a spiritual force have an impact on a material universe to create it?'

'Your question,' replied Mark, having first given some thought to it, 'shows your misconception of God because the God of the Bible is not affected by time, space or matter. If He was affected by it, He would not be God. Time, space and matter all have to come into existence at the same instant because if there was matter but no space, where would you put it? If there was matter and space but no time, when would you put it? You cannot have any one of the three independently; they have to come into existence simultaneously. The Bible provides the answer in this way: "In the beginning (there is time) God created the heavens (there is space) and the earth (there is matter)."' [38]

Loris looked at Mark, his deep-set eyes sinking further into their sockets.

'God is a triune God,' continued Mark steadily, 'and in time, space and matter, you have a trinity of trinities provided as well. In time, you have past, present, future. In space, you have length, width, height. In matter, you have solid, liquid, gas. You have a trinity of trinities created instantaneously, and the God who created them has to be outside of them. The God who created this universe is above it, beyond it, in it and through it – He's not affected by it! With the concept that a spiritual force cannot have any effect on a material body, you would then have to explain things like emotions, love, hatred, envy, jealousy and rationality. If a person's brain is just a random collection of chemicals that were formed by chance over billions of years, how could you trust your own reasoning processes and the thoughts that you think?'[39]

Mark paused for a moment, clearly in thought.

'There's one further aspect about how a spiritual force can have an impact on a material universe to create it,' said Mark, sitting forward and looking intently at Loris, 'and that's in respect to words. You have a spirit within your material body, do you not? Your words are not material, but they influence and impact greatly upon the material world. They influence your work and your family. You use that which doesn't have a material characteristic more than you use your material body, and the impact is far greater and wider than what you can influence with your hands and body. You speak, and people stop and listen. You command, and your children obey. You request, and the shopkeeper or restaurant responds accordingly. This is all influenced by words, which have no material presence to them.'

'But they can see me!' countered Loris strongly.

'That isn't an argument that can be used,' stated Mark, still looking at Loris intensely, 'for what about the phone? This aspect is even more clear when you conduct the examples provided over the phone. Nobody can see you, there's no physical being. They may not even know you or what you look like, but the spirit within you, which is not material, dramatically influences and impacts – creating what it is that you desire, whether it be stock for the lab, clean and tidy bedrooms, combed hair and brushed teeth or a pizza that gets delivered! By your word a house can be built or a wall torn down – and in either action, what influence did your material being have on it? Nothing. It could be done with just the breath of your mouth, with no-one ever knowing who you are, just your name, your authority and your instruction being required!

'The Bible tells us in Genesis 1' continued Mark as he picked up his Bible and opened it at the beginning, 'that God spoke when it came to Creation: "And God *said*, 'Let there be light'"; "And God *said*, 'Let there be an expanse between the waters to separate water from water'"; "And God *said*, 'Let the water under the sky be gathered to one place, and let dry ground appear.' And it was so"; "And God *said*, 'Let there be lights in the expanse of the sky to separate the day from the night'"; "And God *said*, 'Let the water teem with living creatures, and let birds fly above the earth across the expanse of the sky'"; "And God *said*, 'Let the land produce living creatures according to their kinds,'"'

Mark paused briefly as he flipped the thin, delicate pages to another book.

'Psalm 33:6 confirms this,' continued Mark, 'when it says, "By the word of the LORD were the heavens made, their starry host by the breath of His mouth." Verse nine tells us that, "He spoke, and it came to be; He commanded, and it stood firm." Where in all of this was there anything different from the way you operate on a daily basis, with respect to the word of your mouth? Why then is it not possible for a spiritual force to have an impact on a material universe to create it? Man doesn't like this, for it automatically raises a superior authority over him to which he must be accountable. In fact, Psalm 33:8 brings this to our attention in direct link to God the Creator for it says, "Let all the earth fear the LORD; let all the people of the world revere Him." It then goes on in verse nine to say, "For He spoke, and it came to be; He commanded, and it stood firm". When you acknowledge the Creator, you have to acknowledge that He is Sovereign and Supreme.'

Mark paused while he closed his Bible and put it down gently before him on the desk.

'Furthermore,' said Mark, resuming, 'throughout Scripture, spirit beings such as angels and even the Angel of the LORD, who is the LORD Himself and believed to be Jesus, have come to earth in bodily form. So, if they are able to operate in the material world, why could God not have created a material world? Additionally, the gospel of John tells us that through Jesus all things were made, and that without Him nothing was made that has been made.[40] If Jesus, who came in the flesh, was directly involved in Creation, how can we actually question how a spiritual force could impact on a material universe to create it? If the question then changes to how God could create from nothing, why would you raise objection? Criticism cannot be levelled here, for evolutionists believe in the principle of nothing and do not know where the materials came from! However, creationists have a source, being God – an all-powerful, all-knowledgeable God whose wisdom transcends man's understanding. Evolutionists have no source at all, for they claim it *all* came from nothing, but logic should tell you that nobody multiplied by nothing simply cannot equal everything!'

'Tell me,' asked Loris as he quickly stood up, feeling that there was no reason to continue the discussion any further with Mark, 'where do you get your information and resources from with respect to creation and evolution topics?'

'I have a number of resources I turn to,' responded Mark, 'such as Creation Ministries International and Answers in Genesis – CMI and AiG for short. There's also the Institute for Creation Research, and Biblical Science Institute, amongst others who also provide answers in defence of the Christian worldview and analysis of evolutionary claims.[41]

'CMI, AiG!' exclaimed Loris scornfully, the names unfamiliar to him. 'Who are they, and what do they know? What claim to fame do they have? They took science until the 10th grade, I suppose!'

'Your coarse disrespect isn't well directed,' rebuked Mark calmly, maintaining composure in the face of Loris' outburst, 'for they are all graduates, most of them with PhD's in the various faculties of science – biologists, physicists, astrophysicists, geologists and the like.'

'Oh, I see!' said Loris rather disbelievingly, with a great blob of sarcasm. 'I wasn't aware that there were more than about three persons fitting the bill, and I already know all three – Andrew, his father and a certain Professor Burg!'

'I detect your sarcasm, Loris,' said Mark, not too pleased with Loris' manner but keeping self-control. 'Please forgive my lack of respect, but your lack of knowledge in this respect is not becoming of you. There are a great many highly qualified men and woman who stand strongly in favour of the creation account, whose lives are dedicated to the LORD their God and who serve the sciences and related fields honourably. They're also not alone, having predecessors such as Copernicus, Galileo, Kepler, Newton and others – great scientists – who held to the same worldview. I'm no expert in any of the fields of science and couldn't competently stand up in a debate on any subject. However, I do not consult with myself or exalt my own knowledge, I seek it from those who know and understand these types of things, and I screen it through Scripture, as do they, which is the yardstick to measure all knowledge. Science isn't the issue, it's the worldview that is. Proverbs 1:7 says that the fear of the LORD is the beginning of knowledge.

'The same applies to my theology and teaching: I have studied, but I do not consult with myself in that sense or exalt my own knowledge, I seek the counsel of the LORD God by His Holy Spirit as I study and mediate on His Word – His works, precepts, principles, ordinances, etc. I seek that which is from a higher authority than myself and subject all to Him who is a higher authority than man – God's Word being the standard and authority He has given to us, which will never change!'

'Thank you for your time,' said Loris quickly, extending his arm towards Mark to shake his hand and not wanting to discuss it further. 'I appreciated you seeing me at such short notice, even if we disagree on a number of fundamental aspects.'

'My door is open to you, Loris,' said Mark warmly as he shook Loris' hand. 'You may not get from me the answers or responses that you want, but you'll get what I consider to be the truth!' Loris just gave Mark a clipped smile.

'I'll seek to run these issues past other clergy as well,' said Loris as he began to make his way to the door.

'Before you leave,' spoke up Mark, seeing that Loris was anxious to be on his way, 'can I make a suggestion? You mentioned the Ark, and it has just brought to mind a dear friend of mine. He's a Messianic Rabbi located in Brackenbury. Allow me to give him a call. He may be able to see you, and you can put before him what you've put before me. It will be worth your while to hear what that old wise man has to say. He's a stable fellow, you'll not get him to capsize. He will ride out any rough sea with ease. He's calm and easy-going; I've never come across the likes of him before – a great man, full of wisdom!'

'Give him a call,' said Loris, returning to Mark's desk, something having stirred an interest in his spirit. 'I'll go and see him, if he's available.'

Mark sat back down and promptly picked up his phone and made the call.

'He'll be able to see you any time after 12:30,' informed Mark as he put the phone back on its hook. 'He'll be at his home all afternoon.'

Mark wrote down the rabbi's name, contact number and address details on a piece of paper for Loris.

'Here you go,' said Mark, standing up and passing the paper over the desk to Loris.

'Noah Arkesden!' exclaimed Loris in disbelief as he began to laugh. 'You're not serious!'

'Indeed, that's his name,' responded Mark with a smile,

Loris' reaction a common experience when the Rabbi's name had been provided. 'His roots stem from Arkesden, a village and civil parish in Essex, England. To your further amusement, because of his stable and composed disposition, he's affectionately known to his close circle of acquaintances as The Ark!'

'So I'm going to see The Ark,' said Loris, finding it rather funny. 'I suppose he's a large man with three sons!'

'Quite the opposite,' mentioned Mark with a chuckle. 'He's a small man, with five daughters!'

Without further delay, Loris exited Mark's office and greeted his assistant on the way out. Mark accompanied Loris to his car and bid him farewell, with Loris maintaining a degree of friendliness, despite not being too pleased with the outcome of their discussion.

As he would only be able to see the Messianic Rabbi after 12:30, he first made a turn by his house before heading on his way to the small inland commercial town of Brackenbury, a central hub for many of the outlying farming villages and located an hour away by car from Ailensbury.

Chapter 23

The Messianic message

LORIS made the hour-long drive inland to Brackenbury, passing along the way many farmlands. There were colourful patches of labourers working hard out in the fields or groves noticeable everywhere as the warm sun, high and bright, not only brought sweat to their brows but also joy to their hearts as they worked their grounds and harvested their crops. There was not a cloud in the sky above, all having been gathered in by the great Harvester Himself and stowed away in His sky blue barn.

Loris pulled up outside Rabbi Noah Arkesden's small but neat house and parked his car against the curbing. The property was small, with the house occupying most of it. The small patch of grass and few flowers were neat and tidy, with edges trimmed square. It was an old house, but the exterior of it was fresh-looking, with the varnish on the wood of the front door and sash windows smooth and shiny and all other exterior features clean, painted and in good repair.

Having stepped up onto the porch, Loris rang the doorbell, causing a loud melodious chime to ring out inside. He then heard gentle movements coming towards the door after which it was promptly opened.

'Good afternoon,' greeted Loris politely, seeing the small, neatly dressed figure of an old man, 'I'm Dr Loris Lang. Mark Marsh arranged for me to come and see you.'

'Indeed,' said Rabbi Arkesden, his bright face exhibiting a warm and lively smile. 'I'm Noah Arkesden. Please come in, please come in.'

The Rabbi stepped aside, allowing Loris to enter.

'Please take a seat in the lounge,' requested Rabbi Arkesden as he shut the door. 'There aren't many seats, so you'll not get confused nor need fear getting lost in here.'

Loris chuckled to himself, having turned to the Rabbi. He had already noted the small interior, the lounge basically being only a few feet away from the front door, with a rocking chair and two single couches making up the seating. The interior of the house was open-plan, with not much effort required to get from the lounge to the kitchen or from the kitchen to the dining area, which itself merged with the lounge, but it was cosy and pleasant. There was a small guest toilet just to the side of the front door. The sleeping quarters were hidden behind a closed door.

'Forgive any boldness,' said Loris, 'I speak in light jest, but with a name like Noah Arkesden, you must be considered by many as one old man!'

'Quite so, my boy,' responded Rabbi Arkesden with a soft laugh. 'I'm often considered as the "original" Noah from the Ark. Believe it or not, it's a tag I've carried along with my Jewish identity since I was a youth, but I love it, for it often gives me an opportunity to poke one back at those who open its porthole in mockery or jest.'

Rabbi Noah Arkesden was a Messianic Jew, having served a

small community of Messianic believers for six decades. He was a small, slim man, with distinct Jewish features and a neat but thick and full grey beard that matched his still thick mop of hair. His blue eyes were strong, full of life and crystal clear. He was just past his mid-eighties, and although he moved about slowly, carried himself well. He spoke gently, and his generally slow movement seemed more related to his temperament than to any ailment.

'Before we start,' said Rabbi Arkesden, 'I've made some tea and will be having a biscuit or two with it. Can I invite you to join me?'

'I'm fine, thanks,' replied Loris politely, having already seated himself on one of the couches.

'Come, my dear boy,' responded the rabbi light-heartedly, 'it's not an invitation you can refuse an old Jewish man. You don't expect me to provide you with a tale of an old Jew who ate and drank on his own, do you?'

'When you put it that way, indeed not!' responded Loris chuckling softly, instantly drawn to the man, his manner and disposition interesting him immensely. 'I'll happily join you – a little milk and one sugar, please.'

Rabbi Arkesden carefully attended to the tea that was on a silver tray on the sideboard. After handing Loris his cup of tea and a plate with half a dozen different biscuits on it, he sat down. The rabbi first got Loris to tell him all about himself, his work, family and interests, before he got down to enquiring as to the reason for Loris' visit.

'Before I tell you the reason for my visit,' spoke up Loris, 'can I just ask you a question that interests me about yourself?'

'Certainly, my boy,' agreed Rabbi Arkesden, 'what would you like to know?'

'You consider yourself to be a Messianic Jew,' stated Loris, 'which is a believer in Jesus, correct?'

'That is correct,' answered Rabbi Arkesden. 'Yeshua is His name in Hebrew.'

'How can you be both a Jew and a believer in Jesus?' asked Loris curiously. 'Is it not considered giving up your Jewish identity to do so?'

'Ah, my young man,' said Rabbi Arkesden with calm manner, 'there are Jews who believe that by my accepting Yeshua, or Jesus in the English, that I've turned away from God and my Jewish roots. However, there's a lot of hypocrisy in it all too. Firstly, what really makes a Jew a Jew? Is it a religious sect, tradition, birth, nationality? Obviously it comes from a line of birth, a bloodline, with both the Old and New Testaments indicating that a Jew is a physical descendant of Abraham, Isaac and Jacob. However, we also need to note that it's recorded in the Old Testament that people who were not Jewish were able to become Jewish, and in the book of Ester it's recorded that many did as a result of the plot of the enemy of the Jews, Haman, coming down upon his own head.[42] These people were converts to Judaism, they were not descendants. So in order to become a convert, there must be something other than just a bloodline, for you cannot convert physically. Interestingly, Rahab who hid the Jewish spies in Jericho, and Ruth who was a Moabitess, were both Gentiles contributing directly to the royal lineage of King David and ultimately in the direct line of our Messiah, Yeshua!

'In my view, the highest point of issue is who created the Jewish people? The Jews claim their ancestral father as being Abraham, which is correct, but it doesn't stem from him alone. Abraham wasn't a Jew but a Chaldean, yet from him, through his son Isaac, the Jewish people stem. However, there's a source behind Abraham being the father of the Jewish people – God! And Isaac was the fulfilment of a promise of God!

'God called Abraham out of Ur of the Chaldees,' continued the rabbi, maintaining calmness but livening up a little, 'for He had a specific purpose that He wanted to work through Abraham, whose name was Abram at the time – it was the plan to bring through his descendants the Saviour and salvation to all men. This is what is the critical aspect – the call of God and purpose that He had for the nation of Israel.[43] In order to renounce my Jewish heritage, I would need to renounce my God, which I've never done. A problem arose after the time of Christ on earth, when certain sects of Judaism began changing the defining criteria from ethnic based to ethos based. In other words, they claimed that Jewishness was based on theology – namely that a real Jew was one who rejected Christianity and Yeshua as the Messiah. Scripturally this isn't true. This dispute has persisted up until today.

'At that time, Christianity was not a separate religion, but another group within the different groups of Judaism.[44] We need to understand that Christianity in and of itself is Jewish, for who wrote the New Testament? Was it not Jews? Who were the first converts to Christianity? It was 3000 Jews converted under the apostle Peter's preaching on the day of Pentecost! Who is the Christ, the Messiah? Is it not Yeshua, Jesus – a Jew by birth? You cannot take that away from Him nor from me! It's ironic and hypocritical that an atheistic Jew is considered more of a Jew than one who believes in the God of his father Abraham yet also accepts Jesus as the Messiah! I find it hard to accept that there are any atheistic Jews when one considers how Israel was formed as a people!'

Rabbi Arkesden paused momentarily, as though gathering

his thoughts.

'From a spiritual perspective,' said the rabbi, 'Messianic Jews aren't out of place at all, for they are still grafted in to the olive tree of God, which is a scriptural term used. The apostle Paul informs us that the Jews who have rejected Yeshua as being the Messiah are the ones who have been removed from the olive tree, and the Gentiles who accept Him, are grafted in.[45] Furthermore, Nicodemus, a Jewish Pharisee and teacher of the law, visited Yeshua one night. Jesus told him that he had to be born again or in another way of putting it, born from above, explaining that all of us have been born in the flesh but also need to be born of the spirit, as we are spiritually dead due to sin. By accepting Yeshua as his Lord and Saviour, Nicodemus would be born from above, or born again, receiving life to his dead spirit. Now if Jesus told a Jewish teacher that he needed to do this, then it means that it's not unreasonable for me to consider that I would need to do so as well. We know that Nicodemus did accept Yeshua as his Saviour, for he stood up for Jesus when the other Pharisees unduly accused Him and was one of the men who took Jesus' body down from the cross and helped bury Him.[46] Therefore, am I not following what one of our teachers did?'

'But the Jews crucified Jesus!' exclaimed Loris in amazement.

'The Jews had Jesus crucified,' responded Rabbi Arkesden calmly. 'It was the Romans who actually crucified Him, but that is a technicality, for the apostle Peter nonetheless lays the blame at the feet of the Jews when he says, "Let all the house of Israel know assuredly, that God hath made the same Jesus, whom ye have crucified, both Lord and Christ." [47] The reason for them having done so was due to unbelief. When they heard Peter preaching, they were cut to the heart, and many repented in accordance with what Peter had told them to do. As mentioned, the first believers in Jesus were actually Jews! What the world fails to recognise though, is that for 2000 years it has laid the blame of Christ's crucifixion at the feet of the Jewish people, but it was through the Jewish people that salvation has come to the Gentile world! It also needs to be remembered, like any situation in any country, not all the Jews were strongly opposed to Him; it was mainly the Jews in the south, the Judeans, not the Galileans in the north.

'Furthermore, my boy, if you aren't a believer just as they were not when they crucified Jesus, you too are one who stands shouting, "Crucify Him, crucify Him!" Know too that it was also your sins that made Jesus walk the Calvary road. Jesus took all the sins of the world upon Himself! It's needless for man to perish in his sins! Please, young man,' requested Rabbi Arkesden pointing across the room, 'will you bring me my Bible from off the shelf? It's the faded brown leather-covered book on the left side, lying flat.'

Loris sprang to his feet and fetched the rabbi's Bible for him. He did not have far to walk so was back sitting in seconds.

'Listen to this scripture in the book of Proverbs,' said Rabbi Arkesden, having paged carefully through his old and well-used Bible. ""I am the most ignorant of men; I do not have a man's understanding. I have not learned wisdom, nor have I knowledge of the Holy One. Who has gone up to heaven and come down? Who has gathered up the wind in the hollow of his hands? Who has wrapped up the waters in his cloak? Who has established all the ends of the earth? What is his name, and the name of his son? Tell me if you know!"' [48] Isn't that interesting. The writer refers to both God and His Son. Furthermore, he asks who has gone up to heaven and come down, and Jesus told Nicodemus that, "No-one has ever gone into heaven except the one who came from heaven – the Son of Man, who is in heaven." [49] That is Yeshua Himself!'

Loris just listened respectfully, not saying a word.

'Believe it or not,' informed Rabbi Arkesden, paging once again, 'that in the book of Isaiah, which has 66 chapters, there's *one* chapter that is known as the "forbidden chapter", and Jews do not read it – it's chapter 53. Listen to what it says, "Who hath believed our report? and to whom is the arm of the Lord revealed? For he shall grow up before him as a tender plant, and as a root out of a dry ground: he hath no form nor comeliness; and when we shall see him, there is no beauty that we should desire him. He is despised and rejected of men; a man of sorrows, and acquainted with grief: and we hid as it were our faces from him; he was despised, and we esteemed him not. Surely he hath borne our griefs, and carried our sorrows: yet we did esteem him stricken, smitten of God, and afflicted. But he was wounded for our transgressions, he was bruised for our iniquities: the chastisement of our peace was upon him; and with his stripes we are healed. All we like sheep have gone astray; we have turned every one to his own way; and the Lord hath laid on him the iniquity of us all. He was oppressed, and he was afflicted, yet he opened not his mouth: he is brought as a lamb to the slaughter, and as a sheep before her shearers is dumb, so he openeth not his mouth. He was taken from prison and from judgement: and who shall declare his generation? For he was cut off out of the land of the living: for the transgression of my people was he stricken. And he made his grave with the wicked, and with the rich in his death; because he had done no violence, neither was any deceit in his mouth. Yet it pleased the Lord to bruise him; he hath put him to grief: when thou shalt make his soul an offering for sin, he shall see his seed, he shall prolong his days, and the pleasure of the LORD shall prosper in his hand. He shall see of the travail of his soul, and shall be satisfied: by his knowledge shall my righteous servant justify many; for he shall bear their iniquities. Therefore will I divide him a portion with the great, and he shall divide the spoil with the strong; because he hath poured out his soul unto death: and he was numbered with the transgressors; and he bare the sin of many, and made intercession for the transgressors.'"(KJV)

Rabbi Arkesden stopped and just looked at Loris for a few seconds, almost as though he was trying to comprehend the magnitude of the chapter, although he had read it many times before.

'If you know anything about Yeshua's life, death and resurrection,' said the rabbi, 'you can easily see Him in these verses as being the Messiah. It's incredible when you consider that this is a prophecy made by the prophet Isaiah more than 600 years before Jesus' time on earth!'

Loris remembered Mark mentioning that prophecy was a trump card that Christianity had within Scripture, for it proved the power of an almighty, omniscient God.

'Scripture also tells us Jews,' said Rabbi Arkesden, having paged in his Bible to where he wanted to read from, 'that we'll look upon the one whom we have pierced. It goes as follows, "And I will pour upon the house of David, and upon the inhabitants of Jerusalem, the spirit of grace and of supplications: and they shall look upon me whom they have pierced, and they shall mourn for him, as one mourneth for his only son, and shall be in bitterness for him, as one that is in bitterness for his firstborn." [50] It's remarkable that here we have the interconnection of God and the Son – *Me* they have pierced, but mourn for *Him*, with reference to a firstborn. In the gospel of John, we are informed that God gave His only begotten Son, and Jesus told the Jews that He and the Father were one.[51] Messianic Jews are only doing what their fellow Jews will do later. How much better to look upon Him, the Son, now and rejoice than look upon Him later and grieve, having realised what they missed! If any Jew wants to claim that God is One, it is true, but in the application of being united, for right at the beginning of time when God made man, He said, and note my emphasis, "'Let *us* make man in *our* image, in *our* likeness'" and Scripture continues on to say, "So God created man in *His own image*, in the image of God *He* created him; male and female *He* created them." [52] So, right from the start, before there were Jew or Gentile, God is already established as being a unified Godhead of more than one – and we understand Him to be God the Father, God the Son, and God the Holy Spirit. This is in the Torah for every Jew to read! The Messianic message is not just a call to repentance and belief in Yeshua as Lord and Saviour, as the apostle Peter preached to the Jews on the day of Pentecost.[53] It's also that for Messianic Jews, God never changed, only His covenant did, but He told us in His Word that it would!' [54]

Chapter 24

Choose who you believe!

'THANK you,' said Loris quickly, seizing upon an opening to change the direction of conversation, 'that more than answers my question. It seems it all boils down to what or who you choose to believe. Moving on, you've just mentioned the creation account and indirectly how it impacts on your belief in a triune God, but it's a lie, a complete fabrication of myths! How then can you base so much on it?'

'My dear boy,' replied Rabbi Arkesden peaceably, 'it cannot be myth, for God Himself isn't myth. Have you perhaps heard of the late Herbert Spencer, an English philosopher, biologist, sociologist and loyal evolutionist?'

'Yes,' replied Loris, 'he created the Five Manifestations of Natural Phenomena, with everything being segregated into either space, time, matter, motion and force.'

'Come over here?' requested Rabbi Arkesden, gesturing to Loris.

Loris came over and stood next to the rabbi, who opened his Bible to Genesis 1.

'Please read the first verse?' asked the rabbi politely, handing the Bible to Loris.

'"In the beginning God created the heavens and the earth,"' read Loris, and then promptly handed the Bible back to the rabbi.

'Now look here,' said Rabbi Arkesden, pointing with his index finger to the verse. 'Let's apply those same five segregations to this verse. "In the beginning (which is time), God (which is force) created (which is motion or action) the heavens (which is space) and the Earth (which is matter)." [55] Little did the agnostic, Herbert Spencer, realise what he had generated, for within the very first verse of the Genesis account everything fits.'

'That may be fine on paper or in theory,' reasoned Loris as he went to sit down again, 'but not necessarily in practicality! In all confidentiality, and this is what I wanted to present to you today, we're busy with research, the results of which I'm expecting will tear at the heart of your religion and religion as a whole, and as you have clearly indicated that Judaism has religion at its heart, it will tear at the cause of your Jewish roots! We're on the brink of discovering the source of life – the very core of existence. When we do, it will prove evolution and disprove God, shaking religious circles forever! How will you view that, what will you do?'

'Ah, my boy,' responded Rabbi Arkesden with quiet confidence, 'that can never be, for we can never accept evolution replacing God.'

'Why is that?' questioned Loris, a little surprised at the response. 'What real evidence in the world do you have for God?'

'Apart from the universe,' replied the rabbi, 'all living things and mankind—'

'But those are debateable,' interrupted Loris quickly, 'for

there's the widely accepted evolutionary view to consider.'

'Debateable in your opinion, yes,' said Rabbi Arkesden, 'but not in mine and not according to Scripture. However, what I was going to say was that apart from them all, there's us!'

'Us?' queried Loris with raised eyebrows.

'The Jews,' clarified the rabbi. 'The very existence of the Jews is a direct sign of the very existence of the Living God. It may displease you to hear it but it's true. There may be secular and even religious Jews who are happy to accept evolution as a principle, but I cannot accept it purely and simply because we exist as a people. If God did not exist, He would not have called Abraham. Abraham's wife, Sarah, would not have miraculously given birth to a son promised by God to Abraham when they were both passed child bearing age. The miraculous events that followed in the midst of the people of Israel would all be myth, our Messiah and the Saviour of the world too! There's also the present state of the Jewish people and the nation of Israel that influences this for, in all humbleness, we're a miraculous people. After 2000 years the land has been restored to the Jews, our language has been restored, and prophecies about us have and are being fulfilled. It's unheard of and has never happened to any other people. You cannot override this practical outworking with some theory. We need to bear in mind that it isn't about the Jewish people but about God! It doesn't point to the Jewish people but to God – His power, His purposes, His Glory, His Word! And He said that He created the heavens and the earth!'

Rabbi Arkesden paused, not hurried to blurt out words.

'Further to God's word, the Bible,' continued the rabbi after careful thought, 'in defence of it, there's also the numerical structure that permeates throughout both the Old and New Testaments. The number seven is also a long flowing weave that holds it all together from start to finish. Both aspects are what is considered as God's watermark and His signature – you cannot overrule this either!'

Rabbi Arkesden then went into detail, explaining God's watermark and His signature to Loris. (The author does not wish to elaborate here as both God's watermark and His signature were addressed in chapters 24–26 of Book One, *Law and Grace: Journey to Calvary*).

'You can never take away from the source or cause as you put it,' continued Rabbi Arkesden, 'We will always go back to our origins – God, the Living God and Creator, who called Abraham! Allow me to run a quick parallel for you at this point. Genesis 1:1 tells us that in the beginning God... The Hebrew word for God, Elohim, is a plural word, indicating three or more. John 1:1 tells us that in the beginning was the Word. It is expounding upon Genesis 1. The direct Greek translation of John 1:1–2 reads like this, "In [the] beginning was the Word, and the Word was with God, and God was the Word. This One was in [the] beginning with God."(The Interlinear Bible) The full verse in Genesis 1:1 says, "In the beginning God created the heavens and the earth." Continuing on from John 1:1–2, verse three tells us, "Through Him all things were made; without Him nothing was made that has been made." John 1:14 tells us, "And the Word (which is God) was made flesh, and dwelt among us, and we beheld his glory, the glory as of the only begotten of the Father, full of grace and truth."(KJV) Jesus is the one who became flesh, so Scripture is clearly telling us that Jesus is the Word, and the One through whom all things were made. As part of the Trinity, He was clearly the Creator; therefore, there can be no evolution, for He *made* all things.'

'So, you would not renounce,' queried Loris directly, 'or

reconsider your religious view, should we make a great discovery?'

'No!' replied the rabbi definitely.

'Isn't that being rather dogmatic?' responded Loris.

'Dogmatic in the face of what?' questioned Rabbi Arkesden rhetorically. 'The psalmist David said, "The heavens declare the glory of God; the skies proclaim the work of His hands. Day after day they pour forth speech; night after night they display knowledge." [56] Through the prophet Isaiah, God says the following, "To whom will you compare me? Or who is my equal?" Isaiah goes on to say, "Lift your eyes and look to the heavens: who created all these? He who brings out the starry host one by one, and calls them each by name. Because of His great power and mighty strength, not one of them is missing. Do you not know? Have you not heard? The LORD is the everlasting God, the Creator of the ends of the earth. His understanding no-one can fathom." [57] Who do we believe?'

'That's from the Bible,' responded Loris boldly, 'but look at the back of the Bible! There's no list of anything, no significant references, no profound authors of authority! Your question is correct, who *should* we believe? I prefer science to a book without references!'

'My boy,' responded the rabbi gently, 'if you had to make that statement in all sincerity, it would be an ignorant statement worthy of reprimand and scorn rather than being any form of leverage and charge against the Holy writings! For just because a name is not credited or affixed at the back doesn't mean the name isn't affixed to the writing! My boy, please come here,' requested the rabbi, signalling Loris to come over to him once again.

Loris obligingly responded immediately, although he did not

see the reason for it.

'Look at the front of the Bible,' said Rabbi Arkesden, showing Loris, who was now standing next to his couch, 'what do you see?'

'A list of books,' replied Loris.

'What is that name?' asked the rabbi, pointing at a specific entry in the list of books.

'Ezra,' answered Loris.

'And that one?' asked the rabbi, pointing.

'Daniel,' responded Loris.

'And that one,' asked the rabbi, again pointing.

'Luke,' replied Loris, not too impressed with the silly questions but being patient with the old man. He found that he could not be annoyed in the face of the rabbi's quiet, gentle manner.

'Those are names of writers,' said Rabbi Arkesden. 'The Bible isn't a book per say, it's a collection of many different kinds of books – a library of 66 books, with 40 different authors, whose writings span a period of about 1500 years. The writings are in Hebrew and Greek, with some Aramaic. Interestingly, not one of the authors knew at the time of their writing that they were contributing to the Bible we have today. There is variety within the writings but also unity. The variety comes from the fact that personalities and different styles influenced the authors' writings. The unity that runs throughout the Bible is due to there being only one divine editor, God the Holy Spirit. The Bible reflects God Himself.[58] The apostle Paul tells us that all Scripture is God-breathed.'[59]

Loris remembered Mark also mentioning that all prophecy of Scripture had its roots in Divine influence, men speaking from God as they were carried along by the Holy Spirit.

'Now consider some of the authors,' said the rabbi, having motioned with his hand to Loris that he could be seated again. 'You have Moses, who was educated in the Egyptian University and who many believe was heir to the Egyptian throne. David was a king, the best king that Israel ever had. Solomon, David's son, was also a king and considered to be the wisest man alive. Many people came to him to seek counsel or just listen to his wisdom. His proverbs are widely respected and relevant to this day. Daniel was a prophet, but he was also a prince and learned man who excelled in Babylon through his abilities, wisdom and knowledge. Luke was a doctor, and the apostle Paul was highly learned, being a Pharisee expected to become the high priest. You did not have a bunch of monkeys sitting at typewriters under the guidance of a son of a brainlessly evolved rock! Choose who you believe!'

Chapter 25

The Word

'SECULAR society,' said Loris, 'has become too sophisticated for religion and the Bible.'

'That's only because of sin,' responded Rabbi Arkesden. 'The Word of God remains relevant to this present day and beyond. Take for example the fact that people can talk about wars but become uneasy when you mention that the Bible, more precisely Jesus, mentions that towards the end of the age you will hear of wars and rumours of wars, with nation rising against nation and kingdom against kingdom.[60] Why, what is it that makes people uneasy about the Word of God? They can handle heavy conversation, but the Bible brings heavy conviction – this is the issue. You see, Scripture tells us that the Word of God is living and active. It says that it's sharper than any double-edged sword, and penetrates even to dividing the soul and spirit, joints and marrow. It says that it judges the thoughts and attitudes of the heart.[61] This is the bottom line! The reason for this is that Jesus is the Word, and He is living. The Bible isn't some dead book, it's a book of life! It not only begins with the very beginning of our universe, it goes right through to the end of our universe and even beyond. The sin of man steers him away from it so as not to have to account for himself in the face of its conviction. What is sad is that people do not realise that by so doing, their sin holds them in bondage. Yeshua said to the Jews who believed in Him, "If you hold to my teaching, you are really my disciples. Then you will know the truth, and the truth will set you free."' [62]

'What is truth?' asked Loris casually. 'Is it not relative to each person or circumstance?'

'Pontius Pilot asked Jesus that very question,' replied Rabbi Arkesden. 'What he didn't realise was that truth was standing six feet in front of him. Truth isn't a proposal, it's a person. Truth is not something but someone. If you want to know the truth, then you need to have a personal knowledge of this person – this person being Jesus Christ! For then you will know the truth (Jesus) and the truth (Jesus) will set you free.'

'We have science,' responded Loris in opposition, 'which has many different branches, all of which are seeking the truth and the answers as to why things are. We can rely on them!'

'Earlier,' said Rabbi Arkesden, 'I mentioned that John referred to Jesus as being the Word. The Greek word for "Word" used by him is Logos. John wrote his gospel in a town called Ephesus, which is in Turkey, then known as Asia Minor. It's significant because in Ephesus round about 500BC there lived a Greek philosopher named Heraclitus. He coined the term logos, which was basically "the reason why". From this, all branches of science derive their names – bios-logos, biology; meteor-logos, meteorology; socio-logos, sociology; etc. Every branch of science is based on Heraclitus' logos, the reason why. The word crossed the Mediterranean sea to Alexandria, Egypt, where a Jewish philosopher named Philo, who lived at the time of Jesus and the

Apostles, picked up on it. He never deified it but said that the logos was more than an it and personified it in its functionality. John took the word logos one step further and said that you have got to ask about the reason why behind the whole lot – and His name is Jesus or in the Hebrew language, Yeshua! Jesus made all, is the root of all, and He died for all. We need to call on the name of the Lord!'

'Our own scientific investigation,' said Loris confidently, 'will soon provide an answer! We'll find the source, which is all we need!'

'Arrogance only breeds contempt,' said Rabbi Arkesden, paging to a location in his Bible. 'Listen to what God says in the book of Job, "Then the LORD answered Job out of the storm. He said: 'Who is this that darkens my counsel with words without knowledge? Brace yourself like a man; I will question you, and you shall answer me. Where were you when I laid the earth's foundation? Tell me, if you understand. Who marked off its dimensions? Surely you know! Who stretched a measuring line across it? On what were its footings set, or who laid its cornerstone – while the morning stars sang together and all the angels shouted for joy?'" [63] In Job 28, Job says that man searches the depths of the earth for all that is hidden – gold, silver, copper and precious things, but he asks the question, where can wisdom be found? And where is the place of understanding? He says that man doesn't know its value, and that it isn't found in the land of the living. Job goes on to say, "God understands the way to it and He alone knows where it dwells, for He views the ends of the earth and sees everything under the heavens. When He established the force of the wind and measured out the waters, when He made a decree for the rain and a path for the thunderstorm, then He looked at wisdom and appraised it; He confirmed it and tested it. And He said to man, 'The fear of the Lord – that is wisdom, and to shun evil is understanding'" [64] It's very interesting to me that the "Fear of the Lord" is linked to the power of God's hand in creation! God is not to be toyed with nor Him as Creator! Creation itself, which includes the creation of man, testifies to the Creator – and your own findings will prove the truthfulness of this statement!'

'Rabbi Arkesden,' said Loris, standing up, 'thank you for your time, but I must be getting on my way.'

'You're welcome, my boy,' said the rabbi, also standing up.

He went to the sideboard where his box of biscuits was and filled a small plastic container with biscuits.

'I hope,' said Rabbi Arkesden, handing the plastic container of biscuits to Loris as they walked to the front door, 'that our discussion has been of benefit to you in more ways than I can understand. Please take these to your children, and I'm sure your wife will enjoy one too.'

'Thank you,' said Loris, graciously accepting the rabbi's generosity, 'I'll pass these on. Even though you and I don't see eye to eye, the discussion has been very insightful to me. Ordinarily, I would have pitied you for being a fool to believe what you believe, but I've seen that you're a man who possesses wisdom in respect to your beliefs.'

'Ah, my boy,' responded Rabbi Arkesden, 'I on the other hand pity the one who says in his heart there is no God for therein is stupidity in great measure. I hope you find the answers you're looking for – search for them objectively.'

Loris gave a brief smile. Even though he strongly disagreed with the rabbi, he was drawn to him, his relaxed but confident disposition causing Loris to be careful not to permit aggression on his own part.

'By the way,' said Rabbi Arkesden, having opened the front door for Loris, 'before you go, answer me this: you mentioned at the beginning my name in relation to Noah's Ark. Do you believe in the Flood?'

'No,' replied Loris, a little surprised at the question.

'Then I must just tell you,' said the rabbi, putting his hand on Loris' shoulder, 'that your very denial of its occurrence is a confirmation of Scripture and of a prophecy, for the apostle Peter tells us that in the last days scoffers will come. He says they wilfully forget that by the word of God the heavens were of old, and the world that then existed perished, being flooded with water.' [65]

Loris gave the rabbi a clipped smile, remembering that the rabbi had said he often used the joke about his name as an opportunity to poke one back at those who mentioned it. He promptly turned and headed to his car and was soon on his way home.

The afternoon sun was burning brightly and directly into Loris' eyes, blinding him slightly. Even with his dark glasses on, he had to pull the sun shield down to help. He could not, however, escape its penetrating heat against his chest, his black shirt not helping the cause. Only the coolness from his vehicle's air-conditioner relieved some of the discomfort, but the sun's powerful effects remained unrelenting upon that which housed his heart.

As Loris drove along, he considered the adamancy of both Mark Marsh and Rabbi Arkesden, particularly the robustness and buoyancy of the man known as The Ark. He felt that it was total bigotry but could not deny their steadfastness in what they professed, as though it was truth to be believed and accepted. The outcome of the two visits had not yielded the results he was expecting, and although he stood opposed to what they believed, he knew in his heart that if he had to accept creation, it would automatically be coupled to him acknowledging the need for repentance and the acceptance of Jesus Christ as Lord and Saviour. Loris' heartbeat raised its tempo at the acknowledgement, and he breathed a little heavier, but this was not a thought that he wanted to consider.

He pooled his internal resources and rallied to his cause, using these two meetings to further fuel his determination to disprove God and proclaim the evolutionary source of existence. He knew that at present it ultimately boiled down to his word against what the rabbi had termed *the* Word. Loris felt the pressure – he had to make his discovery, and quick!

Chapter 26

A summer break at Ailen Oak Lake

'**I** WOULD love to come!' exclaimed Sarah over the phone, delighted at being invited by June to join her, Andrew, Tim and July the next day at Ailen Oak Lake for fishing and a picnic. 'I'm sure the girls would too!'

'So you'll come then?' asked June, pleased to hear Sarah's interest. 'We'd love to have you all join us.'

'The only problem is Loris,' said Sarah, suddenly a little downcast. 'As tomorrow is a public holiday, he's already planned to take the girls sailing at the lake, but that's in the afternoon when the wind is expected to pick up. I'm not sure if he'll want to join everyone in the morning, particularly not just at my request. Considering that I've now accepted Jesus as my Lord and Saviour, he sees me as a little problematic in the pursuit of his cause, having mentioned that he now not only has to deal with others who pursue the Christian belief but me as well! If I tell him that you have invited us, he may feel that we're ganging up on him.'

'Maybe Andy can invite him directly?' suggested June, the

thought popping boldly into her mind. 'I can ask him to do so, if you like?'

'I would like!' sang out Sarah, her eyes brightening again and the tone of her voice clearly expressing her appreciation. 'That would leave him free to answer as he wants to – the decision is up to him, no obvious pressure from me! But I really would like to go and picnic, things have been so tense and hectic with the research and everything. I could really do with a break, even if it's just a visit to the lake.'

'Hold on one second,' said June, 'here's Andy now, I'll ask him. Andy,' called June, seeing him disappear into the kitchen, 'please come here a minute?'

'What is it, dearest June?' responded Andrew, approaching her.

'Would you call Loris directly,' asked June, 'and invite him to join us tomorrow? Sarah is concerned that he might see it as us ganging up on him if she informs him of our invitation.'

'Sure, no problem,' replied Andrew agreeably. 'I have to speak to him shortly anyway about some lab details that were just brought to my attention, so I'll invite him in the course of our conversation.'

'That will be grand!' exclaimed Sarah delightedly, having heard Andrew's answer. 'I'll leave it to him and wait to see what happens.'

'Okay,' said June, 'let's see what happens.'

June ended the phone call, a bright smile on her face as she considered Sarah's manner, but in her heart she felt for her as well. She realised that there was likely much she was going to have to go through with Loris, particularly considering that he stood strongly against her now professed faith in Christ. It was not that Loris did not love Sarah, for he did, but what she now stood for bothered his conscience, compromised his convictions and put a hurdle before him that he felt he had to overcome.

June went to Andrew and taking his hand, mentioned her disquiet to him. Andrew patiently listened, aware of the concerns that troubled her heart. When she had finished speaking, they lifted a prayer to the Lord that if it was from Him that the Lang family join them the next day, that Loris would be receptive to the invitation. They also prayed for the family, specifically lifting Loris to the Lord, begging God for mercy and to open his eyes to the truth and reality of the Gospel before tragedy struck. Andrew then headed back upstairs to phone Loris.

'Loris,' said Andrew, having concluded briefing him about the lab details, 'tomorrow we're going fishing and picnicking at Ailen Oak Lake. Would you and the family like to join us?'

'Who all is going?' enquired Loris, not particularly wanting to spend some recreational time with George.

'Tim and July will be joining June and myself,' replied Andrew. 'We'll be leaving at about 9 a.m. Tim and myself have plenty of fishing tackle, if you don't have, and the twins are preparing plenty of eats!'

'I've already planned to take the girls sailing at the lake early afternoon,' replied Loris, 'so let me check with Sarah if they would like to make it an early start and join you. It sounds like fun! I'll call you back in a few minutes.'

'I'll wait to hear from you!' said Andrew, a broad grin on his face, knowing the outcome but not daring to tell.

'Hi, Sarah,' called June out Andrew's car window, with July waving happily from the back seat. 'Are you all ready to go?'

It was the next morning, and Andrew and June had fetched Tim and July. As the Lang family lived in the next street, they had pulled up outside their house less than a minute later.

'Nearly,' called back Sarah energetically, having just lifted a large basket of food into the back of their SUV, 'just two more things to pack in – Mika and Abigail! Loris is fetching them now.'

Sarah closed the back of the SUV as Loris and the two girls appeared at the front door. The two girls were quick to run down to Andrew's car to give June and July big hugs. Loris arrived soon after, having first locked the house. After brief, jovial greetings with their fellow companions, the Lang family wasted no time in getting into their vehicle.

July, June's twin sister, was also of medium height and delicate build, with a healthy complexion and animated expression. She had long, straight golden-brown hair and bright blue eyes. Just like her sister, she had a bubbly character that was natural and pleasant, not brash or attention seeking. Both of them were qualified physiotherapists, having also completed a special supplementary nursing course after graduation.

The large and posh, white SUV with its dark tinted windows was shortly in tow with Andrew's small dark-blue sedan as they headed on their way to Ailen Oak Lake. The town was a hive of activity when they passed through, with cars and people moving in and out of parks and shops like busy bees. They were soon out onto the main highway that would take them past the open farmlands to the lake, calmness resuming the throne after the brief encounter with the chaotic town. The pastoral lands were always sedate, the slow-moving herds never in a frenzy or care. The scene of restfulness and peace always induced a sense of tranquillity to passers-by, with the abundant green pastures infused with vibrant summer colours pleasant to even the least discerning.

The sun had risen early, bringing a bright morning with pleasant weather. A clear sky and the faintest of breezes left the day-trippers pleased and in joyous spirits. The conversation in Andrew's sedan was light and calm, while Loris' SUV was filled with giggles and chit-chat, the two girls occupying themselves with all the sights their eyes could take in.

The old rusty signpost with its somewhat faded and peeling brown lettering indicating the turnoff to Ailen Oak Lake had finally been put out to pasture, to the satisfaction of some and sadness of others. The new, gleaming pole and larger, green board with white lettering was far more noticeable even from further away.

Andrew slowed his vehicle and turned onto the gravel road that wound its way up to the lake. The tall, densely-packed trees shadowed the entire road, instantly dropping the temperature as they suppressed the sun's influence. Loris followed suit but hung back a little once they were on the gravel road, not wanting to inhale the dust cloud coming from Andrew's car nor have a rough piece of gravel fly up and chip the paint on his SUV or crack his windscreen.

'Here we go,' called Andrew, glancing at June and the other two in the back as they were about to exit the trees into the manmade clearing just in front of the lake area.

'Wooooo,' chorused the other three, their youthfulness expressing itself in one of their traditional practises over the years. 'Waaaaa,' they then sang together before bursting out with laughter as Andrew's vehicle was belched from the mouth of the gravel road and out into the clearing.

'Surely,' howled Andrew with laughter as he headed across the clearing to the edge of the grassed area, 'we're getting too old for that now!'

'Never!' exclaimed Tim emphatically. 'It's become tradition!'

'You would spoil all the fun of us girls coming fishing,'

responded July, before wiping some tears of laughter from her eyes.

'I see,' said Andrew. 'Then if June says "aye", then it's voted in for the next few years.'

'Aye,' said June keenly, taping Andrew gently on his forearm.

Loris' SUV soon hurtled out from the gap in the trees, and he followed Andrew, parking next to his car at the edge of the grassed area. They all climbed out briskly, pleased to have arrived safely and ready for some fun.

The natural wonder that had stood for millennia was picturesque in its glory. Beauty exuded everywhere you looked and as far as the eye could see. The trees, thick and green, climbed high up the sides of the hills all around the lake and into the distance, with peace and tranquillity etched upon every branch.

'A summer break at Ailen Oak Lake,' rhymed July with effervescence, her bubbly character overflowing at the pleasant surrounds. 'Let it begin!'

Chapter 27

A real cracker

'**I**'M anticipating a cracker of a time!' exclaimed Andrew, lifting the box of fishing tackle from the trunk of his vehicle. 'The weather is perfect!'

'Perfect for fishing, yes,' responded Loris, helping the girls with their stuff, 'but not for sailing – not yet anyway.'

'The forecast did predict that the wind would pick up in the early afternoon though,' informed Tim, 'so who knows what may happen later on!'

'That's what I'm banking on,' said Loris upbeat. 'I'm all for some fishing but sailing – that's my game!'

'We'll worry about that later,' said Sarah, standing holding her basket. 'Let's first enjoy the pleasant morning hours – it's so peaceful that it's uplifting!'

'I love it here,' said July, hugging her basket of goodies.

'You should,' jibed Andrew, 'for you have fond memories – ones that, euhm, others would rather forget!'

'That's mean!' snapped July as the others laughed, pursing her lips at Andrew the way she always did when he teased her. 'I have no doubt that you're referring to my hooking that sailing boat when I cast out my line for the first time. If you're not careful I'll set my husband on you!'

'Ouch, Tim!' joked Andrew as he locked his car. 'You up for a duel? With what we have at our disposal, it'll have to be fishing rods!'

'Oh, you nasty tease!' exclaimed July, flicking her head at Andrew as she began to walk away with Sarah. 'And to think that I'm pleased to have you as a brother-in-law! If we had a dog, I would secretly teach him to bite you every time you visited, and I'd invite you round more times than I do now!'

The others just laughed, and they all made their way across the grassed area to the water's edge under the trees, the two young girls skipping merrily all the way.

'Tell me, Tim,' said Loris as they placed their belongings in the shade under the trees, 'I've heard that your father used to live in some cabin in these forests, is that true?'

'Indeed it is,' replied Tim, unfolding his and July's brown camping chairs. 'The cabin, called *Forester's Cabin*, was formerly used by the forester many decades ago. Through contacts, my father had access to it and used it for quite some time before he remarried my mother.'

'Who uses it now?' enquired Sarah, interested in the tale.

'No-one,' replied Tim. 'My father is still the caretaker, and from time to time he and my mother spend a weekend there, just to get away and be quiet.'

'Sounds interesting,' said Sarah, her bright face not dulled by the shadows.

'Interesting if you don't mind a few multi-legged "crawlers"!' responded July, her face showing displeasure at the thought. 'There always seems to be a few out and about that like to stop by for a chat!'

'Have you stayed there?' asked Sarah, amused at July's expression.

'Twice,' replied July, 'and it's beautiful up there – restful and peaceful – until the "visitors" arrive!'

'That's when tranquillity bids goodbye,' responded Tim with a smile, looking at July. 'The poor blighters are then deafened and stunned by a shrill war cry, followed by an attack from whatever will flatten their miserable bodies into the surrounding woodwork or landscape. It's quite a sight!'

'Shame on you, Timothy Nicholls!' moaned July, blushing slightly but smiling nonetheless. 'And to think that I married you! You're worse than Andrew. Now if we had a dog—'

Everyone burst out laughing, knowing what July was going to say. She chuckled as well, clutching her husband whom she dearly loved around his waist.

After having placed everything the way they wanted it, the ladies settled down to chat, the men baited up their fishing rods, and the two girls began frolicking at the water's edge.

It was a glorious morning, warm and full of life. The birds whistled their merry tunes, quite contended to play amongst themselves in the tree-branches above, while the sun leapt and danced across the surface of the rippling water created from the few rowing boats out.

The morning was passed pleasantly, with each of the men managing to make a catch. June, as usual, wrapped up the catches in newspaper and placed them carefully in the cooler box with ice bricks. July also willingly spent a bit of time at Tim's side, plying her hand at fishing. She was successful, pulling in a nice catch, but as always, Tim had to release it, thus giving it a second chance at life. Snacks and cold beverages were enjoyed by all, with Sarah having also baked some small cupcakes for everyone, which the girls had beautifully decorated. A stiffer breeze began to drift in just past midday, with soft, cirrus clouds beginning to blemish the pristine deep-blue expanse above.

'Looks like predictions are going to be correct,' observed Loris, looking up at the sky and taking note of the change in the breeze. 'Sarah,' called Loris, turning towards her, 'I would not delay getting a sandwich into the girls, for I may soon be able to take them sailing.'

'It might not be a bad idea,' voiced Andrew, 'to get a sandwich into us as well. We've enjoyed the snacks, but for some reason I'm beginning to get hungry!'

'You're not alone on that one, cousin!' exclaimed Tim, also looking up at the sky. 'I'll happily use the changing weather as an excuse to grab a bite to eat, but then for some reason, when we come fishing, we always like to eat!'

'And since the days when the two of you started dating June and I,' remarked July, 'you've always been provided with plenty of dainties too!'

'That's true,' responded Andrew, 'and we're ever grateful that's for sure, but in all fairness to my mom, I do recall her provisions being equal.'

'Yes, dear brother-in-law,' said July in a comical manner, 'but hers came with a mother's touch, ours with a loving touch.'

'I see,' poked Andrew, amused at July, 'so the butter was spread a little more affectionately across the bread!'

'You pest!' groaned July light-heartedly, puffing her cheeks at Andrew in an attempt to show disapproval. 'You should be trampled on like a bug! You spoil everything! Next time I'll make you a few sandwiches with mouldy bread!'

'Grand idea,' quipped Andrew as the others laughed, 'I'll take them to the lab, and who knows what Loris and I may discover!'

'If you're not careful,' responded July, unable to hide a smile, 'I'll get Tim to take me to the cabin beforehand and provide you with some multi-legged "flatters"!' July softly flicked one of her flip-flops at Andrew, which he caught.

'Now what are you going to do?' asked Andrew, waving it at her. 'You'll have to either hop over on one foot or put your delicate toes on gritty sand and get them all dirty or worse, tread on an earthworm!'

'Help, Tim!' cried July laughing. 'I know I married you for a reason!'

'Quick, Don Quixote,' called Andrew, turning to Tim, 'your damsel's in distress!'

'I'm married, you nit!' scorned July, Andrew throwing her flip-flop back to her. 'I cannot be a damsel, even if I'm in distress!'

They all had a good chuckle, July going and giving Andrew, whom she loved like a brother, a gentle one-armed squeeze round his waist.

The two girls were given another quarter of an hour to play in the water before they were called. Loris reeled in his line and packed away his fishing gear at which time it was unanimously decided that they all should enjoy lunch together. The group sat in a circle quietly enjoying the tasty food. Cheese and tomato sandwiches, rolls with sliced beef and mustard, potato salad, spinach quiche, savoury biscuits and sweet treats were in plenty supply, along with soft-drinks of cola, crème soda, lemonade and bottles of water.

The breeze steadily stiffened, causing the lake's forehead to wrinkle and the ripples to lap harder against the embankment. The soft cirrus clouds increased their footprint across the expanse before gathering into clumps of cotton wool as they moved more hastily along in turmoil.

'I think we must get going, girls,' said Loris about an hour after they had all eaten. 'The wind is coming up beautifully, we'll be able to race around the lake.'

'If it's okay with the others,' said Sarah, 'I'll wait for you here. You can fetch me afterwards.'

She looked at June for approval.

'That's fine by us,' affirmed June. 'We'll still be here as Andy and Tim want to walk up to the cabin.'

'You can leave all your stuff here if you like,' suggested Andrew, 'and pick it up when you fetch Sarah. That way you can get going right away.'

'I'll do that,' said Loris, liking the idea as Sarah would have company while he and the girls were out on the lake. 'Look out for us, we'll sail past.'

'Not too close though,' warned Andrew jestingly, looking at July.

'Brute!' objected July. 'Don't forget that you once left one of the trees with a Christmas decoration!'

'I'm done in,' conceded Andrew raising his hands. 'You've truly got me there – hook, line and sinker, and float! It's probably still up here somewhere.'

'Okay, we're off then,' said Loris, picking up his set of car keys. 'We'll see you later on.'

'Be careful, girls,' cautioned Sarah, drawing them to herself and giving them a big hug, 'and enjoy yourselves.'

The two girls acknowledged their mother's request and promptly headed off with Loris, leaving the rest to fish, chat, relax or do whatever they wanted to do. Loris and the girls climbed in the SUV and made the short trek around the perimeter of the lake to the sailing club.

The sailing club's large parking area was overlaid with blue-grey stones, which were rough on bare feet, but they kept down the level of mud being walked into the small clubhouse located between the parking area and water's edge. The small, whitewashed clubhouse was rectangular, with a flat roof that doubled as both a recue lookout and gathering spot for general observers. Inside it was divided into three areas – the main clubhouse hall, storeroom for equipment and boating essentials, and a First Aid room that was capable of handling small emergencies until adequate help could arrive. Attached to the side of the building was a small office. During the summer season and vacation times, the clubhouse was open every day, with a mix of volunteers and paid staff manning the facility. The rest of the year it was only open on weekends and run by the members who had access to the facilities. To the right side there was a boatyard, with many different boats carefully positioned on trailers or dollies, idly waiting for their owners to come and release them from their bonds and set them free upon the cool, fresh waters of the lake.

Loris had a GP14 dinghy, which he had sailed with his father from before he was a teenager. His father had given it to him as a university graduation gift. He took pride in the little boat and cherished it greatly, having contracted a company to maintain its upkeep, as he never had the time to spend on its maintenance. He would never let it fall into disrepair in the slightest.

'Good afternoon, Dr Lang,' greeted Alex cordially, a young 20-year-old volunteer who spent much of his time at the sailing club, his father being one of the club's committee members. 'I'm sure that I'm the one you're looking for.' He produced a grin, knowing that Loris was going to need some help to launch his boat.

'You're never wrong on that one, Alex,' responded Loris, handing Alex a set of keys as he and the girls walked up to the clubhouse's main entrance. 'Please give me a hand with the dinghy, the girls and I are raring to go!'

Alex, who made money from gratuities, knew exactly which was Loris' boat, and while Loris signed in, he went to the boatyard to bring his boat round to the launch ramp. After signing in, Loris assisted Alex to make it a little easier for him. Once they had the dinghy at the launch ramp, they carefully removed the cover, and Alex folded it up.

Loris' GP14 was in immaculate condition, with not a spot of damage to be seen anywhere. The white hull was smooth and sparkling clean, with the varnish on the clear wooden decking polished and gleaming in the bright sun. The dinghy's name, *Mikail*, a Franken word derived from Mika and Abigail, was neatly written on both sides of the hull at the front in a colour that matched the deck's wood, the boat having been renamed after a complete overhaul. The rigging, pulleys, ropes and sails looked brand new.

Loris quickly checked everything, to see that all was in order, then removed the lifejackets that were kept inside. The girls promptly put on the bright-orange jackets, and Loris ensured that they were properly fastened before putting on his own.

'All set,' said Alex, raising his hand to Loris, having put on his chest-high waterproof suit. 'Ready when you are.'

'Let her roll,' said Loris after conducting a few more checks and finalising his preparation.

The aluminium dolly was eased down the slipway and into the water. Alex assisted in loosening the dingy from her bonds, and the dinghy happily shook herself free, instantly bobbing up and down on the water.

Loris and the two girls were soon out on the water and underway, Alex having brought the boat to the mooring embankment so that they could get in without having to get themselves wet. The wind had picked up even more, and the occasional gust was felt. The water became a bit choppy, but it was good sailing weather for the little dinghy that raced pleasantly along, the wind full in its sails. Mika and Abigail assisted Loris, having been taught the basics of sailing, but he did most of the work, particularly that which required some muscle.

On the other side of the lake, Andrew and Tim had packed up, the wind and waves making fishing a degree unpleasant. They had all put on their windbreakers and been sitting chatting pleasantly together, with Andrew and Tim now about to head off on their walk up to Forester's Cabin.

The sky began to cloud over in places, with large white clumps now everywhere across the blue expanse. One clump cast a nasty shadow over the lake as Loris headed in the direction of where the others were located. He had the dinghy whistling along, the girls loving it as the GP14 cut through the water, causing the water to peel at the bow, the wind whipping it into the air instantly.

Sarah had been on the lookout and spotted them coming. She took her phone from her bag and began filming.

Loris did not want to come too close in-shore, just in case there were fishing lines in the water, so at about 250 yards out, he planned to tack and sail parallel to the embankment. He warned the girls and began to shift his weight, slackening his hold on the sail in preparation for the manoeuvre. As he did so, a mighty gust of wind suddenly charged over the tree tops and down the hillside like an invading army, rushing at the little unsuspecting boat.

Loris was momentarily distracted by something in the water when the gust hit them. It wrenched the control of the sail out of his hand, flicking it violently. As Loris turned back, he was in time to see out of the corner of his eye the beam of the main sail snap round towards his head, but he could not react fast enough, and the beam collected him right across his temple with a cracker of a blow, sending him unconscious overboard as the dinghy listed heavily to starboard!

Chapter 28

Help and mercy

'Loris!' cried Sarah anxiously, jumping up from her chair as she watched the dinghy capsize, the sail landing right on top of him. 'Oh, no! Have mercy!'

Both girls managed to jump into the water, clear of the boat.

'Tim!' 'Andy!' yelled July and June simultaneously, the cousins having just started off on their trek up to the cabin. 'Help!'

Adrenalin rushed through Tim and Andrew's systems as they swivelled round, having been so startled by the blood curdling cry of their wives. They instantly ran back, looking to where July and June were pointing and seeing the capsized dinghy.

'Loris isn't surfacing!' wept Sarah, almost beside herself. They could hear the two girls yelling in distress for their father.

Tim ran straight for the water's edge, yanking off his windbreaker and shirt on the way and flicking off his moccasins just before entering the water. He ran into the water and began swimming with all his might.

Andrew had followed Tim's lead but had quickly made a

detour and grabbed the safety buoy from Loris' stuff, which indicated to other boats the location of someone in the water. He put the rope over his shoulder and was soon in Tim's wake palming the water with as much strength and intensity as he could.

The three ladies had run to the embankment, their hearts beating profusely as they stood there, Sarah with her hands over her mouth and nose. With bated breath they watched Tim and Andrew swim like champions but knew inside that it was a race against time they would not likely win.

The two girls in shock and bewilderment kept screaming as they paddled for dear life in the water, unable to see their father and not realising that their lifejackets were keeping them afloat.

'Hurry!' begged Sarah, bobbing on her toes, tears streaming down her face.

June sympathetically put her arm around her in an attempt to console her, but she knew it was nothing more than a gesture and prayed silently to God for help and mercy.

Tim reached the scene first, and seeing the bulge in the sail, knew instantly where Loris was. He ducked under the water and pulled Loris out from under the sail, his lifeless body limp and offering no resistance.

'He's not breathing,' informed Tim in a plosive manner, Andrew arriving a few seconds after he had surfaced, and trying not to alert the girls. 'Go round to the girls. See that they're alright and keep them distracted.'

'Okay,' responded Andrew, not wasting time. 'Here comes the rescue boat!'

The volunteer on duty at the clubhouse lookout had spotted the commotion and instantly dispatched a vessel. Tim turned, having heard the high-revving motorboat approaching. He dragged Loris around to the other side of the dinghy, away from the sight of the girls and in direct observation of the approaching craft. Within 20 seconds of him having done so, it pulled up alongside them, having raced across the water at top speed.

Andrew tried to calm the girls and keep them distracted while the two rescuers, their bright orange suits and lifejackets noticeable from a far off, lifted Loris' lifeless body on board. They placed him on one of the side benches and having a bottle of oxygen at hand, pumped half-a-dozen mouthfuls into him. The one man, having already tilted Loris' chin and head back slightly, conducted CPR, pumping his chest with the base of the palms of his hands. The other rescue worker quickly checked if further assistance was needed, Tim confirming in as few words as possible that he and Andrew would get the girls back to land. Without delay the rescue worker turned the boat around and raced back to base, intent on getting Loris into the First Aid room as fast as possible.

Sarah wept bitterly as she stood on the embankment and watched the boat race off, seeing the rescuer still pumping profusely at Loris' chest. She put her hands over her eyes and buried her face on June's shoulder, almost feeling that she was about to collapse from shock and horror.

Andrew and Tim managed to calm the girls a little, getting them to hold onto their shoulders, and they swam breaststroke next to one another back to shore. The girls had light frames, and the task was made easier with the fact that they were also buoyant as a result of the lifejackets, so they made good headway back to shore, the girls whimpering all the way.

Two small sailboats pulled up alongside them to see if they needed assistance, but the lads were close to land and managing, so it would have just been a delay in transferring to the boats.

The boats then followed as support. July and June had towels ready and waiting, with mugs of cola and some chocolate for the girls, knowing their likely condition.

'We're almost there,' said Andrew as he felt soft, slushy ground beneath his feet.

The moment he and Tim could walk, they swivelled the girls around, their little hands now clinging tightly to their necks, and carried them out of the water in their arms. Tim gently shook his head dejectedly, seeing July's questioning look. Her heart pained at the thought, and she had to swallow hard but dug deep to quell her own emotion, knowing that there were two little ones that needed attention and care.

'Give her to me,' said July to Tim, holding out a towel. June had said the same to Andrew.

They had the lifejackets off and the two girls warmly wrapped and lovingly in their embrace in seconds, speaking tenderly and consoling them as best they could.

'It's okay, girls,' encouraged Sarah as bravely as she could, bending down and kissing each of her precious ones generously, her heart throbbing with pain, 'you're safe now, thanks to Andy and Tim!'

'What about Daddy?' they cried, their fragile bodies still trembling from fright and shock as they drank some cola. 'What's happened to him? Where is he – they took him away!'

'The rescuers took him to the sailing club,' said Andrew gently, 'to give him urgent medical attention. I'll take your mother there now to see what's happening, okay?' Andrew gave June a despairing look but lifted his eyes to heaven.

Tim and Andrew quickly dried themselves and put on their shirts, windbreakers and shoes. July and Tim then took care of both girls, while June assisted Andrew with Sarah. He took her aside and quickly briefed her on what had taken place, only confirming what she had observed from a distance but had hoped may have been different. She dug deep, not wanting her girls to hear her, but she could not contain her emotion, and her body shook as she silently wept. They hurried to Andrew's car, and the three of them raced round to the sailing club. Sarah jumped out of the car and ran into the clubhouse.

'I'm sorry, ma'am,' said the man in charge, when Sarah enquired at the desk, 'this was a most unfortunate incident, but these things happen.'

Sarah nearly fainted and had to clutch the desk with all her might.

'Were they not able to resuscitate him?' asked Sarah tearfully, Andrew and June walking in just then.

'I don't yet know,' replied the man sympathetically. 'They have him in the First Aid room, and the door is shut. I haven't heard from them yet, but you can be assured that they're doing the best they can to save him. We've telephoned for an ambulance, which we expect to arrive from Ailensbury Medi-Clinic any moment now.'

Sarah turned away, putting her hand on her forehead as the riverbanks of her eyes burst full force. June embraced her warmly but was unable to contain her own tears at what Sarah was facing. Andrew just turned and walked back outside, feeling heart-sore for Sarah but also unable to see his own wife in such pains without it affecting him emotionally. He let out a heavy sigh as he looked up to heaven, crying out to God in prayer.

The wind swirled round, and the clouds covered the sun, causing the area to darken. Andrew felt an instant drop in temperature, and a shiver fill his body as the wind caught his wet pants and hair. He walked out to the edge of the embankment and just gazed out over the choppy water, his mind above the clouds in the throne room of God at His mercy seat.

He could see in the far distance a rescue boat at the location of Loris' capsized GP14 dinghy, helping to salvage it. They soon had it upright and after taking down the sails, began towing it back to shore.

Andrew returned to the clubhouse, entering just as the First Aid room's door creaked open. One of the rescue workers stepped out in front of him and promptly entered the main hall, heading with purpose directly to the desk. He was a short, stocky fellow, with heavy-set jaw. His brown curly hair pressed bountifully out from the sides of his cap, and his dark-brown eyes had a shine to them like the lustre on freshly varnished wood. After looking for confirmation from the man at the desk, who motioned with his hand towards Sarah, he turned towards them.

'Ma'am, I'm sorry for the wait,' said the rescuer solemnly. 'These things are never pleasant, but we have managed to pull him through.'

Sarah did not know whether to sing or cry for joy, so she did both – crying and half laughing with joy at the same time.

'He's very weak,' continued the stocky fellow, 'but slowly stabilising. We cannot tell if there will be any damage or not, that will only be determined later. However, we did manage to resuscitate him quite quickly and get oxygen into him, which in itself was a great help. He just didn't respond very well and is taking time to stabilise. We can do no more. We're expecting an ambu—' He stopped speaking, hearing a siren in the distance. 'I hear the ambulance coming now,' resumed the rescuer. 'They will take him to Ailensbury Medi-Clinic for further assessment and monitoring.'

'Thank you so very much for your effort,' said Sarah with deep gratitude, trying to dry her eyes with a tissue but failing miserably. 'I cannot express my gratefulness to you.'

'You're welcome, ma'am,' responded the rescue worker, tipping his cap to her and the other two. He promptly turned and headed back to the First Aid room to prepare for the arrival of the ambulance.

The ambulance arrived, and the medics were soon wheeling Loris out on a stretcher, his mouth and nose covered with an oxygen mask and a drip attached intravenously to his arm. They carefully loaded him into the ambulance. Sarah decided to go with him in the back, leaving Andrew and June, who had volunteered to sort things out for her in her absence. Without delay the ambulance pulled out of the parking area and headed for the hospital.

By the time Loris was taken off to hospital, his GP14 dinghy had been moored against the embankment. Alex and another volunteer kindly assisted Andrew in retrieving Loris' keys and other belongings that were stowed in the waterproof box on board the boat. They had the boat on its dolly and out of the water in no time at all. Alex declined any money when Andrew asked how much Loris usually gave him, but Andrew insisted and after obtaining the amount, quickly went to his car and got the cash for the young man for which Alex was very grateful. The cover was put on and the dinghy locked away in the boatyard. Andrew and June promptly left.

'Where's Mommy? What's happened to Daddy?' cried the girls, running up and clutching June as she climbed out of the car.

'Your daddy is going to be okay,' assured June tenderly, embracing the two girls simultaneously. 'They had to take him to hospital, and your mommy has gone with him.'

Tim and July, who had cleared all the stuff from their camping spot and placed it at the edge of the parking area, were greatly relieved, and their spirits lifted upon hearing the news after being on tender hooks until then.

'I'll brief you later,' said Andrew, taking Tim and July aside momentarily, 'but we can thank God! Here are the keys to Loris' SUV. Can the two of you take care of the girls until evening? June and I will stop by the hospital and take Sarah home.'

'All in a day's work,' assured Tim having first looked at July.

'We'll bath and feed them,' said July willingly, 'and bed them down in our spare room. They are clearly exhausted after this ordeal.'

After all had been agreed upon, the adults packed the two vehicles and headed on their way. Andrew and June went straight to the hospital to provide Sarah with support, while Tim and July travelled slowly home in Loris' SUV, the two girls having fallen asleep in the back before they had even reached the highway.

'Look at the two of them,' said July quietly to Tim, having turned and beheld them in the back. 'Little princesses! How quickly and easily their little lives could have been turned upside down today. What would they be facing if it hadn't been for God's help?'

'Indeed, that's true,' said Tim softly, but soberly, 'but where would Loris be, and what would he be facing if it hadn't been for God's great mercy!'

Chapter 29

In the hands of the Potter

THE two girls spent the night with Tim and July, Sarah only getting home very late and not wanting to disturb them if it could be helped. She was also extremely emotionally drained and was grateful for the additional assistance with the girls that Tim and July had kindly provided.

Under the watchful eyes of the medical profession, Loris managed to fully recover, suffering only from a hoarse throat, which he was told would eventually heal. He was discharged from hospital two days later, having been cleared to resume work after the weekend for which he was very grateful.

'Come in, you two,' greeted Sarah joyously, having opened her front door to Tim and July. 'I'm truly glad that you could make it.'

'So are we!' exclaimed July with animation, promptly giving Sarah a quick hug. 'Tea and cookies are always a draw card.'

'Hi, Sarah,' greeted Tim agreeably, 'glad to see colour in your cheeks and that you're more lively.'

It was Sunday afternoon, Sarah having invited them round

for tea in gratitude for the help they had been during the ordeal with Loris and the girls on the Wednesday just prior. Even though Tim and July lived in the next street, it was the first time that they had been invited to the Lang's home.

It was a beautiful house, full of character. Its lattice windows and high-pitched roof with attic windows gave it a feel from a fairy-tale storybook. It was a mixture of Sarah's decorative touch and Loris' lab-style orderliness; practical but homely.

'I told Loris that I'd call him when you arrived,' said Sarah, closing the heavy wooden door after Tim and July had entered. 'He's in his pottery studio, pottering about. People laugh when I sometimes refer to my husband as a potter!' Sarah chuckled lightly at her own joke.

'If it wouldn't be a nuisance,' said Tim, 'I'd like to see his studio.'

'No hassle at all,' assured Sarah politely. 'It's in the room behind the garages. Loris would actually like it if you took an interest! It'll give July and I a chance to talk about embroidery for a while without being frowned upon.'

Sarah gave July a knowing look, and in high spirits she quickly showed Tim out through the kitchen and pointed to the room.

'Afternoon, Loris,' greeted Tim as he stepped up into the outer room, seeing him sitting at the back at his potter's wheel, trying to work a piece of clay.

'Hi, Tim,' greeted Loris with his hoarse voice, looking up, 'nice to see you. Come on in. What do you think of it?'

Loris' pottery studio was another of his prized possessions. He ensured that it was always tidy, with his lab-mentality embossed on every shelf and work station. The studio shared a common wall with the garages along which were all the shelves and cupboards. Two large lattice windows with boldly pronounced mullions were separated by the stain-glassed door. Pot plants were hanging in all four corners, with small pot plants on each of the windowsills. Under each of the windows was a thick, sturdy wooden bench. Some tools were lying on the work benches but the majority were stored neatly on the shelves against the back wall, with bags of clay in storage totes stacked next to it. A washing trough was located in the corner at the back, just next to the potter's wheel, which had a purpose-built counter with a cut-out for the wheel. There was a firing kiln in the other corner at the back with a ventilation system, and rubbish bins were placed strategically around the studio. There was also one large shelf against a side wall that housed a number of Loris' carefully crafted creations. Lighting above all the work areas and terracotta floor tiles finished off the studio nicely, giving it a bright and pleasant ambience.

'It's impressive,' replied Tim with a smile, looking round. 'In all honesty, I like it a lot!'

'Thanks, Tim,' said Loris, his hoarse voice making him sound horribly sick. 'I love to spend time out here.'

'I can see why!' remarked Tim, walking over to where Loris was working.

'I'll finish up now,' said Loris, thumping a piece of clay that was on the wheel. 'I've been struggling with a batch of clay that just will not work nicely. This happens at times.'

'Carry on for another few minutes, Loris,' said Tim quickly. 'I'm interested to see you work the clay.'

'With this lump of clay,' said Loris, looking up at Tim, 'I'm not sure that I'll be able to produce anything decent! To my annoyance, it's likely to land up in Sarah's box!'

'What's Sarah's box?' enquired Tim.

'It's the box where all the unworkable clay gets dumped,' replied Loris. 'I shape it into medium-sized rocks, which Sarah then paints and decorates. She uses them for a rockery she's busy creating at the back of the garden. To me it's a waste when the clay cannot be used for something decent and useful, but so be it – that's life!' Loris sighed and promptly began spinning his wheel again.

Tim watched with great interest as Loris plied the clay with water, trying hard to work it carefully and draw it up into the shape he had in his mind. Twice more it failed miserably, breaking off out of Loris' hands.

'It's no use!' exclaimed Loris frustratingly, scraping off the clay from the wheel and adding it to the chunk already broken off. 'It's consigned to Sarah's box!'

He quickly shaped it into a rock and placed it on one of the drying tiles at the side of his work station.

'Come, Tim,' said Loris, getting up from his pottery wheel, 'it's time we joined the ladies for tea! I just need to wash up.'

'Loris,' said Tim a little reservedly while Loris was washing up, 'I don't want to seem like I'm bombarding you with the Bible, but having watched you trying to work that clay, I'd like to give you a very relevant analysis.'

Loris turned his head and looked at Tim, his arms up to the elbows in white soap suds as he scrubbed purposefully.

'Both you and I have been granted a great mercy,' said Tim seriously, 'for it could have been final for both of us – you, in fact, actually being brought back from the dead, if I may be so blunt!'

'That's the luck of the draw, Tim,' responded Loris, still scrubbing his arms, 'that's all. It's what happens in evolution – you heard Professor Jack Mertin, dean at Ailensbury, speak at Professor DeRoach's memorial. And that's what I believe it to be.'

'It may be what you believe,' said Tim, 'and in fact, it was what I used to believe too! Yet, what hope does it leave you with? What hope did Professor Mertin provide in his speech?'

Loris was suddenly conscious stricken, remembering his thoughts directly after the memorial service, having noted the empty vacuum within himself due to the very absence of hope.

'If anything,' continued Tim, 'the only thing that the dean emphasised was a hopelessness within mankind. Yet, why does man seek a hope? The heart automatically wants a hope. Why? Where does it come from? Is it from man's own inadequacies or is it actually divinely instituted because man has lost that which he should have had?'

Loris stopped washing and stood up, just looking at Tim and not saying a word.

'The Bible tells us,' said Tim, a little nervous in himself but not showing it, 'that man is appointed once to die and then the judgement.[66] Where would I have been if God hadn't pulled me through? Where would you be today? If we hadn't made it, what would we be facing?'

There was momentary silence between the two men as they looked at each other, Loris aware that these were thoughts he had previous considered but discarded.

'Before I read the scripture that I want to use as analysis,' said Tim, 'kindly allow me to give you my story and testimony. I'll not take long.'

'That's fine,' agreed Loris, bending down to carry on rinsing his hands and arms, a clean, fluffy towel lying on the counter next to him waiting patiently for him, 'go ahead.'

Tim explained what had happened to him, and how Mark Marsh had used the situation to bring to his understanding the reality of God and need to accept Jesus as Lord and Saviour (as per *Law and Grace: Journey to Calvary*). He went on to explain what had transpired between himself and July, and how God had mercifully prevented him being sucked into a vacuum of no return outside the pub, Down and Out's, when he had rebelled (as per chapters 22–24 in *Law and Grace: Divine Intervention*). Loris politely afforded Tim the opportunity to speak but reserved his own thoughts and opinions.

'There's an account in the Bible,' said Tim, scrolling through the Bible on his phone, having concluded his story and testimony, 'about the potter and the clay. It's in the book of Jeremiah. It reads like this, "This is the word that came to Jeremiah from the LORD: 'Go down to the potter's house, and there I will give you my message.' So I went down to the potter's house, and I saw him working at the wheel. But the pot he was shaping from the clay was marred in his hands; so the potter formed it into another pot, shaping it as seemed best to him. Then the word of the LORD came to me: 'O house of Israel, can I not do with you as this potter does?' declares the LORD. 'Like clay in the hand of the potter, so are you in my hand, O house of Israel. If at any time I announce that a nation or kingdom is to be uprooted, torn down and destroyed, and if that nation I warned repents of its evil, then I will relent and not inflict on it the disaster I had planned. And if at another time I announce that a nation or kingdom is to be built up and planted, and if it does evil in my sight and does not obey me, then I will reconsider the good I had intended to do for it. Now therefore say to the people of Judah and those living in Jerusalem, "This is what the LORD says: Look! I am preparing a disaster for you and devising a plan against you. So turn from your evil ways, each one of you, and reform your ways and your actions." But they will reply, "It's no use. We will continue with our own plans; each of us will follow the stubbornness of his evil heart.'"""' [67]

Tim shut the cover on his phone and looked up at Loris.

'Firstly,' continued Tim, 'God can and will work that clay, yet—'

'That's exactly one of my objections!' interrupted Loris hoarsely, his facial expression displaying his displeasure. 'Your God does what He wants, irrespective of man!'

'You miss the point,' said Tim. 'God does what He wants because He's sovereign and powerful! However, He also acts on the obedience or disobedience of man. That's exactly what God is saying here. He's giving man the chance to repent, even when He has pronounced disaster upon him, and if man does so, God will withdraw from carrying out His intention. God mentions the reverse for those who turn to evil after He has pronounced their good. That tells me that man has a direct influence upon what God does, and it's all centred around obedience and disobedience to Him.'

Tim paused, taking a deep breath.

'The second part,' continued Tim a little more calmly, 'a direct parallel that I wanted to draw in respect to your inability to get that clay to form into what you wanted is this: your hands were trying to create what your clever mind had in its vision for a messy, useless lump of clay. On your potter's wheel was clay without form or use, yet in your mind and through the working of your hands, you wanted to transform it into a vase or other beautiful creation useful to man. However, the clay wasn't pliable, it wouldn't allow you to create what you wanted. It objected, rebelled, was stubborn – whatever you want to call it, but it would not allow you to create with it what you wanted. That's exactly what God was showing the prophet Jeremiah. He was saying that He wanted to create something good from the people, but they wouldn't allow Him to. God ends by saying that the reply of the people will be, "We will continue with our own plans; each of us will follow the stubbornness of his evil heart."[68]

'That is the bottom line of the matter! God wants to create what is good, but evil men resist – like the clay in your hands – and rebel against Him, following their own stubbornness. What did God then declare? Destruction! What did you do with that lump of clay? Consign it to being a useless rock, when you wanted it to be something useful and of value. Men cannot stand and blame God for the outcome of their lives when they stand in defiance and stubbornness against Him. The Bible tells us that God hardened Pharaoh's heart, but before this took place, God told Moses that He was sure that the king of Egypt would not let the Israelites go, not even by a mighty hand. Scripture tells us that Pharaoh's heart grew hard – it was a progression – and that he sinned even more, hardening his heart more.[69] When the Israelites rebelled in the desert, God eventually said so far and no further!'

Tim opened his phone and scrolled to another passage.

'In the book of Numbers,' said Tim, 'God said to Moses, "How long will these people treat me with contempt? How long will they refuse to believe in me, in spite of all the miraculous signs I have performed among them?" Further on God says, "How long shall I bear with this evil congregation, which murmur against me? Your carcases shall fall in this wilderness."[70] This is why Scripture says, "Today, if you hear His voice, do not harden your hearts." [71] God deals with both the unbeliever, in Pharaoh, and the believer, in the Israelites. He knows the heart and what is thought and said in private chambers. To the Christian, God also tells us that we are not to conform any longer to the pattern of this world, but to be transformed by the renewing of our minds[72] – basically moulding to His ways and image, which is only done through the Holy Spirit, whom God gives us when we repent and turn to Jesus Christ. We have to yield ourselves to His hands. God has given you a second chance, Loris. Seek Him, for He says that today is the day of salvation! I pray that you'll submit to the true Potter, heed His warning and respond to His call. Do not allow yourself to be consigned unnecessarily to the waste bin of eternal damnation.'

'I appreciate your concern, Tim,' said Loris with a clipped smile, 'as much as I appreciate what you did for me and my girls, but at present I have something else to seek, which I anticipate starting first thing on Monday morning. It will give me the answer that I need! Come now, the ladies are waiting!'

Chapter 30

FLEA

'FLEE, you buzzard!' complained Loris angrily, waving his hand wildly at a small insect flying in front of his face. 'Go and harass someone else!'

'I see you're worked up and ready for action,' said Professor McKenzie Smyth, coming up behind Loris in Microlab Industries' parking area.

Loris was a little startled, having been so focused on this little menace that would not relent from pestering him that he was not aware of the professor until he spoke to him from behind.

'Indeed!' exclaimed Loris, waving at the little insect once more. 'A pure little pest.'

'Still struggling with your voice, I hear,' said Professor Smyth more seriously as they entered Microlab's building. 'How are you feeling? It's only been a few days since your unfortunate incident. Do you think you're up to the stresses of research?'

'The doctor said that I could return to work today,' replied Loris, stopping and looking at the professor. 'Kenny, BEAFT has arrived and is to be commissioned today. I wouldn't miss it for the world! I have a task to fulfil – an objective that I do not want delayed. Last Wednesday's incident was a blow to me, but I'm bouncing back. My body still feels a little weak, maybe it's the trauma of what happened, I don't know and don't care – our discovery is of utmost importance and urgent!'

'I understand,' said the professor. 'I'm with you on this one!'

'Thanks, Kenny,' said Loris, grateful for the professor's loyal support. 'In recent time I've also been up against Christian philosophy and creationist dogma. I haven't mentioned it yet to anyone, but Sarah recently became a Born Again Christian, basically throwing all my papers in the air as I now have to deal with her too! I've got to discover the answer and proof and silence the evolutionist critics once and for all! The drive in me to pursue this discovery is unyielding – more so now! We must succeed!'

'You've got my backing,' said Professor Smyth as the two men resumed their walk down the corridor towards the laboratory. 'I'll do whatever I can to assist. Your success is in all of our interests, mankind as a whole as well! I'm here to assist with the commissioning of BEAFT, having had a long chat to Professor Burg on Friday last week after it was delivered by the courier. He highlighted a few points and to put a flea in your ear, he's already working on a hunch he has that may provide an improvement to the already remarkable machine, can you believe it!'

'I can,' said Loris with a smile. 'After what I saw in his rooms at Bramford, the man has the brains to improve the improvement! It's just his blasted beliefs! He—'

'Let's not go down that road yet,' cut in the professor quickly. 'He's a good man, and your discovery will put paid to all dangerous and harmful beliefs. You'll be able to thank him afterwards for contributing!'

'You're right,' said Loris, the two men chuckling conspiratorially. 'Talk about digging a hole and falling into it! We need to focus on the task at hand. They will all be shocked when we're done!'

'But thankful too,' added Professor Smyth, 'for what you discover and reveal to them – don't you forget it!'

The two men entered the main laboratory area and headed for Dr Whyte's office. Andrew was already busy in Pepe unpacking the crate housing the new fluorescent microscope, BEAFT.

'Good lad,' said Professor Smyth upon entering Pepe, pleased at seeing what Andrew was doing. 'You've beaten everyone to it!'

'Morning, Professor, Loris,' greeted Andrew with a smile, having stopped and looked up at them. 'I'm as eager as anyone to get this apparatus operational. I think it's a tossup between Loris and myself who has the more itchy fingers!'

'Don't kid yourself,' said Loris lightly, placing his laptop on his desk. 'I beat you hands down on this one!'

'Never mind that,' said Dr Whyte enthusiastically, having come along after first having a quick briefing with Loris and Professor Smyth in his office, 'let's get this big boy operational!'

'Sounds like you have itching fingers too!' quipped Professor Smyth, his deep voice booming as usual. 'I think I'll hold my tongue and not let any of you know how I feel!' The others just laughed, knowing that the professor was as keen as them all to see this new piece of valuable equipment in operation.

By early afternoon they had BEAFT up on its shiny stand and slotted into the vacant spot on the lab floor that had been there since Pepe had been given life. All the cabling had been carefully connected according to the instruction manual and rechecked just for safety sake. Dr Whyte had the pleasure of switching it on and seeing his newly acquired apparatus open its eyes and wake up. After a few further checks, a briefing was held, George also being called in to attend. Once all the important procedures had been discussed, Loris and Andrew were left to begin the next phase of their research.

'Andrew,' said Loris, coming over to his desk after having packed away all the papers and operational manuals for BEAFT, 'just a word.'

'I'm all ears,' responded Andrew, looking up from his work.

'I'm sure you recall,' said Loris seriously, his voice a little grating to the ear, 'that when we discovered Midge we received a number of calls from universities around the globe.'

'I recall,' confirmed Andrew, having shifted his chair so that he could look directly at Loris.

'I mentioned to you at the time,' continued Loris, 'that there would soon be a number of players hankering after what we're looking for. Well, it's happened – and sooner than I thought. I had a quick meeting this morning with Dr Whyte and Professor Smyth, and they both confirmed having independently received news of a number of universities and research labs having put into place a program similar to ours. One such university is Bridgetown, with the appointed head of operations being my former colleague and good friend, Professor Dudley Kensington! Duke will stop at nothing if he feels that he has a chance to beat the world!'

'You seem concerned, Loris,' observed Andrew, taking note of Loris' facial expression. 'Anything in particular?'

'No,' replied Loris, 'just caution. We just need to be cautious with what we do and say that's all. This issue isn't my main concern however, for although they have some information, they are playing catch up. With this new apparatus, I'm sure we have a further advantage now!'

'I agree on that!' said Andrew emphatically. 'I know that we've got a lot of work to do and much to find out when it comes to Midge, but Professor Burg's machine is a timely acquisition in our favour for sure!'

'This is what I want to mention to you, Andy,' said Loris. 'We may have months ahead of us before we see the light of day, but we must keep pressing on, as I mentioned before. We need to do the best we can, it's important. Additionally, you know my intention. I'm here to do scientific research, this is my goal, but I'm also aiming to prove the truthfulness of Donald Browning's fictional novel, *Beginnings*! This may clash with your worldview and current Christian belief, but the results will be my defence.'

'Loris,' said Andrew, sitting up in his chair, 'my interest is the science behind the research. We'll both be working on this aspect with equal interest and importance. My worldview and Christian beliefs will not abandon anything in this regard. However, it will be different when it comes to how I personally view the results for to me it can only point to God. You're seeking some sort of nucleus-type organism that's basic in all its forms of functionality and has no further source, but in my opinion, what we'll find is something complex yet simple and efficient in its functionality. Are you familiar with the Mandelbrot set?'

'Yes,' replied Loris, a little put out by Andrew's attitude. 'It's the set of complex numbers for which the function does not diverge when iterated from, and it creates the most fascinating and intricate picture when plotted.'

'My observation,' said Andrew confidently, 'is that just the same as the Mandelbrot fractals never come to an end no matter how small you go [73] so too will our findings be. We'll never be able to find the beginning of that cause when there's an infinite God behind that beginning. Science has already proved this with what we have discovered. With technology we're able to find smaller and smaller things within things on the one side and on the other side, an ever-larger universe. I don't see it being any different now! The prophet Isaiah tells us that the LORD God's understanding is unsearchable!' [74]

'That's fine,' said Loris abruptly, 'you stick to your opinions for now. I just want you to know that we have pressure on one side and I have additional purpose on the other, which I'm determined to pursue for I want the answer!'

'I comprehend both,' assured Andrew devotedly. 'I'll be on my guard, and you can be sure that I have every interest in us making the discovery before others do!'

The two microbiologists spent the rest of the afternoon calibrating BEAFT and creating their plan of action. The following day they extracted a stock of kinesin from which they extracted a number of Midges. They began investigations and in between, finished up the work that had been held over by Dr Whyte while they were on holiday.

Day after day the two men ploughed away methodically at their task, exerting themselves in an effort to locate what they felt existed within this micro nano-cell. The difficult and exhausting task, however, progressed slowly, some days dragging sluggishly on. From day to day, week to week and month to month they worked away. The two men became experts at using BEAFT, corresponding on a weekly basis with Professor Burg to update him on how they were doing and to provide him with valuable feedback on the apparatus. Loris' statement that it may take months was proving to be correct, as once again the leaves changed colour, the weather began to turn, and the ambience outside lab life gave way to late November frost and rain.

'No go, Loris,' called Andrew, scratching his head in thought and frustration as he lifted his face away from BEAFT's eyepiece. 'I have a strong impression that I'm looking at something, but it's operating in camouflage. I cannot make it out or distinguish it clearly from the rest of the organisms in the cell. I've tried once again with the super nano-tweezers, but as I cannot see distinctly due to the "camouflage", I've been unsuccessful every time. We need something extra!'

'I'm ahead of you on this one,' said Loris, putting his hand over the mouthpiece of his phone, his voice having now fully recovered. 'I was watching on the monitor, and the same thought crossed my mind. I'm trying to get through to Prof— Hi McKenzie!' exclaimed Loris, turning away from Andrew when he heard Professor Smyth's voice. 'I've been trying to get through to you before you head off to give your lecture! The line's been engaged though. Have you got a minute?'

'I've been trying to get through to you!' said Professor Smyth. 'I have a few minutes. You go first, you sound more anxious!'

'Have you heard anything from Professor Burg lately?' asked Loris impatiently.

'I thought you communicated with him every week?' said the professor questioningly, his deep voice being clearly heard by Andrew.

'We do,' replied Loris quickly, 'but I'm referring to the advanced part that you mentioned months ago!'

'Oh,' said Professor Smyth with a light chuckle, 'that flea that I dropped in your ear.'

'Come, Kenny,' said Loris, deep expression in his words. 'I

can hear from the tone of your voice that you're keeping something from me. You know that Professor Burg has been cagey about what he's been doing – he'll not share it with us, the blighter! He keeps leaving us in suspense!'

'Only at our request,' said the professor. 'We haven't wanted communication flowing regarding what he's been doing. They also had some concern from their side.'

'We're desperate now,' informed Loris. 'As you well know, we've been leading up to this point. Andrew and I have come to the same conclusion – some things are operating in camouflage. You know that we've segregated everything that we could over the past months, but there's something there that we're looking at but cannot get at it. It's either too smart or too well hidden. I prefer the second option for I don't expect it to be too smart! We've both tried multiple times again today with the super nano-tweezers but it's useless, we just cannot define it clearly enough.'

'The very reason I was trying to get through to you, Loris,' said Professor Smyth. 'Professor Burg has been taking all our correspondence, which includes your weekly feedback, into account, and I have one word to tell you, FLEA!'

'Flee!' exclaimed Loris, baffled by the response from the professor. 'Why must we flee? What are you referring to?'

'Not flee as in take flight,' said the professor, greatly amused by giving Loris a little run around, 'but flea as in F.L.E.A!'

There was silence on the phone.

'Professor Smyth,' said Loris seriously, 'are you taking the mickey out of me? What the heck is flea?'

'FLEA,' said Professor Smyth with a big grin as he laughed to himself, 'has been scheduled to *jump* on a plane and be brought over by a technician in the second week of December.'

'And what is flea?' enquired Loris again, confused at this

point.

'FLEA,' informed the professor smartly, 'stands for Fluorescence Light Enhancement Attachment!'

235

Chapter 31

Security breach

'Is it possible!' burst out Loris, his voice raised. 'What animal did the professor use this time?'

'He told me to tell you not to ask,' replied Professor Smyth, his laughter booming through the phone and filling Pepe's internals. 'He said that you might not like the "animal abuse" – him stealing their design properties once again!'

Loris just laughed, Andrew too as he could hear the whole conversation.

'The professor told me that it was a hunch that he had had,' continued Professor Smyth, 'so he worked on it, and it's paid off. He was only prepared to mention that it was a very small parasite that did it for them this time. He said that the improvement isn't in resolution but in light sensors. Being very sensitive to green-yellow light, it can now detect changes in light and dark better. Specific details will be included with the attachment when the technician brings it.'

'You mentioned they had some concern on their side,' enquired Loris with interest. 'Have they had specific reason for it or was it just general concern?'

'They had noticed a potential breach of security,' replied the professor, 'with certain of their research files being tampered with and a possible confidentiality leak.'

'That's not good!' said Loris with concern. 'Any serious information?'

'No,' informed Professor Smyth assuredly, 'just a disgruntled student snooping and putting his IT intelligence to bad use. They also raised the same red flag that you did when it came to Bridgetown as this student had studied there before, but they dismissed it as coincidence. Information accessed was generally unimportant, so nothing serious for them to have worried about it.'

'I see,' said Loris thoughtfully, 'but it does mean that we need to remain on our toes.'

'Indeed it does,' agreed the professor. 'We cannot be careless and need to keep pressing.'

'The day BEAFT was commissioned,' informed Loris, 'I discussed this very issue with Andrew. Let's hope nothing arises here!'

'Let's hope!' seconded Professor Smyth.

'Thanks, Kenny,' said Loris, 'I assume Llewellyn is aware of all this?'

'Up to date on everything,' confirmed the professor. 'I spoke to him before I spoke to you, but as he had some things to attend to before being able to inform you, I volunteered. We'll keep in touch.'

'Were you able to hear, Andrew?' asked Loris, having ended the call.

'Every word,' replied Andrew, a serious look about him. 'We just have to be sensible and careful.'

'We cannot really do more than that,' agreed Loris. 'I'll discuss it with Dr Whyte later and hear what he has to say.'

Loris promptly changed his focus and did a little research by means of his laptop on flea eyes, Andrew looking on. When he read the information to Andrew, they both laughed quietly. The last thing either of them wanted troubling Pepe were fleas, but they were both most anxious to get the FLEA, with a short wait before them.

The rain had fallen consistently for two weeks, but a break in the clouds came at Thanksgiving time. Loris decided that this year his family would celebrate it at home, not accepting any invitations irrespective of who they came from.

The anxious wait for the Fluorescent Light Enhancement Attachment finally came to an end, with the technician from Bramford University arriving on a cold, blistery day just before mid-December.

'You're not going to believe it!' exclaimed Loris, a large grin on his face as he entered Pepe.

'Whatever I'm not going to believe must be good,' said Andrew looking at his watch, 'considering how long you've been away. Were you able to fetch the technician alright?'

'Mitchell!' said Loris, placing a big reinforced box on one of the work benches. 'Yes, he's fine. I had no problems meeting up with him. He's a very pleasant chap, not very talkative but good-natured. I've dropped him off at the Boulevard Inn already so that he could check in and rest – he did look rather tired after the long flight and the trouble at the airport!'

'Trouble?' questioned Andrew, perking up at Loris' comment. 'What happened?'

'It was this box that caused all the trouble!' exclaimed Loris with annoyance, patting it gently on the top. 'Or should I rather say that it was likely Professor Burg who caused it!'

'Why,' queried Andrew with interest, 'what did he do?'

'Read what's on the box,' requested Loris. 'It'll tell its own story.'

'"FLEA – TAKE EXTRA CARE / CONFIDENTIAL,"' read Andrew, a little puzzled as to why it should be of issue.

'Now take our customs officers,' said Loris, 'who have their work cut out for them with all the laws and environmental safety checks they have to deal with!'

'Ah!' responded Andrew, seeing where this was going.

'You guessed it,' said Loris. 'Professor Burg's sense of humour caused customs to want to investigate the box, thinking it was some sort of alien parasite enclosed inside!'

'What happened when you told them what it was?' asked Andrew, laughing quietly as he pictured the scene with Loris and Mitchell trying to explain.

'They said they couldn't take a chance,' answered Loris. 'I had the feeling that they were inquisitive, but then I suppose it's their job to be!'

'Why didn't you just open it?' asked Andrew sensibly.

'Because it's a sealed crate,' replied Loris, 'which isn't easy to just open at an airport, and besides, Mitchell would have none of it. He said that the lenses are very sensitive due to the wiring in them and if damaged, it would be a major setback.'

'How did you sort it out?' asked Andrew, slightly amused at the undesirable dilemma but glad that he did not have to deal with it.

'I didn't,' replied Loris. 'I phoned Professor Smyth, and Mitchell phoned Professor Burg. We then went and had some coffee while the two professors had to phone the airport's customs security to explain and ensure them that it was no breach.'

'Surely,' said Andrew in disbelief, 'you cannot confuse a highly sophisticated piece of electronic equipment with some type of fauna or parasite!'

'Beats me,' responded Loris, shrugging his shoulders, 'but there you have it – a story for the record books! I'll be fetching Mitchell first thing tomorrow morning, and he'll fit the FLEA!'

True to plan, the technician was fetched first thing in the morning and brought to the lab. Special care was taken to open the crate and remove the delicate part from it. There was no rush in attaching it to the unique fluorescent microscope for there was no room for error at all. Tests were carried out by him before signing it off to Microlab Industries. The task was completed in a day, with both Loris and Andrew upbeat about its prospects after observing the tests. Mitchell was soon on his way home, anxious to get back before a severe snow storm that was expected to pound his homeland set in.

'Now we have something!' exclaimed Andrew, peering in BEAFT's eyepiece, having wasted no time getting stuck into investigation once the technician had left. 'Can you see what I'm seeing, Lori?'

'If you're referring to slight colour variation,' replied Loris, looking at the large monitor, 'then yes! That gives us a hope of breaching the little guy's camouflage and segregating further.'

'That's exactly what I'm thinking!' voiced Andrew enthusiastically. 'Now we'll get him!'

Andrew worked the machine, looking attentively into the eyepiece, impressed by the distinctions that the Fluorescent Light Enhancement Attachment now provided.

'I wonder,' said Andrew thoughtfully, still looking into the eyepiece, 'how long before we— Did you see that!' exclaimed

Andrew excitedly, pressing his face hard against the eyepiece.

'I did!' cried Loris jumping up off the stool he was sitting on and quickly moving closer to the digital monitor. 'Where did it go? It came and went so quickly!'

'Play back the recording,' requested Andrew, hastening to Loris' side.

'I can't!' groaned Loris, smacking his forehead with the palm of his hand. 'I forgot to switch it on!'

'Oh dear!' said Andrew dejectedly. 'We'll just have to continue searching and hope that we find it or that it reappears – soon!'

'Sorry, Andy,' apologised Loris, feeling the weight of his blunder. 'I shouldn't have forgotten that!'

'Never mind,' assured Andrew, 'these things happen. Let's just take encouragement from what we briefly saw, even if we couldn't make it out. It means that the FLEA is working, and our assumptions are somewhere on target. It won't be long before we've caught up with the object of our interest again!'

Loris switched on the recorder, and he and Andrew worked late into the night, hoping to find what they had briefly seen, but they were unsuccessful. It remained withdrawn or hidden under camouflage.

Andrew eventually called it a night, but Loris was determined to press on as if there was no tomorrow. He worked tirelessly, searching, probing, checking. Eventually, with the clock hands falling just passed midnight, he spotted something that moved when he accidently prodded an area he was not focused on.

Loris focused in with the new FLEA attachment. With intense concentration, he pressed against the fluorescent microscope's eyepiece, his eyes fixed purposely on the area in search of his target. There was specific movement once again, and this time Loris could see a fairly distinct colour variation just beneath the surface he was investigating. He moved in with the super nano-tweezers but was suddenly startled, hearing the cold, dark night's silence penetrated by two car doors being slammed shut!

Chapter 32

The chancers

LORIS stood upright, a little puzzled at hearing the car doors. He wondered who would arrive there at that time of night, with Andrew not likely to return without phoning him first. He went over to the window but suddenly stopped, his heart skipping a beat, as the lights went out. Loris recoiled and a cold shiver ran down his spine at the thought of the possibility that a breach of security was being attempted and a break-in was in progress. He instantly wondered if they were just a bunch of chancers or there with a specific purpose related to the research taking place.

The generator immediately kicked in, with the lights coming back on within seconds. Loris shifted the one window blind slightly and peered out, seeing an unfamiliar black sedan parked outside of Microlab's public entrance, the company's main parking area closed and requiring a security pass to access it. He let go of the window blind, and as he went to his desk, he heard the generator outside in the yard splutter and stop, the lights flickering before going out permanently. There was silence.

BEAFT went into provisional standby mode before

performing an automatic shutdown. In seconds it had closed its eyes and left Loris' investigation abruptly interrupted. Thankfully there were emergency lights at all desks and work stations that ran on batteries, so Loris was not left in utter darkness.

Loris reached his desk just as Microlab Industries' alarm went off, causing him to recoil once again, leaving him on edge. He knew that Pepe would not be easy to access, as it was a lab within a lab, and it had a secure entrance. Nevertheless, this was not the only concern.

He hastened in his efforts to call for help, trying not to fumble with the phone as his hands began to lightly shake from nervousness and insecurity, but the landline was dead. Loris grabbed his mobile phone and promptly called the police and Microlab's security company.

A minute later Loris could hear commotion outside Pepe's walls, but he dared not go to investigate, keeping well out of sight of the mantrap security door that was the only see-through frontage into Pepe. As he stood around the corner, behind one of the partitions, his heart was pounding profusely, but he hardly breathed he was so on edge.

His heart skipped a double-beat when he suddenly heard a bang against the trap-door's reinforced glass, realising that an attempt was being made to enter. He dared not peek around the corner but remembered that his laptop was lying open on his desk, which could be seen from the door. There were another few bangs, Loris feeling the shudder as the glass of the door stood defiantly firm against the attack. He took a deep breath, looking at his watch continually, wishing with all hope that the police and security would make haste.

Just then Loris heard a faint noise in the distance. He

stopped breathing to listen, and joy rose in his heart that his ears had heard correctly – it was the sound of sirens!

There was a sudden flurry outside Pepe, followed by silence.

Loris raced to the window, hearing the heavy six-cylinder motor of the sedan parked outside roar to life.

Two men ran out of the building's entrance with bulging bags and jumped in. The vehicle pulled away before they had even shut the doors, the sirens of two police vehicles bearing down upon them with speed. The sedan managed to get away just before the police arrived, skidding its way out of the parking and down the road. Loris watched the two police vehicles chase after it, their sirens deafening and lights flashing menacingly as they rushed past and into the distance. His heart leapt at the sight, hoping that the pursuit would pay off.

On the heels of the police was a vehicle from the security company, clearly noticeable by its insignia all over the car. Two security men hopped out with purpose, their grey clothing blending in with the dark, cold and wet surrounds. They cautiously looked around out front, alert and on the ready for any surprises.

Loris carefully opened the window, not wanting to create alarm and called to them, informing them of what he had seen.

Despite Loris' communication, the men made their way systematically inside, beams from their strong flashlights piercing through the darkness into every corner, checking on the way and not taking any chances.

When Loris saw them outside Pepe's trap-door, he went out to survey what had transpired outside Pepe's walls and to speak to the security personnel. They first made their way downstairs to switch the electricity back on.

'Are you okay, Loris?' asked Dr Whyte who had arrived

shortly thereafter, the security company having given him a call after Loris had alerted them.

'Yes, thankfully,' replied Loris, his face pale from the ordeal. 'A little shaky inside but okay. Pepe kept me out of harm's way.'

'At least there's no excessive damage,' observed Dr Whyte, looking around. It seems that the bulk of what was targeted are tools and small apparatus.'

'When we switched the electricity back on,' informed Loris, 'I noticed that at reception the laptop and printer were missing.'

'What a pity,' said Dr Whyte, 'but no great inconvenience, thankfully. At least the main lab computers and laptops are in security housings or locked away!'

'Evening, sirs,' greeted a policeman, having just arrived on the scene along with one of his colleagues. 'We're here to make a survey and take statements, but I can tell you that we've just been informed that our two chase vehicles have managed to arrest the offenders in the black sedan.'

'That's great news!' exclaimed Dr Whyte, Loris also well pleased with the news.

'It always is when we do,' mentioned the policeman, his plump face grinning brightly. 'The vehicle overran a turn and spun off the road. We were able to nab them quickly and without trouble. We'll need a statement from the eye-witness.'

'Certainly,' said Loris, happy to assist. 'I'll head off down to the station as soon as we're done here.'

'Very good, sir,' said the policeman, he and his colleague promptly withdrawing so that they could make a survey of the place.

'I can read your thoughts, Loris,' said Dr Whyte looking at him. 'It's a question on my mind too! Any connection between this break-in and your research is unproven at present.'

'It may be,' said Loris, 'but I have my concerns. The closeness of this security breach to the installation of the FLEA is unnerving, also taking into account the concerns and experience that Professor Burg and his team have had. We've got to make this discovery soon!'

'Come,' said Dr Whyte, seeing Loris' peaky face, 'I'll drive you down to the station quickly, and you can make your statements and head on home. The security company will take care of this place, just ensure that Pepe is inaccessible. We'll deal with all this in the morning, which isn't that far away now! We'll beef up security around here.'

Dr Whyte and Loris were soon at the police station, the process going smoothly and quickly as it was the only case they had to deal with at that time. Through cross-examination, it turned out that the offenders were just a small, independent group of chancers, looking for an easy haul.

'You should be able to rest easier with that little bit of information,' said Dr Whyte, pulling up outside Microlab Industries after their visit to the police station. 'Just a group of chancers! One good thing that came out of this is that I wasn't aware the alarm system is so old that it's still connected to the telephone line and not on a wireless system! Had you not been here, our unwanted visitors may have created more trouble than they managed!'

'That's one way of looking at it,' said Loris without much enthusiasm, his eyes heavy with tiredness. 'I've certainly had my full of them, so whatever you do to keep such corrupt scoundrels away will be welcome.'

Loris headed home, leaving Dr Whyte to arrange with the security company temporary measures to secure the building until daybreak, when they could deal with the issues properly.

He arrived home and quietly entered, not wanting to wake anyone. Worn out but a bit hungry, Loris headed for the kitchen, knowing that Sarah would have left a plate of food for him on the counter that he could just warm up and pick at as he wanted to. There next to the plate of food lay an envelope with "Dearest Daddy" written on it. Loris instantly recognised Mika's handwriting, and although he was extremely tired, he could not resist the desire to open it. While he waited for his food to heat in the microwave, Loris carefully opened the envelope with a knife and slipped the small piece of paper out.

Dearest Daddy [said the letter],
We know that you do not like to go to church and don't want to be asked. However, as you know, we're both playing a part in the production called *The Gift* taking place on Christmas Eve at the church. Please, Daddy, will you come? We very much would like you to attend, please?
Love you lots,
Mika and Abigail

Loris put the letter down on the counter, emotion and love for his girls welling up inside of him. He could not help smiling at it, knowing that if they had asked him any other way, they would have received a definite answer of no. He could also see Sarah's hand in it though.

'Truly!' thought Loris with amusement, as he took his plate of food out of the microwave. 'A real bunch of chancers!'

Chapter 33

Who would have believed it possible?

'Come, Daddy,' chorused Mika and Abigail together. 'We don't want to be late, we're in the play you know!'

Mika ran up to Loris just as he had finished coming down the stairs, grabbed his hand and started pulling him with all her might.

'Give me a chance, my dear child,' objected Loris, 'I've only been home for five minutes. According to your mother's information, I still have another 20 minutes before we have to leave to get you there on time. I'll see to it that you're not late!'

'That should be fine, dear,' confirmed Sarah, coming down the stairs behind Loris. 'We must just remember that it is what they are terming a "Special Christmas Eve Service", so they are expecting a lot of people. The earlier we leave, the better.'

'Yes, Daddy,' chorused the girls.

'The sooner the better,' added Abigail.

'I'll be ready in 20 minutes,' confirmed Loris a little edgy, 'so please don't press me! If I'm hassled, I'll just not go!'

'You cannot do that, Daddy!' complained Mika strongly. 'I

have our letter in my pocket, where you wrote on it to us, agreeing to go!'

'Who would have thought it possible,' said Sarah, taking Loris lovingly by the arm, 'that you would agree to go but you did!'

'You cannot break your promise,' drummed home Abigail, grabbing Loris around his waist, 'I won't allow it! If you don't go, then I won't go, and if I don't go, they'll be short of one angel who sings!'

'The whole play will be a mess,' sang out Mika with animation, throwing her arms in the air, 'and you would be responsible for it!'

'They're definitely your girls, Sarah!' said Loris, bursting out laughing. 'Okay, I'll be ready as soon as I can. Now let me alone; otherwise, I *will* take a full 20 minutes!'

Loris quickly made his way to the kitchen to grab a bite to eat, his plate of food faithfully waiting there for him. After a few hurried mouthfuls of brown basmati rice, savoury mince and some steamed vegetables, he returned upstairs to finish up.

'Okay, girls,' announced Loris, bouncing down the stairs with his thick rain jacket flung over his shoulder, 'I'm ready to go and with more than five minutes to spare. Have you got your rain jackets? Heavy showers and a storm have been forecast for later tonight.'

'Everything's at the front door,' confirmed Sarah, getting up slowly from the sofa, the advancement of her pregnancy not permitting her to do otherwise. 'You'll just need to help me with the bags.'

It was drizzling outside, so everyone put on their rain jackets and promptly headed out, Loris assisting the girls with their bags. They were soon in the SUV and on their way to the church.

The core of winter was true to its word. It had faithfully brought its cold and wet conditions, with the grey world dark and unpleasant outdoors. Heavy rain clouds hung about ominously above, their dark, swollen faces angry and menacing. Everything around was sodden from the consistent rains, that afternoon having been no different. Heaven's liquid gift shined under every street lamp, the many puddles reflecting the light strongly and in some cases, creating colours of brilliance amidst the dark, grey melancholy hue that encompassed the natural world.

'Look, girls,' said Sarah as they drew near to the church, pointing to the coloured lights in the parking area belonging to Ailensbury Christian Fellowship. 'Don't they make the area look pretty?'

'They are beautiful,' agreed the girls, having leaned forward and placed their chins next to the headrests on the top of the two front seats as they looked out the front window. The quaint old black Victorian-style parking lot lamps were filling the parking area with a colourful array, having specially been fitted, as they usually were, with coloured bulbs for the Christmas season.

Loris turned in at the entrance, vehicles before and after him filing in as well, as a stream of cars began filling the parking lot. He found a parking bay without difficulty and promptly parked the SUV. There was a lot of movement, with people hurriedly getting out of their cars. "Beeps" were heard, and vehicle indicator lights were flashing all over the parking area, as vehicle alarms were being switched on. People scuttled along with purpose as it continued to drizzle, trying to avoid the liquid landmines just waiting to soak a shoe and dampen the bottoms of trouser legs.

The Lang family were soon doing the same as everyone else, as they made their way to the church entrance's two wooden doors. Once inside, they stopped hunching and threw back the hoods of their rain jackets.

The interior was bright and warm as usual, the white teardrop lights hanging from the roof faithfully burning brightly, like angels looking down from on high. It was a pleasant welcome from the miserable world outside. Fresh flowers had been faithfully arranged, bringing colour and life, but the platform at the front stole the show, having been transformed into a scene dating back 2000 years.

It had been modelled after the Nativity, with the props providing great colour and detail. The area had been divided into two sections – the shepherds out in the fields and the inn where Mary and Joseph were to seek shelter. In order to draw the audience into the play, small straw bales had been placed around the outside of the pews, with loose straw being scattered on the floor between pews and on the seats of the pews.

People began seating themselves, while others milled around and chatted, many going forward to get a close-up view of the stage props.

'We must go to the hall,' informed Mika, taking Sarah's hand, 'as the cast is gathering there. We must join them now.'

'Off you go then,' said Sarah with a happy countenance and cheerful smile. 'Do your best, you two. We're proud of you.' She promptly hugged them both, and they sped off. 'Where do you think you're going?' questioned Sarah, tugging objectingly on the sleeve of Loris' jacket as she frowned upon him.

'I'm taking a seat!' replied Loris, looking surprised at having been questioned. 'What does it look like I'm doing?'

'In the very last pew?' queried Sarah, chuckling lightly as she took him by the arm and began walking forward. 'Really, Loris! At least half way down – I want to be able to see my girls!'

Loris was not too pleased with the closeness to the stage and worse, the nearness to the pulpit, but he did not want to make a scene and followed Sarah to a pew about midway down the aisle. They took off their jackets and sat down.

'Hello, you two,' greeted June pleasantly, slipping into the pew alongside Sarah, with Andrew following suit. 'Do you mind if we join you?'

'Not at all!' exclaimed Sarah lively, pleased to see her.

'We saw you move into the pew,' said June, 'so thought it would be nice to slip in alongside.'

'Always agreeable company,' confirmed Sarah warmly, taking June's arm, 'and I'm sure Loris will at least appreciate having someone close by that he knows.'

'No hassle to me,' said Loris, feeling quite out of sorts as he looked around, 'I'm here specifically for the girls – you know they're in the play?'

'Yes,' replied Andrew, seating himself next to June, 'but we didn't know you were coming. Glad you could make it, Loris.'

'I have a feeling,' responded Loris, 'that I'd rather be at the lab, but we'll have to wait and see. I promised the girls, and I'm interested in their activities and to see how they do, so I'll just have to stick it out!'

'Oh, you pessimist!' objected Sarah, leaning against him gently. 'Can you imagine if that was his attitude towards his research?' she added, looking at June and Andrew, who were quietly amused at Sarah's observation.

It was not long thereafter that everyone in the church settled and seated themselves. Tim and July found Andrew and the other three and seated themselves next to them. They all watched as the stage performers took their places before the congregants, the two Lang girls having morphed into little angels, with white flowing garments and shiny silver tinsel fastened into their black, curly hair, making it stand out beautifully.

The church lights were switched off, and the temporary stage lights turned on. The pianist and accompanying musicians began playing and singing commenced. The whole play was created with song rather than dialogue. It was well choreographed and clearly evident that all participants had prepared and rehearsed well. The production went off smoothly and transitioned between the different scenes flawlessly. Mika and Abigail were part of a quartet for the one song. Sarah's heart swelled as she watched her two poppets, and she clapped heartily when they were finished, her face alight with delight and joy. Forty minutes later the play concluded with all the performers singing in melodious harmony to the glory of God for the heavenly gift of His one and only begotten Son.

The congregants stood in appreciation of the performance and effort made. Deafening applause filled the church as the cast bowed and curtsied, Sarah being amongst the most passionate clappers. Although Loris did not embrace the story, he too was touched by the performance, particularly the effort by his girls, who he felt not only looked but sang angelically. After a few minutes, the applause abated and the people sat down again.

The performers left the stage and went to sit down. Two men carried the bland pulpit back onto the platform and placed it where it usually stood so that Mark could give his sermon, the people waiting in anticipation for him.

'Surely!' exclaimed Tim with amusement, whispering in July's ear as loud laughter broke out when Mark, the shepherd of God's sheep, made his appearance through the side entrance. 'Who would have believed it possible?'

Chapter 34

The Shepherd's message

Mark entered dressed as a shepherd, carrying his Bible and notes in one hand and a crook in the other. He had a broad smile as he stepped up to the pulpit, not surprised at the peoples' laughter, looking particularly unusual to the regular church attendees.

'I was asked if I would be a part of the cast,' said Mark, putting his Bible and notes on the pulpit and the crook against the side of it, 'so I've been accommodating – not in the form of an actor for I'm not one. However, as a shepherd of God's sheep, I can play my part, and I hope to do so well this evening.' 'There's no such thing as a secular job,' continued Mark after opening his notes. 'Those of us who are Christians are all ambassadors of Christ's redemptive work, irrespective of place or time or season. A doctor, a plumber, a fitter and turner, pilot, accountant, fisherman or shepherd – it makes no difference. Therefore, I can stand before you dressed as a shepherd, although it may be considered beneath a person and unconventional. Granted, it's not something I would normally do, but then I do not stand before you improperly nor irreverently before my holy God, whom I fear with a godly fear.'

Mark looked out across the audience, pleased to see the attendance, the mixture of sheep and goats sitting quietly awaiting the shepherd's message.

Loris looked on, not too impressed with the whole scene, but then if Mark had been dressed in suit and tie he would have had the same perspective and attitude anyway. He was concerned, even sceptical, about what he was about to hear.

'Some congregants approached me,' said Mark, 'wanting to know if they could stage the Nativity in song. I thought it would be quite a good thing to do, for although I'm not one who holds strongly to Christmas festivities, the Biblical account of the coming of the Messiah, even if not the focal or important aspect of the saving grace of the Gospel, is relevant and holds in itself a message to man – it was the physical provision and appearance of hope and mercy.'

Mark paused and took a deep breath as he scanned the people before him, aware that the strong message he was to deliver would fall on the ears of many strangers. He hoped before God that they would have ears to hear.

'Tonight I want to give a threefold message,' informed Mark calmly. 'It encompasses mercy, repentance and hope. The three fit together and through Jesus Christ, culminate in salvation and true eternal life. At the outset of mankind, Adam and Eve sinned, as recorded in the book of Genesis. The judgement that God had indicated to Adam would be manifest for the penalty of that sin was to come into effect. However, God's first act of mercy is immediately evident, for He provides a hope, a restorative solution, even before He institutes the judgement upon Adam and Eve. This is an incredible act of God – before the punishment is declared, the atonement is proclaimed. That is mercy!'

Mark opened his Bible to the first of his markers.

'"To the serpent," read Mark, "God said, 'I will put enmity between you and the woman, and between your offspring and hers; he will crush your head, and you will strike his heel.'" [75] This is the declaration that God would provide a Saviour for mankind, who would destroy the cunning and catastrophic work of the evil one. This was before there was Jew or Gentile. The Saviour to be provided was for all mankind, not just Jew or Gentile – one Saviour for *all* mankind. This mercy provides man with hope, and this hope is obtained through repentance. This Saviour, whom God proclaimed would be born of woman and would crush the devil's head, was then born 4000 years later.'

Having put his first marker next to his Bible, Mark promptly opened his Bible at his second marker. Loris listened but did not like what he was hearing.

'Luke tells us,' said Mark and began reading, '"Then the angel said to them, 'Do not be afraid, for behold, I bring you good tidings of great joy which will be to all people. For there is born to you this day in the city of David a Saviour, who is Christ the Lord.'" [76] Why do we need a saviour? Firstly, because the sin of Adam is uninterrupted to all his offspring, for the apostle Paul tells us that, "Sin entered the world through one man, and death through sin, and in this way death came to all men, because all sinned." [77] Secondly, the prophet Isaiah tells us that, "We all, like sheep, have gone astray, each of us has turned to his own way." [78] When God revealed that the Saviour had been born, I think it was appropriate that the angel should address shepherds, for God had made known His physical process to bring the lost sheep into His fold.'

Mark briefly paused, as though separating points.

'There's one relevant point,' continued Mark purposefully, 'which is a great marvel – Mary's conception. Isn't it ironic that people will believe that God created the heavens and the earth; that He brought multiple plagues upon Egypt; that He brought the Israelites out of slavery, provided a cloud by day, a pillar of fire by night, parted the Red Sea and led them through, supplied their needs in the wilderness for 40 years, parted the Jordan river, smashed down the walls of Jericho and gave them the Promised Land. Yet, a virgin birth isn't believable – even though the prophet Isaiah prophesied it saying, "Therefore the Lord Himself will give you a sign: The virgin will be with child and will give birth to a son, and will call Him Immanuel." [79] Immanuel means God with us.'

Mark gently shifted the pages in his Bible with his next marker.

'This is recorded and confirmed,' he continued, having opened at the location, 'in the book of Matthew, "An angel of the Lord appeared to him (Joseph) in a dream and said, 'Joseph son of David, do not be afraid to take Mary home as your wife, because what is conceived in her is from the Holy Spirit. She will give birth to a son, and you are to give him the name Jesus (which incidentally means, the Lord saves), because He will save His people from their sins.' All this took place to fulfil what the Lord had said through the prophet (Isaiah): 'The virgin will be with child and will give birth to a son, and they will call Him Immanuel' – which means, 'God with us'." [80] Joseph could never have been the father, because sin, which is transferred from man to man, would still be present – and Jesus had to be sinless because sin cannot overcome sin. Mary couldn't have been born with "seed" already in her, as some have suggested, for it would have still represented the same situation. In order for the term "God with us" to be practically visible and for sin not to be present, Mary's conception had to be a sovereign work of God, which was by the Holy Spirit. This made Jesus both man (born of woman) and born of God (a work of the Holy Spirit). He's both fully man and fully God. Jesus couldn't have been born of "seed" as we understand it, He had to be born of the work of the Holy Spirit or else He too, like man, would need to be redeemed from sin, but He didn't have to be, He's *the* Redeemer! There has been no other person on the face of the earth, either before or since, who could fulfil the role of the Saviour in such a sovereign capacity, and this isn't taking into account the other prophecies spoken about the Messiah, which Jesus also fulfilled.'

Loris felt a little uneasy as Mark paused briefly once again, opening his Bible to a new passage and looking across the audience.

'In Psalm 107,' said Mark, continuing on, 'there's a call to the redeemed of the Lord to give thanks to God. It explains why they should, for it tells us what God has done for them and what He will do for mankind. I'll read three quarters of the Psalm to you. Psalm 107:1–32, "O give thanks unto the LORD, for He is good: for His mercy endureth for ever. Let the redeemed of the LORD say so, whom He hath redeemed from the hand of the enemy; and gathered them out of the lands, from the east, and from the west, from the north, and from the south. They wandered in the wilderness in a solitary way; they found no city to dwell in. Hungry and thirsty, their soul fainted in them. Then they cried unto the LORD in their trouble, and He delivered them out of their distresses. And He led them forth by the right way, that they might go to a city of habitation. Oh that men would praise the LORD for His goodness, and for His wonderful works to the children of men! For He satisfieth the longing soul, and filleth the hungry soul with goodness. Such as sit in darkness and in the shadow of death, being bound in affliction and iron; because they rebelled against the words of God, and contemned (scorned) the counsel of the Most High: therefore He brought down their heart with labour; they fell down, and there was none to help. Then they cried unto the LORD in their trouble, and He saved them out of their distresses. He brought them out of darkness and the shadow of death, and brake their bands in sunder. Oh that men would praise the LORD for His goodness, and for His wonderful works to the children of men! For He hath broken gates of brass, and cut the bars of iron in sunder. Fools because of their transgression, and because of their iniquities, are afflicted. Their soul abhorreth all manner of meat; and they draw near unto the gates of death. Then they cry unto the LORD in their trouble, and He saveth them out of their distresses. He sent His word, and healed them, and delivered them from their destructions. Oh that men would praise the LORD for His goodness, and for His wonderful works to the children of men! And let them sacrifice the sacrifices of thanksgiving, and declare His works with rejoicing. They that go down to the sea in ships, that do business in great waters; these see the works of the LORD, and His wonders in the deep. For He commandeth, and raiseth the stormy wind, which lifteth up the waves thereof. They mount up to the heaven, they go down again to the depths: their soul is melted because of trouble. They reel to and fro, and stagger like a drunken man, and are at their wit's end. Then they cry unto the LORD in their trouble, and He bringeth them out of their distresses. He maketh the storm a calm, so that the waves thereof are still. Then are they glad because they be quiet; so He bringeth them unto their desired haven. Oh that men would praise the

LORD for His goodness, and for His wonderful works to the children of men! Let them exalt Him also in the congregation of the people, and praise Him in the assembly of the elders."'(KJV)

Mark stopped and closed his Bible. The storm that had been predicted now began to make its first impressions as the rain began to fall a little harder.

'It's very clear,' said Mark, looking directly at the people sitting on the straw-strewn pews, 'the mercy that God exhibits to mankind, but what comes through in each case is the following: they cried to the LORD. Each time they cried to the LORD, He worked a heavenly, merciful work in their situation, even though it's clear in certain instances that their affliction was due to their sin and disobedience to God. This is mercy, God's mercy to mankind, but it's based on mankind who are now the redeemed of the LORD – as per verse one – having cried out to God, which is repentance. But what does Scripture tell us about repentance? In speaking to the Athenians about them worshiping many gods, the apostle Paul said, "And the times of this ignorance God overlooked; but now commandeth all men everywhere to repent." [81] At the time Paul spoke, the angel's announcement of the born Saviour had been heard, the Saviour's redemptive work on Calvary's cross had been completed, and the Saviour had already ascended into heaven. God now no longer overlooked ignorance, and the Gospel of salvation went out to all men, commanding all people everywhere to repent. One of *the* great dangers of the modern Gospel is the exclusion of the fundamental requirement of repentance. Many of you, both Christian and those of you who are not Christian, may have heard it. This terrible error corrupts the foundation of Salvation, waters down the power of renewal and wears away the core of true righteousness. In modern-day societal circles there's often the notion of no true right or wrong, no true black or white and no true principle of absolute. Sadly, the modern church today has embraced this perspective and incorporated it into the underlying philosophy and fabric of church growth. However, what isn't being considered is spiritual uprightness. The biblical instruction to walk in God's righteousness and to perfect holiness isn't seen as significantly relevant but simply relative. Its form takes on a fake righteousness that's nothing more than a tattered garment worn around the shoulders of the New Cross and New Gospel Christian. This should be to the annoyance of the godly saint.'

A serious look came over Mark's face, and his tone of voice seemed to match his serious look.

'The warning is this,' continued Mark. 'In reality, this fake righteousness only represents a cloud of mist, rendering the wearer unable to see into the distance and the danger of what lies ahead. When the heat of trial arises, and the scorching wind of tribulation begins to blow, that which they thought covered and shielded them, will leave them standing bare, exposed to the elements and incapable of standing spiritually strong against the onslaught of its cold-hearted, relentless force. For it is only repentance that brings about a renewal, a cleansing, a redeemed soul and a changed heart, covered by the blood of Jesus and kept in the bosom of God. Without repentance there can be no forgiveness; without forgiveness there can be no cleansing; without cleansing there can be no change; without change there can be no spiritual growth. Such people stand in a dangerous and undesirable position, with hearts still blackened by the continuous inheritance handed down from Adam. They remain unredeemed, though they may not recognise it. Repentance requires a recognition of one's sin and encompasses the deep sorrow for one's conduct and the wish that it had never been so. Repentance also embraces the determination not to continue in a manner that represents the wrongdoing; it's a determination to change and do what's right!

'Sadly, filled parish pews are seen as providential power and approval from the Almighty God. What is failed to be realised is the misunderstanding of God's requirement for true salvation and the foundational platform for spiritual wellbeing. Through His prophets, God called the people to repent. John the Baptist called people to repent and to bear forth fruit in keeping with repentance. Jesus, when speaking about the tower of Siloam and to the woman caught in adultery, called for repentance. Peter called the people to repentance at Pentecost, when he informed them about what they had done, and Paul informed the people of Athens of God's command to repent.'

Loris did not like this at all, for it challenged his very position. He sat with his arms folded, a stern look on his face as he brooded.

'God isn't a cowardly and timid God,' said Mark as he concluded the first section of his sermon, 'who drifts like man on the tide of fashionable change in order to maintain the approval of men. He is God – a holy, righteous, just, upright and powerful God. He does not change His requirements to suit men. This is His message: He commands all men everywhere to repent!'

Chapter 35

The Gift of salvation and life

OUTSIDE, the rain began to fall even harder, with thick, heavy drops pelting down from heaven upon the earth, drenching even further that which was already wet and sodden. The wind began to pick up and swirl, causing the trees to sway in all directions and the small shrubs and bushes to be harassed unpleasantly. The colourful sheep and goats, however, kept their focus on the shepherd before them as he continued unrestricted in the delivery of his sermon.

'Let's now take,' said Mark, continuing steadfastly on, 'one of the instances in which Jesus spoke about repentance. Jesus said, "Likewise, I say unto you, there is joy in the presence of the angels of God over one sinner that repenteth." [82] The presence of angels automatically stirs a strong ethereal feeling within the being of mortal flesh, and although angels play a part throughout Scripture, this heavenly presence, in respect to joy, is twice expressed most notably. The first is when Christ is born. Heaven's realms are brought to earth and there's an angel's announcement and a multitude of the heavenly hosts expressing joy to man and praise to God for the Saviour born. The second is when the Saviour, through explanation to the multitudes, transports man to heaven's realms and reveals angels' joy at the repentance of a sinner. There's no expression of rejoicing or joy over men, but only in respect to redemption and *redeemed* men – the Saviour who would redeem and the sinner who after having repented becomes redeemed, through Christ's atonement at Calvary. There's praise and joy at the Gift given to man by God, and there's joy expressed when man receives that Gift given. Through deduction, it implies that the angels understand the eternal implications such repentance has upon the soul of man and the importance that such a step means in that soul's present and everlasting wellbeing. It shows that repentance, even if it takes place in the darkest dungeon, is revealed throughout heaven's bright expanse. Repentance from sin and salvation through Christ's substitutionary sacrifice, lifts the spirit of man and grants him entrance into heaven's residence, generating great joy in the ranks of angels.

'Men's works and good deeds do not generate this joy amongst angels. Goodliness, religion, devotion, social standing, intelligence and the like never reach the realms of eternal influence in man's favour, only repentance before the Eternal God. Scripture doesn't say that there is joy when a sinner attends church, nor when a sinner embraces religion, nor when a sinner does charity, but only when a sinner repents. True repentance tears the heart, not the clothes – it's a deep internal work of the heart that changes the life of the person, setting them on a new path, a path unto righteousness in the footsteps of their now embraced saviour, Jesus Christ. Sin is renounced and removed, and although the new white garments of justification through faith may become dirtied through stumblings, they're quickly washed when the face of Christ is beheld and His hands grasped through the repentant heart that earnestly seeks forgiveness and mercy.'

Mark paused as he looked intently at the audience, their faces brightened from the lights above. He knew that what he now had to say was of critical importance; it was the core of his message, the gospel message. He let out a quiet sigh as he lifted his eyes heavenward, his inward cry, "LORD God have mercy, and open the eyes of the blind", pressing upon his heart.

'Know this day,' boomed Mark above the stormy noise coming from outside, 'that rejoicing only takes place and joy is only present upon the new birth of the sinner, upon him being Born Again – and not otherwise. For unless you repent, turn from your wickedness and seek God through Jesus Christ, heaven's realms will remain silent. The joy bells will not ring, the angels will not sing, and the Lamb's book of Life will remain shut, with the ink pot of eternal glory and happiness never being disturbed by the Omnipotent's finger – your name will not be written down in the record book as one of God's redeemed saints. Jesus said, "What will it profit a man if he gains the whole world, and loses his own soul?" [83] and "Fear Him (God) who is able to destroy both soul and body in hell." [84] The apostle Paul said, "Behold, now is the accepted time; behold, now is the day of salvation."' [85]

Mark ceased from his intensity but kept a sober tone as he continued.

'To the sinner I ask,' said Mark questioningly, 'would you turn away the promise of a heavenly mansion for habitation in the fiery pits of eternal torment? Would you turn away coexistence with the Eternal King for the company of wretched hypocrites? Would you turn away a realm wherein righteousness dwells for a place far worse than streets of evil, great oppression and cruelty? Is your pride so strong that it cannot repent of what is wrong? Would it not be wise to have your sins removed rather than spread across the skies for all the world to consider and be to your own condemnation? Is your heart so stubborn and sin so valuable that it's worth giving up salvation? I beg you to hear and to heed the words of Christ – *Repent*; the words of Peter – *Repent*; the words of Paul – *Repent*! Turn to God that He may freely forgive. Give your life to Jesus, let Him take control. Let Him hold you in His hands and make you whole. And as you surrender your life to Him, He will set you free, that through Him you will be able to walk in true, God-given liberty. Through Christ you *can* be righteous! Through Christ you *can* overcome sin and temptation! Through Christ you *can* live free from bondage! In Christ you *can* please God and live for Him!

'To the saint, the redeemed of God, I say: honour God, hold Him in the highest regard, obey His commands and serve Him faithfully. Rejoice in the LORD – for what great knowledge it is that your name has been carried on the melody of angelic voices in joy and praise to God for redeeming you from damnation and for giving you eternal life! What a Gift! What a glory! What a God!'

Sarah could sense Loris' disquiet, and she dared not even glance at him, the tension in her own body from his uneasiness already strong.

'The ability of man to be able to repent gives man hope,' said Mark continuing on, 'hope of forgiveness, hope of amends, hope of a future, hope to change, hope of a second chance. What is man without hope? Without hope, man is lost. One of the worst states for man to be is in a state of hopelessness.'

Loris recalled his thoughts just after Professor de Roach's

memorial service, the emptiness that he realised was there – the lack of hope, which he had never understood before. He trembled.

'Where there's no hope, there's no life,' informed Mark, pressing faithfully on, 'but God *has* given us hope, so let me explain this hope further. The apostle Paul says, "Therefore if any man be in Christ, he is a new creature: old things are passed away; behold, all things are become new." [86] New Year is a week away, and it's a wonder for many! Its arrival is often long awaited, as though it contains a healthy quality that was non-existent in the year about to be cast into extinction. As the past morphs into the future when the clock hands are at their most erect, New Year's arrival is celebrated with energy by the masses of faithful festival enthusiasts. What power does this festival possess that it's long awaited? Is it the hooliganism that it affords or the indulgence that it allows to flow with liberal tolerance free from scorn and criticism? This may present the lion's share of the reason, but there sits in the back corner of the conscious mind something other, something more which is actually far greater – hope!'

Mark quickly moved to the following page in his notes.

'It's a hope,' said Mark persistently, 'that the future will be better than the past; that the failures will be overcome by successes; that the fears and insecurities will be erased by peace and stability; that the heartaches and sorrows will be soothed by joy and gladness; that the burdens of the past will be slain by blessings; and that plans, longings and desires will be fulfilled. For many, it's the hope of being able to start anew. Old resolutions are erased from the board without question as to how successfully they were fulfilled or how soon after they were made that they were broken, and new resolutions are written. It's almost as though a feeling of freshness and a cleansing from the old sweaty self sets in as the grip of the Old weakens and quietly slips into history on the back of the setting sun, with the rising of the New dawn a seeming lifeline, and so to say, "second chance". In the reality of the secular world, however, this is a gross lie. Of further sobering knowledge is the fact that sin in an unbeliever's life builds up, no matter what that person does. Yet, in Christ, there is a new hope and a cleansing from the old. In Christ, there is a "second chance". In Christ, there is a complete erasing from the slate, and in Christ, there is true hope – true salvation. Man can start anew, but its right and sound foundation rests upon Christ alone, no other. Temporal New Year's resolutions rest on man's strength, but eternal salvation rests on God's supremacy.'

Loris did not like this at all, for he felt the burden of its conviction. Internally he began to burn at what he was hearing – he had to make his discovery and thus rip from the grip of Christianity this convicting power that influenced the lives of men and woman. He had to prove it untrue, unfounded, created directly from the mind of man, for if he could not, he knew that he was facing an authority and sovereignty far beyond his ability to oppose. He knew that if he could not, he would then have a lot of questions he would have to answer.

'And with Christ's continuous washing,' continued Mark, 'through our continuous repentance, we need not wait for the New Year, for He continually picks us up, enabling us to keep going. Dear listener, what a confidence, what an encouragement – with Christ you can! For unto us that fear God's name shall the Sun of Righteousness (Jesus) arise with healing in His wings.[87] And for us who have repented and accepted Christ as Lord and Saviour, God has made us alive with Christ,[88] forgiving all our sins, having cancelled the written code (Old Testament Law), with its regulations, that was against us and that stood opposed to us; He took it away, nailing it to the cross.[89] Beloved saint, you who has been cleansed by the blood of our blessed Lord, it is not only advantageous to heart and soul to ensure such a cleansing continues through ongoing repentance and washing through the word of God, but it's a necessity – and each day that dawns will then be a New Year for you in Christ. What a joy worthy of celebration, singing and praise, even this Christmas Eve.

'Yet, there are those who only know of the temporary offerings. Listener, do you not know the cleansing power of eternal mercy? Have you not yet experienced the sweet celebration that comes from the hand of divine salvation? If not, what a glory you are then missing, what a hope you are losing and what a blessed assurance you are separated from! Would you not jump at any opportunity of gain in this world? The cleansing blood of Jesus through acceptance of Him as our Lord and Saviour is true gain indeed – for this life and the life hereafter. Rid yourself of the sweaty film of sin that covers the body and makes it stink. Rid yourself of the black-stained heart, sick with sin. Rid yourself of the life-threatening parasite called wickedness that builds up and clings to the walls of your arteries, restricting the flow of life to the heart as it hopes, with all the delight that hell's demons can muster, for your slow or even swift departure to the bottomless pit of eternal hopelessness – hell. To rid yourself of such a condition, would this not be considered gain?'

Loris could not deny the reasonableness of this, should it be true. His heart pounded inside, and he itched to get back to the lab.

'The portion of Psalm 107 as read earlier,' said Mark, his tone changing automatically as he moved on to his next point but maintaining a seriousness as to the reality of what he was saying, 'is a beautiful insight into God's loving-kindness, mercy and provision to those who cry out to Him. As mentioned, it provides man with hope – for God delivers, saves and sets free. However, it's a hope provided while man has breath in his body. Scripture tells us that man is appointed once to die and then to face judgement.[90] Man will be able to cry out when he's on the other side, but it will be to no benefit, he'll have no hope. This is revealed to us in the story, given by Jesus Himself, of the rich man and Lazarus as recorded in Luke 16. It informs us that a time came when a rich man and Lazarus, a beggar who sat at the rich man's gate, both died. Lazarus went to Abraham's bosom, which was a waiting place for the redeemed souls until Jesus' work on the cross had been completed, but the rich man was cast into hell. He was in torment and cried to Abraham to have mercy on him, but there was no help available to him, his lot was secure. He could see heaven's pleasant place but could not get there. He could call to Abraham but could not receive from there. He could cry out for mercy, but it was no longer available to him there. He could plead for help, but there was none forthcoming there! What a terrible and frightening expectation, to call out and be denied! What a dreadful thing to wake up to the realisation that there is now no longer hope!'

Mark paused as he scanned the audience, his heart going out to them. Just then a flash of lightning lit up the stain-glassed windows, and a peel of thunder spoke emphatically to the world.

'If God has made a provision to overcome the devil's deceitfulness and destruction,' said Mark questioningly, 'why is man so determined on being needlessly eternally damned? God warns us severely when he says, "The wicked shall be turned into hell, and all the nations that forget God."[91] Sin against an eternal

God requires eternal punishment, but we have a hope, and that hope is Christ Jesus the Lord. That hope is Him whom the angel declared to the shepherds, Him whom the shepherds told about to all the people, and Him whom this shepherd standing here tonight declares to you. The psalmist David said, "When I consider your heavens, the work of your fingers, the moon and the stars, which you have set in place, what is man that you are mindful of him, the son of man that you care for him?" [92] God in His mercy has considered and cared for us and made a way for us. Why then do we reject Him? Hear God's cry to you this night, and it comes from His anguished heart, "'Say to them, 'As surely as I live, declares the Sovereign LORD, I take no pleasure in the death of the wicked, but rather that they turn from their ways and live. Turn! Turn from your evil ways! Why will you die, O house of Israel (O people)?'"' [93] "'I will judge you, each one according to his ways,' declares the Sovereign LORD. 'Repent! Turn away from all your offences; then sin will not be your downfall. Rid yourselves of all the offences you have committed, and get a new heart and a new spirit. Why will you die, O house of Israel (O people)? For I take no pleasure in the death of anyone, declares the Sovereign LORD. Repent and live!'" [94] Allow then the cleansing blood of Jesus to flow through your veins, expelling all rot and infectious pus and making new. Allow Him, who rose from the dead and shattered principalities and powers triumphing over them by the Cross,[95] to raise you up into life and hope and purpose and meaning. Allow Him to breathe true life into your nostrils and to get your deadened heart pumping again with energy. Is this not gain? Hurry, dear friend, to Calvary's hill and have all your sins nailed to the Cross. Look up to heaven's gates and see the risen Christ, now seated at the right hand of

God the Father. Let God raise you up in Christ and become a temple of the Holy Spirit. Let not your heart be hardened, for Today is the day of God's calling; Today is the day of salvation;[96] Today is the day for old things to pass away and all things to become new. Listen and pay attention to the words of the prophet Isaiah, "Seek the LORD while He may be found; call on Him while He is near. Let the wicked forsake his way and the evil man his thoughts. Let him turn to the LORD, and He will have mercy on him, and to our God, for He will freely pardon." [97] The apostle John sums it up neatly for us when he says, "And this is the testimony: God has given us eternal life, and this life is in His Son. He who has the Son has life; he who does not have the Son of God does not have life." [98] Give your life to Jesus this day, I pray, and let heaven's blessed gift of salvation be yours!'

Chapter 36

Pepe's gift

LORIS sat stewing as Mark concluded with a prayer. He was angry with himself for he did not know what had possessed him to give in to his daughters' request to attend the church service, even though they were in the play. He was enraged by what he had heard but also shaken, which annoyed him terribly, for he knew that only his discovery could counter what had been said, nothing else. Mark's words rang in his ears, almost in his conscience, and he could not remove them no matter how he tried. They had tackled his pride, his standing, his very belief, and he wanted revenge, not just vindication. He wanted to be able to throw criticism in the face of creationism, spit in the face of Christianity and mock in the face of intelligent design – for he did not believe any of it to be true. He knew there was but one way that he personally was going to be able to achieve all this in one go, and he had to get working on it, now with more determination and firmness than ever. He knew that if he could not do this in the face of all three, he would have to recognise the sovereignty of an Almighty God and with that, the need to embrace the Saviour of mankind, Jesus Christ.

This Loris did not see as an option, although it presented itself as large as life. His research would give him the answer and provide his route of escape from any form of conflict or confusion, of this he was sure. The truth of his findings he would not deny or turn away from, but he firmly believed they would cement evolution in the depths of his heart! With this perspective, he had to find an answer, he had to make the discovery! Without it, he would not have anything concrete to stand upon, but with it, religion and particularly Christianity, would have to shut its books. The words that now greatly troubled his soul and angered his spirit, would be burned by the lively embers of science forever, and his mind could then rest at ease. He was sure of this too! He was sure that the book by Donald Browning, *Beginnings*, was no sham – evolution and an ultimate discovery of the origin of origins would nullify and neutralise this Christian nonsense and dismiss all power and authority attached thereto.

What bothered Loris, however, was that he could not argue against it rationally. He could not override the principle of hope, even within his own heart, but to him it was not a realism, just an emotion that had somehow come on board over the millions of years of evolvement. Loris remembered Mark's comment when he had visited Mark at his office, about how he would have to explain feelings and emotions to Mark if a spiritual force could not have any effect on a material body, including how he could trust his own reasoning and judgement if our brains had just evolved from a random mix of chemicals over billions of years. But he could not adequately answer or explain it – he had to get to Pepe, he had to get his discovery, he had to obtain his answer, and he had to dismiss the lies that were now plaguing the very core of his existence.

'Loris,' said Sarah, reaching out and touching his shoulder, seeing that he was adrift in thought, the sheep and goats slowly stirring with Mark having finished his prayer, 'Loris!'

'Yes,' responded Loris, a bit startled and quickly turning towards Sarah as he noticed the movement of the people around him, 'what is it?'

'Would you like a mug of hot soup?' asked Sarah reservedly, the fiery, determined look on Loris' face troubling her. 'Perhaps a cup of tea or coffee and a piece of Christmas cake?'

'I'd like you to get the girls,' replied Loris somewhat strongly, 'for I want to get you home. I want to head back to the lab!'

'This evening?' questioned Sarah, taken aback. 'It's now pouring with rain, and the storm has begun to make itself manifest! Haven't you done enough? It's Christmas Eve!'

'I'm not concerned about a storm,' said Loris dismissively, 'or what day it is. I have work that I want to do – work that needs to be done! I must just press on, and tonight I have the strength and desire to continue!'

The others just looked on, aware that Loris was in a bit of a bad mood, even though he was trying to suppress it somewhat.

'If you would like,' offered Tim kindly, 'July and I can take Sarah and the girls home. We have to help with kitchen duties, which will end at about 11 p.m. We can take them home afterwards, if they would like to stay?'

'I'd like to stay,' responded Sarah, looking at Loris, 'and the girls would love to stay up. We can manage it. You can head straight to the lab then. The only thing, Loris,' added Sarah with a concerned look on her face, 'is that I'm scared with you working late like this after the recent break in at the lab.'

'No need to worry,' assured Loris confidently, 'we have added security now, with security personnel on the premises at all times. Andy' said Loris, turning quickly to him, 'are you perhaps interested in joining me?'

'I am, actually,' replied Andrew. 'I feel that we're very close now to finding that evasive "little fellow" that I'm eager to keep at it, but I'm on kitchen duty with June and the rest.'

'We could manage,' said June, seeing Andrew's interest in going and knowing that he wanted to support Loris as well. 'If you go with Loris, I'll pick you up after we've finished here – just after 11 p.m. I'll send you a message when I leave.'

'I'd be greatly appreciative,' said Loris, softening a little in his manner. 'Andy's help is always welcome.'

Tim and July headed off to assist with kitchen duties while June and Sarah quickly went to make Andrew and Loris some coffee that they could take with them.

'Don't forget Pepe's gift,' reminded Sarah upon return, as she handed Loris a transportable mug of coffee, 'it's in the box in the back of the SUV.'

'I won't forget it,' said Loris, 'I packed it in!'

'What gift is this, may I enquire?' asked June with interest, having given Andrew his coffee.

'I made some beautiful lilies out of clay,' answered Sarah with a bright smile and bubbly manner, 'and painted them before glazing. I arranged them carefully in one of Loris' large vases.'

'That sounds like a nice gift,' complimented June. 'It'll add a little colour and feature to the lab, I'm sure!'

'That's what I said,' responded Sarah, quite pleased with June's approval. 'I actually wanted to provide a small painting, a copy of something from Rembrandt, Michelangelo or Leonardo da—'

'I told Sarah that there's no place for that sort of thing,' interrupted Loris, eager to be on his way, 'but we have a spot where we can safely put the vase and flowers.'

'I'll have to find another place for a da Vinci,' said Sarah, pulling a naughty face as she quickly gave Loris a hug. 'Take care. Andy, please look after him!'

'Go on!' moaned Loris as he departed with Andrew, the ladies and Andrew chuckling. 'Just listen to it!'

Loris and Andrew were soon on the other side of the two wooden doors that separated the warmth and brightness of the church from the cold, black outside world. It was still pouring with rain, with the wind swirling and blowing it directly into their faces. Loris made his way quickly to his vehicle, with Andrew close in tow. They were soon in the shelter of the SUV and on their way to the lab.

The past two weeks had been frustrating for both of them. They had worked long hours right up until Christmas Eve in an attempt to find the object of their interest they had so nearly seen on the day the Fluorescent Light Enhancement Attachment had been installed on BEAFT. It was to no avail though for they just could not locate it. It was almost as though something was riding along nano-microtubule filaments, but they could not locate it, only briefly having seen a shadow of it when it appeared near Midge's surface. The power of BEAFT was being used to its maximum, but its sophisticated capabilities just could not penetrate deep enough into Midge to give them a clear form of imaging; they needed Midge to comply and assist them in some way.

Loris was particularly frustrated for he sensed that he was so near yet so far from the discovery that he so badly wanted. Each day up until then had been one of near misses. Loris knew, however, that a miss was as good as a mile – he had no data, he had no discovery, he had no success! Nevertheless, his motivation did not dwindle, for he knew that if they could be close before, they could be again, and he wanted to be there when that happened, with the hope that between himself and Andrew they would get it. This night, his energy and enthusiasm were peaking!

'Back again for more testing, sirs?' queried Franz after greeting Loris and Andrew at the security entrance to Microlab's parking area. 'Rather a chilly night. I'd have thought cosying up at a warm hearth would be more desirable!'

'It's the perfect night for work!' exclaimed Loris with a smile. 'I wouldn't want to be anywhere else!'

With a closed-lip smile the security guard tipped his cap and watched Loris pull into the empty parking area.

The two microbiologists were soon in the building, having quickly dashed out of the rain. They greeted another security officer at a second check point inside before promptly making their way to the lab.

'What weather!' exclaimed Andrew, switching on the lights after entering Pepe and hearing the rain suddenly come torrenting down. 'I'm beginning to wonder if Franz isn't the wiser of us!'

'Nonsense,' responded Loris, rubbing his cold hands together after putting Pepe's gift down in a noticeable but safe spot, his zeal bubbling over and desperately anxious to get started, 'this is pri-soup weather, just what we need!'

'Pri-soup?' queried Andrew, a puzzled look on his face. 'I've never heard that word before!'

'Primordial soup,' informed Loris, 'I'm sure you've heard of that! I've coined a new word by merging the two that's all. When I look at Midge and see the movement just under the surface, it's like yellow primordial porridge to me.'

'Oh,' said Andrew as he went over to switch on BEAFT, disinterested in Loris' connection. 'I'll leave your imagination to work on that one.'

Just then the window blinds flashed brightly, closely followed by a deafening clap that ripped through the night's sky in stereo. It startled both Loris and Andrew, who looked at the windows, having heard them shudder.

'The sooner we start the better,' said Loris, fetching the sample he wanted to investigate. 'We have to maintain persistence if we're to succeed.'

Loris promptly set up the sample in BEAFT and let Andrew take charge at the apparatus while he stood and closely followed on the large digital monitor, giving pointers to Andrew as he worked.

Andrew worked solidly, tuning out the disturbing stormy weather that was lurking around the coast and stirring up nature. There was no sign of what they were looking for, but Andrew was able to locate a nano-microtubule filament, which up until then they had only been able to partly identify due to the shape beneath the surface. He held it firm with the super nano-tweezers but could not bring it up to the surface without breaking it.

'That's encouraging progress,' said Loris, installing another sample in BEAFT, 'even if you couldn't raise it up. We just have to keep trying – there must be a way!'

'I'll give it another go,' said Andrew, 'unless you want to try this time?'

'You keep your steady hand at it, Andy,' said Loris, 'I'll watch the monitor. I admit that I'm actually learning a lot from seeing what you're doing.'

Andrew smiled briefly, heartened by what they had managed to do and by Loris' comment. He worked steadily once more, carefully searching systematically and following the process that he had just used.

The weather continued to worsen as time continued to tick. Andrew's concentration was kept at a peak by the adrenalin pumping through his system, and he was not even aware of the time. He managed to locate another nano-microtubule filament, this time securing it at the surface.

'That's your phone,' said Loris, looking at his watch. 'Would you believe that it's already 23:10!'

'It must be June,' said Andrew, lifting away from the eyepiece. 'Thankfully I've just managed to secure that filament – it certainly is interesting. I really need to keep going though!'

'You've done exceptionally well, my dear colleague,' said Loris with a smile, taping Andrew on the side of his arm as he walked past him to fetch his phone. 'You head off home with June. I'll take over from here and see what I can manage to do. I'm still feeling fresh!'

Andrew saw that it was a message from June informing him that she was just leaving Ailensbury Christian Fellowship so would be there in five minutes. He promptly handed over to Loris and exited Pepe, making his way to the building's main entrance to wait for June, who arrived a minute later.

Loris, having heard June arrive outside, looked out the window. He watched as one of the security guards saw Andrew to his car, shielding him from the heavy rain with a large umbrella. Andrew and June wasted no time in heading on their way, and the security guard hastened back to firm shelter. Loris stared momentarily out the window, consumed in his thoughts. In the distance he saw the lightning flash brilliantly across the expanse and sink its powerful bolts deep into the ocean caldron. He let go of the window blind and went back to BEAFT, ready to continue on where Andrew had left off.

Loris looked into BEAFT's eyepiece and studied what Andrew had done. He then went and looked on the monitor before pulling up some photos that he had remotely taken of Andrew's work that evening and studied them carefully. Once he was happy and confident, he went back to BEAFT and set his face against the eyepiece again. Loris left Andrew's work untouched for a while, working another area of the sample and making his observations.

About an hour later the eye of the storm hit the coast. Gale-force winds ripped between the buildings, rattling windows heavily as the rain pelted down with energy and might. The eerie sough of the wind raised its voice and cried tormentingly loud as it swirled and haunted everything while the anguished sea broke heavily on the rocks, its thunderous roar powerful and striking. This did not deter Loris one bit as he went back to working on what Andrew had done. It actually energised him, and he felt something urging him to keep going.

Loris worked carefully and systematically, despite the cracking of lightning and deafening thunder all about him. From the photos he had taken of Andrew's work, he was able to see what may be needed in order to lift the nano-microtubule filament. Loris' concentration intensified as he tackled this task, hoping that it would pay dividends.

'Come on you pri-soup!' cried Loris, careful not to be hasty in his excitement as the filament began to surface.

He paused momentarily to steady his hand and nerves, desperately not wanting to break it. He eventually managed to lift it above the surface and secure it. Just as he had done so, to

Loris' amazement, something began to stir just below the surface, right on the line of the nano-microtubule filament. He watched in awe, hardly believing his eyes.

'BEAFT, you beauty!' cried Loris, almost shaking with delight when he realised what was following along the filament and about to surface. ' Pepe this is a wonderful gift!'

Chapter 37

Da Vinci

'**W**HO is it?' asked June half asleep as she turned over to face Andrew. 'It's just past 3 a.m.!'

'It's Pepe!' exclaimed Andrew through bleary eyes, trying to wake himself up as he switched on his reading lamp and picked up his mobile phone. 'It must be Loris. I hope nothing's wrong!' Andrew answered the call without delay.

'Andy!' exclaimed Loris in a plosive manner, hardly able to speak. 'I found him!'

'Found who?' asked Andrew, not understanding what Loris was referring to, having been in a deep sleep.

'H–Him!' stammered Loris, unable to get his words out due to his delight.

'Who is him, Lori?' enquired Andrew, sitting up. 'I'm not with you!'

'Da—Da,' managed Loris, then there was momentary silence on the phone, Loris hardly able to speak as he trembled with excitement and almost fear at what he saw.

'Is he alright?' asked June worriedly, also sitting up.

'Loris, are you okay?' asked Andrew. 'Is something the matter?'

'Da Vinci!' blurted Loris loudly, eventually able to get the words out. 'Da Vinci! Da Vinci! I managed to capture da Vinci! Come quickly!'

The call suddenly disconnected, Andrew realising that Loris had put the phone down.

'What's da Vinci?' enquired June, having been able to hear Loris cry out the name.

'I really don't know,' replied Andrew as he hastily jumped out of bed and made his way to the bathroom, 'but whatever it is, Loris is so excited that he cannot contain himself. He's asked me to get there quickly. I must go! Could I perhaps ask you to make me a cup of coffee?'

'I'm on my way,' answered June warmly, already putting on her gown, having anticipated Andrew. 'You get yourself warmly dressed, and I'll have a small flask of coffee and some oat biscuits ready for you.'

'Thanks,' said Andrew, quickly poking his head out of the bathroom, deep gratitude and love in his heart for June, 'you're always good to me, you know that?'

June quickly kissed him on her way passed and made her way downstairs to switch on the kettle.

Within 10 minutes Andrew was downstairs and ready to go, his tangled hair combed, face washed and teeth cleaned. He grabbed his thick, warm winter jacket and put it on as he made his way to the front door, June following him.

'Thanks, Precious,' said Andrew, taking the little parcel that June had prepared for him. 'I'm not sure what I'm in for, but I'll make every effort to be back for the family lunch. If anything, I like holidays and need some rest.'

'Keep me posted,' said June. 'I'll be praying for you.'

Andrew quickly embraced June and kissed her affectionately before heading out into the dark, bitterly-cold morning wondering what he was about to see. His nose, face and hands instantly whitened the moment he penetrated the glacial outdoors and once on the way to the lab, had to turn on his car's heater to stop the windscreen from misting up, his condensed breath not helping things.

The tail of the storm was still present, visibly displaying the last vestiges of its power. However, the heavens had cleared slightly and a few bright stars could be seen peering down through the leaden sky.

Andrew wasted no time in getting to Microlab Industries nor when passing through the security checks. He hastened down the corridor to the lab, eager to discover what Loris had been on about, and raced into Pepe.

'Come, Andy!' cried Loris, signalling anxiously with his hand before Andrew was even properly through Pepe's mantrap security entrance.

Andrew put his little food parcel on his desk and swiftly made his way over to BEAFT, where Loris had gone back to.

'It surfaced!' said Andrew with big eyes, looking at the large monitor and suddenly realising what Loris had been on about. 'You filmed it?'

'I captured and filmed it!' exclaimed Loris, unable to contain his emotion and near to tears. 'You were right, Andy, it is complex in design! I began sketching it after I called you.'

'Its design is far more complex than I had even imagined!' acknowledged Andrew, his heart pounding at the sight, the long gruelling months of research and investigation making the discovery even more impactful. 'This is incredible! Tell me what happened.'

'I basically carried on from where you left off,' informed Loris energetically, quickly bringing up on the monitor a file that he had made containing static images he had taken. 'I was able to lift the nano-microtubule filament above the surface and secure it. Just then, to my great amazement, I watched our target rise up above the surface as it followed along the filament. You can see that it moves along by means of a cogwheel. The only way I can describe it is that it rides on a single-wheeled Segway! I managed to put a barrier in its way and stop it. Remarkably, I was able to capture it first go, without destroying it! It's a marvel and a marvel how it seems to work – looks to be so simple! I got it all on film!'

Loris left Andrew to look over all the data and images that he had created while he went to the staffroom to make himself a mug of coffee. He returned a short while later and sat silently sipping at his coffee, his mind focused solely on the recent success. He looked at the monitor, the new discovery frozen upon the screen as if it had been there for eons of time, untouched, unmoved, untroubled by man, and he wondered where it would all lead to.

'This is just fascinating,' commented Andrew, turning to Loris after having gone through all the data and photos, 'not to mention thrilling! We need to do a complete study on this "little guy" to see how it really works and functions.'

'I fully agree,' affirmed Loris putting his coffee mug down on a work bench, 'but we first need to backup all data and details that we have. It's nearly 4:30 a.m. now. If we get started, we can have it completed by sunrise. What are your plans for the day?'

'We have a family lunch,' replied Andrew, 'so if possible I need to be back by 11 a.m. I should be free by late afternoon, early evening.'

'I need to be back just after sunup,' informed Loris. 'The girls always like me to be there when they open their gifts, and they never want to wait! We're also having a family lunch, but it's just the four of us so not a big deal. I need to get some sleep though. Maybe I'll get a chance after lunch. I'll be back here at 5 p.m.'

'I'll plan to do the same,' said Andrew, 'and we can get stuck into the investigations pronto! What about Dr Whyte and Professor Smyth?'

'As they're both away with their families for the Christmas long weekend,' said Loris, 'I don't want to bother them, for there's nothing they can do. We'll leave them in peace and give them a surprise present on Monday.'

'They will moan for sure,' responded Andrew, 'for not telling them straightaway, but then they'll jump for joy!'

'Most likely,' agreed Loris, amused at the thought of it, 'but as today is Friday, it gives us the weekend to get stuck into our research. If we work hard at it, we'll then have all that we need. On Monday, Professor Smyth can arrange a press conference. I'd be highly pleased if it could be arranged for Tuesday afternoon. It's short notice, agreed, but if there's anyone who could have it arranged, it's the professor. Anyhow, I want it announced before New Year!'

The two microbiologists promptly got on with their task and made detailed reports of all their work done since the night before, ensuring that nothing was left out. They backed up and secured all data and records of the discovery, with each of them double checking the other's work just to ensure there were no mistakes. They managed to complete it all just as the sun yawned and stretched its long arms across the sea, lighting the window blinds and sneaking in through the sides. They both headed off home and later met back at the lab as agreed. They worked tirelessly till late that evening, continuing again on the Saturday and Sunday, conducting further investigations and capturing valuable data and details from their research.

'Okay, Loris,' said Andrew, well pleased with their efforts over the weekend, 'I think that's about it from my point of view. I've written up all the data and secured it. We just need to run backups now.'

'I'm about done too,' responded Loris, coming over to Andrew. 'I'll run the backups and then check everything again, just in case. I think we've covered a lot this weekend and gained a mound of answers and insight. We can definitely be satisfied!'

'If you need my further assistance,' said Andrew, looking at his watch, 'I'll stay; otherwise, I'm going to head off, for I would like to attend church if possible. By the way,' added Andrew with a questioning look, 'I keep forgetting to ask. What have you named this "little fellow"? When you phoned me in the early hours of Christmas morning, you kept saying, "Da Vinci". What was that all about? I didn't understand it at all!'

'That's the name I've given it,' answered Loris, a little amused and embarrassed at the recollection of his own conduct. 'At the time, I was so thrilled and awe struck by the whole thing that I could hardly speak, let alone answer you sensibly. I just wanted you to get here!'

'Has the name da Vinci come from Sarah's influence?' asked Andrew, remembering what Sarah had said about the paintings.

'Not actually,' replied Loris. 'I named it from a comment your own minister, Mark Marsh, made. When I went to see him at his office, after we got back from Bramford, he mentioned to me that Leonardo da Vinci had once said, "Simplicity is the ultimate sophistication." When I first viewed this nano-kinesin, I could see the complexity of it. I was convinced, however, of its operating with complete simplicity and greater efficiency than anything else, which we've been able to confirm over the past two days. That was the reason for naming it da Vinci!'

'I see,' said Andrew. 'Interesting how you came about the name. Well, it's going to cause quite a stir!'

Andrew switched off his computer, and quickly packed up.

'I'm on my way, Loris,' said Andrew, taking his thick jacket from off the back of his chair and heading for the exit. 'I don't want to delay if I can help it – tonight is the last church service for the year!'

'Enjoy it,' called Loris, 'for it will more than likely be your last church service, period! If we have the press conference as I've planned, Tuesday your religion dies!'

Chapter 38

The universal truth

ANDREW whipped around, his countenance having changed in
an instant. Loris recoiled as he looked directly into Andrew's face
of fire. He had not intended to stir a broth of confrontation nor
actually reveal his thoughts. They had just slipped out before he
knew it and he could not back down now.

'"How long, O men,"' fired Andrew, filled with a righteous
anger as he quoted from the Psalms, '"will you turn my glory into
shame? How long will you love delusions and seek lies?" [99] The
very words of a holy God!'

'I don't see it as falsehood,' defended Loris, not liking
Andrew's demeanour one bit, 'I see it as truth! Nor do I see my
cause as worthless or being contradicted by reality or rational
argument!'

'When I see da Vinci,' said Andrew, walking up to Loris, 'I
marvel at what I see because I see the powerful creation by an
Almighty God at work – and nothing less.'

'That's your opinion,' informed Loris, 'but not mine. It's
everything I've been searching for – and it points directly to

evolution! The nano-kinesin may be more complex than kinesin, but it operates far simpler and is 10 times more efficient. That indicates to me that the beginning was from a simpler operation and developed from there. Within the body of da Vinci is the heart of simplicity, irrespective of what may seem to be revealed on the outside, for it's so efficient and simple in its operation. That's what is sought and that's what evolution presents – a simple start! The heart of da Vinci has to be connected to that start for mankind. You've also seen the energy supply pack on da Vinci's back that feeds everything! It's shaped in a golden spiral – exactly after a galaxy's spiral! Da Vinci represents the origin of origins!'

'You either speak ignorantly or deceitfully, Loris,' responded Andrew, 'for as a scientist you know and understand complexities. You know that complex mechanisms cannot be considered simple operations, and high efficiency never functions because of simplicity. There's usually something exceptionally intelligent within its system – and in this case, that "something" is the LORD God!'

'That's rubbish!' snapped Loris aggressively. 'You creationists are a bunch of knuckleheads, that includes your father!'

'You and I are both microbiologists,' said Andrew, unimpressed by Loris' criticism, 'and my father too! Which part of my evolutionary brain did I use to discover and extract Midge? You insult my intelligence, mock my family, ridicule my God and Saviour and on what basis, what grounds do you have? Only the idea that your body and brain came from rocks – and that those rocks originally came from nothing!'

'We came from the Big Bang, not from some god!' retaliated Loris sharply. 'All things have had millions of years to hone and fine tune!'

'Tell me, Loris,' questioned Andrew, 'what is 0 x 0?'

'Confounded nonsense!' said Loris with irritability. 'You don't expect me to answer that, do you?'

'Yes, Loris,' said Andrew, a little disdainfully, 'it's nought! And 1 x 0 and 2 x 0?'

'What ridiculousness is this,' spat Loris, 'an idiot's guide to beginner maths?'

'Answer me!' said Andrew forcefully.

'It's all nought!' replied Loris, not pleased with Andrew's insistence. 'Are you struggling with kindergarten mathematics or are you just being dumb!'

'What is $0 \times 1 \times 10^{79}$?' asked Andrew, ignoring Loris' mocking comment.

Loris just stared at Andrew, understanding exactly what he was trying to imply, as it is estimated that all the atoms in the universe amount to 1×10^{79}, and that this figure multiplied by nought will equal nought!

'Now please tell me,' continued Andrew with guns blazing, his internals still burning with hot anger, 'this vast and expansive universe that we have, with large amounts of matter, how was it made, considering that the foundation of the evolutionary model indicates that there was nothing and it exploded and formed the universe? Taking into account your answer,' added Andrew, being a bit sarcastic himself, 'maybe evolutionists need to go back to playschool! So tell me, how was it all formed, if nothing cannot equal something? How much time do you need for 0×0 to equal 1 or will it always equal 0?'

'Don't waste my time, Andrew!' retaliated Loris, not prepared to answer him. 'I have better things to do! Da Vinci may be complex in appearance, but then biology is the study of complicated things that have the appearance of having been designed with a purpose.' [100]

'But you're not prepared,' responded Andrew, 'to consider that these complicated things *are* designed by an intelligent designer – this is just not an option? Great scientists such as Kepler, Newton, Pasteur, Faraday, Kelvin, Copernicus and others all believed strongly in the Bible and in the biblical account of creation. They had no difficulty engaging in science with a biblical outlook!'

'That may be,' bit back Loris, 'but modern science doesn't deal with supernatural explanations because they aren't scientifically testable. There's no way to gather evidence that would help us determine whether or not the explanations are accurate! The biblical account of creation doesn't meet this standard, so it's disqualified!'

'But you believe,' said Andrew, 'that evolution does meet this standard!'

'Evolution is happening all around us,' replied Loris, 'it has been observed, just hasn't been observed while it is happening.' [101]

'Consider what you are saying, Loris!' exclaimed Andrew in disbelief. 'That's unintelligible – garbled junk! If it hasn't been observed while it is happening, how could it have been observed? And if it is not observed, then it is just pure guesswork and belief – pure faith! Your statement is baseless and ultimately wicked, not to mention hypocritical, for in itself it's accepting that for which there's no way to gather evidence that would help us determine whether or not the explanations are accurate! Wake up Loris!

'Before you get on with those "better things",' added Andrew, taking his mobile phone from his jacket pocket and scrolling quickly through it, 'you mentioned that all things have had millions of years to hone and fine tune. Maybe the following will interest you: the universe is finely-tuned. Listen to a former leading physicist and cosmologist, who was an atheist and evolutionist, "Most of the fundamental constants in our theories appear fine-tuned in the sense that if they were altered by only modest amounts, the universe would be qualitatively different, and in many cases unsuitable for the development of life. Our universe and its laws appear to have a design that both is tailor-made to support us and, if we are to exist, leaves little room for alteration. That is not easily explained, and raises the natural question of why it is that way." [102] You know exactly what he's saying – just slight changes in the makeup of the universe and we're doomed! He admits that it raises the question of why it is that way, but he was also not prepared to consider God!'

'That may well be,' said Loris, 'but I'm working in the micro-world!'

'This fine-tuning,' responded Andrew, 'extends even to the features of individual atoms – how small do you want to get! Listen to this from a former leading astronomer and cosmologist, "Some super-calculating intellect must have designed the properties of the carbon atom, otherwise the chance of my finding such an atom through the blind forces of nature would be utterly minuscule. A common sense interpretation of the facts suggests that a superintellect has monkeyed with physics, as well as with chemistry and biology, and that there are no blind forces worth speaking about in nature. The numbers one calculates from the facts seem to me so overwhelming as to put this conclusion almost beyond question." [103] But God is not to be considered as the "superintellect"?

'Some years back, scientists attempted to calculate how finely tuned the Big Bang had to be, if such an event had actually produced our universe. It was calculated that if it had created just *one* grain of sand more than is currently in our universe, then we wouldn't be here, because our universe would have collapsed into a black hole long ago. On the other hand, if the Big Bang had created just *one* grain of sand less than what is currently in our universe, then the universe would be completely empty today because space would have expanded too quickly and galaxies could never have formed. Therefore, the idea that a Big Bang created our universe, that a random event could be so precisely finely tuned down to a single grain of sand, is ridiculous. However, when they added dark energy to the equation a while later, the fine-tuning got even worse! Now it had to be accurate to far, far less than even one hundredth of one atom within a grain of sand! That's how accurate the alleged Big Bang had to be! [104] It's absurd, Loris!'

'That may be one side of things!' said Loris.

'Indeed,' agreed Andrew, 'but you should be concerned for it leads on a downward spiral – and this is my point. It has led to the multiverse, which you know is the concept of multiple universes.'

'The concept of multiverses are theories,' said Loris.

'They aren't even theories,' responded Andrew, 'they're science fiction, theologies, works of the imagination unconstrained by evidence.' [105]

'It's a very real possibility,' objected Loris, 'and widely accepted!'

'A very *real* possibility?' questioned Andrew sceptically. 'How can it be *real* if it can never be discovered? The word universe means "all that there is". Scientists now redefine it as being "everything we could ever see". Other universes are defined as being "everything we could never see". So in order to overcome the preciseness of our universe, non-biblical science has conveniently concocted something that can never be seen!'

Andrew quickly scrolled through his phone.

'It's confirmed by the following,' he continued, '"Our universe may be but one of perhaps infinitely many universes in an inconceivably vast multiverse. Commonly accepted today in cosmology, yet the existence of other universes cannot be proved or disproved. Advocates argue that, like it or not, the multiverse may well be the only viable non-religious explanation for what is often called the 'fine-tuning problem' – the baffling observation that the laws of the universe seem custom-tailored to favour the emergence of life." [106] But the insanity continues, with it having been said in as many words, that there's another Milky Way just like ours, with a solar system that's the same, with a planet that's exactly like earth, with a house that's identical to yours, with people who look just like you and your family, who are doing exactly the same things you and your family are doing right now! And there are an infinite number of such copies! [107] And this you consider as a very real possibility? It's all an attempt to get away from God for it's been clearly mentioned, "If there is only one universe, you might have to have a fine-tuner. If you don't want God, you'd better have a multiverse." [108] Truth isn't determined by what gets the greatest number of votes! I wouldn't worry about the golden spiral – here you have man's downward spiral! God says, '"Woe to him who quarrels with his Maker, to him who is but a potsherd among the potsherds on the ground. Does the clay say to the potter, "What are you making?" Does your work say, "He has no hands"?"' '"It is I who made the earth and created mankind upon it. My own hands stretched out the heavens; I marshalled their starry hosts.'" [109] The psalmist also says, "Why do the nations rage and the peoples plot in vain? The kings of the earth take their stand and the rulers gather together against the LORD and against His Anointed One. 'Let us break their chains,' they say, 'and throw off their fetters.' The One enthroned in heaven laughs; the Lord scoffs at them.'" [110]

'That's all religion,' objected Loris, 'supernatural!'

'The Big Bang model,' observed Andrew, 'denies supernatural explanations but at the same time requires supernatural explanations! And you want to lay claim to "observational science", whereby the biblical account is excluded? When you deny the truth, you must believe a lie! Listen to this,' added Andrew, quickly scrolling through his phone. 'Scripture says, "How many are your works, O LORD! In wisdom you made them all; the earth is full of your creatures. There is the sea, vast and spacious, teeming with creatures beyond number – living things both large and small. These all look to you to give them their food at the proper time. When you give it to them, they gather it up; when you open your hand, they are satisfied with good things. When you hide your face, they are terrified; when you take away their breath, they die and return to the dust. When you send your Spirit, they are created, and you renew the face of the earth." [111] God is continually busy with His creation. When you deny God, you must end up in foolishness, and the downward spiral continues.'

'That's rubbish,' opposed Loris strongly. 'It's folly to hang on to the failing letters of religious writings!'

'It's not rubbish!' pressed Andrew firmly. 'The multiverse has led directly to Boltzmann brains. The mathematical improbabilities of creating a whole universe by chance has led scientists to grasp at it all being an illusion, with just naked brains floating around in space thinking that it's all real! Welcome to the Boltzmann brains – nothing exists, just brains, and they are not even sure that there is more than one brain! And again, this is all because man wants to suppress the truth and deny God!

'Then you also have something called the Oort Cloud,' added Andrew, scrolling through his phone once again, 'which you may have heard about. Evolution cannot provide a decent answer for long-period comets, so they've invented the Oort Cloud – a fictitious creation. It has never been seen, and can never be seen, for it is make-believe – yet it has location, size, functionality and stock. It apparently is the most distant region in our solar system, lying far beyond Pluto. It's so far away that it would take NASA's Voyager 1 spacecraft, travelling at about a million miles per day, 300 years to reach it, and it would take it about 30,000 years to exit it on the other side! Apparently, unlike the planets, objects in the Oort Cloud can travel in all different ways, much like lazy moths around a porch light! Furthermore, there may be hundreds of billions, even trillions of icy bodies in the Oort Cloud. And this detail is provided for something that has never been seen nor can be – pure fantasy! It has been written that most known long-period comets have been seen only once in recorded history because their orbital periods are so long. It goes on to say that countless more unknown long-period comets have never been seen by human eyes. Some have orbits so long that the last time they passed through the inner solar system, our species did not yet exist! [112] If they have never been seen by human eyes, how could anyone know there were countless that haven't been seen? If our species apparently did not exist, how could anyone truly know that they actually passed through the inner solar system? Pure guesswork, pure assumption, pure fantasy and based on what – belief, not observation! Although it's a theory, it's spoken of as though it should be believed to be true, for it is needed in order to assist with evolutionary processes. Where's observational science here? This wild fabrication isn't considered a fairy-tale but sound science! Isn't this unreasonable, not to mention hypocritical also?'

Loris did not answer Andrew, his deep-set eyes just glared at him.

'"The heavens declare the glory of God," read Andrew from the Bible on his phone, '"the skies proclaim the work of His hands. Day after day they pour forth speech; night after night they display knowledge. There is no speech or language where their voice is not heard. Their voice goes out into all the earth, their words to the ends of the world."' [113]

Andrew looked directly at Loris, momentary silence etched forever in history.

'So from "non-religious" science,' concluded Andrew frankly, 'we have the Oort Cloud – something never seen or that can ever be seen, designed and functioning as if it were real. How is this possible? We have the multiverse, which again can never be seen or discovered, for whatever we discover that can be seen has to fit within what is termed our universe. So the widely accepted, unseen, unknowable, multiverse, whereby you and I are also replicated in another universe or even in more than just one, with everything acting exactly the same because it apparently "aids" the evolutionary concept, is considered reasonable and accepted science! And then we have Boltzmann brains – where in fact, instead of our universe, solar system, planet and everything about us including what we are currently doing being replicated, now nothing exists! Now you and I don't even exist, this conversation is illusionary, the imagination of some distant brain that has it all made up in its mind. I'm not angry, you're not irritated, our emotion isn't getting involved, because it's all make-believe and we don't actually exist! Madness of madness! And you claim there's no faith, only science? You claim you're an atheist; you claim you only believe in science, why then are you filled with so much speculative belief that is so outlandish it's unreal – literally! The more we discover, the more it astounds the mind as to such sophistication and orderliness that man cannot rationalise it away with anything sensible or sane. Why is this possible? Because we suppress the truth!

Chapter 39

Andrew's assertions unfold

'LISTEN to Scripture, Loris,' said Andrew, having nimbly found the verses he was looking for, '"The wrath of God is being revealed from heaven against all the godlessness and wickedness of men who suppress the truth by their wickedness, since what may be known about God is plain to them, because God has made it plain to them. For since the creation of the world God's invisible qualities – His eternal power and divine nature – have been clearly seen, being understood from what has been made, so that men are without any excuse. Although they claimed to be wise, they became fools and exchanged the glory of the immortal God for images made to look like mortal man and birds and animals and reptiles. They exchanged the truth of God for a lie, and worshipped and served created things rather than the Creator – who is for ever praised." [114] When you remove the power of the immortal God from being the creating, sustaining hand and replace it with self-creation, this is exactly what you are doing, making gods in the images of the created.

'One of man's greatest offences is his self-exultation against

God, and when he does so, he is following right in the footsteps of his father, the devil, who was the originator of this hateful transgression. This is what the LORD said to the Babylonians who exalted themselves, '"Your wisdom and knowledge mislead you when you say to yourself, "I am, and there is none besides me."'"[115] The result was God's wrath and judgement upon the people. Should man believe that God views such an attitude differently today, and that His anger should not burn against those who seek to rob Him of His glory? In answer, God says, "I am the LORD; that is my name! I will not give my glory to another or my praise to idols."' [116]

'You're just a religious fanatic!' said Loris disdainfully.

'I'm not religious,' replied Andrew, 'I'm a Christian. True Christianity is based on a relationship with God through Jesus Christ, not based on religion. There's a big difference.'

'It's all the same to me,' snapped Loris, 'twaddle!'

'In da Vinci,' said Andrew, ignoring Loris' comment, 'we have the most incredible and profound discovery, no doubting it! Yet, you wouldn't consider the discovery to be revealed by the hand of God, nor the object of the discovery to be created by the hand of God! It would be considered a ridiculous consideration because it refers to an omnipotent God with infinite wisdom, unsearchable knowledge and unmatchable intelligence performing the task! It's better to consider the creation of da Vinci as chance, coincidence, luck, fluke and the achievement of discovery as good fortune or better still – man's brilliance, which he somehow managed to attain to from rocks by way of pond scum! This is despite the fact that you cannot make one hair on your head white or black, and Scripture reminds us of that! [117] Scripture is correct when it says in Romans 1, that although they knew God, they neither glorified Him as God nor gave thanks to

Him, but their thinking became futile and their foolish hearts were darkened.[118] This is where you stand, Loris! Where will man stop in his attempt to run from God?'

'I'm not running from anything!' bit back Loris firmly. 'I seek the truth, and in my opinion, truth doesn't point to a creator God!'

'The wrath of God comes upon men because they suppress the truth,' said Andrew. 'You cannot suppress that which you do not have, and God has provided it for everyone to plainly see and understand – as was mentioned in the scriptures already read to you. Man is without excuse, as Scripture has said, for we have the revelation of God in Scripture. We have everyday existence as evidence to testify at our trial, that a design has to have a designer, and a creation has to have a creator! God has inlaid the evidence of spiritual and moral truth, and of His own existence and His greatness and His power, in the very fabric of man's being. We cannot plead ignorance, for everyone has some knowledge of God – in the mind, in the conscience, in the reason, in the soul, in the very makeup of man! [119]

'Solomon said, "He (God) has set eternity in the hearts of men; yet they cannot fathom what God has done from beginning to end." [120] There's something within the very being of man that will lead him to God. Why is it that man asks the questions: where did I come from? Why am I here? What happens to me or where do I go when I die? It's because God has set eternity in the hearts of men. The apostle John says, "God is light; in Him there is no darkness at all." [121] This means that God isn't hidden, He has revealed Himself to man. However, John also says, "This is the verdict: Light has come into the world, but men loved darkness instead of light because their deeds were evil." [122] The problem isn't that man cannot find God or recognise God. Nor is his problem that he cannot find or recognise the truth. Man's problem is that he doesn't want to and will not!'

'I seek answers, not God,' said Loris firmly, 'and in those answers I'll find truth – and I have found it in da Vinci!'

'Seek God,' stated Andrew, 'and you'll find the truth, for God is truth! Your answers found outside of God may not necessarily reveal or lead you to the truth, but God will always point man to the truth! God has revealed Himself to man, and man has received the truth. Yet, men have turned from the truth and rejected God, suppressing the truth under their iniquities because they love darkness rather than light. Man plunges downward, believing that he can live his life any way he wants without any consequence at all, thus leaving himself under Divine judgment! For you to acknowledge God and honour Him would instantly cause you to recognise that you're accountable to Him and His law, which would place you also under His judgement! [119] As a result, man does anything to bypass this possibility – and evolution is one extremely ugly and vile means used!'

Loris fell silent.

'For example,' noted Andrew, pulling up some more information on his phone, 'isn't it interesting that the list of vestigial organs in humans, the once-critical support for evolution, shrunk from 180 structures in 1890 to 0 just before the turn of the twenty first century! Now scientists are trying to use an amended definition in order to resurrect the use of "vestigial" in evolutionary claims! [123] Additionally, in Darwin's day they hadn't even discovered the cell, which you're well aware of. Since then, we have discovered infinitely more than just a cell. How then can we consider keeping evolution as the foundation, with the equation of impossibility stiffening continually? Would you bet on a lame donkey in a pack of 30 thoroughbred horses? Not in a million years. You would also not bet on it winning three times in a row in a billion years, yet you gamble your very life and soul and that of others on worse odds! That's insanity! That's having an elephant hide! You wouldn't gamble mere pennies on such odds, but your soul, which will endure forever, you gamble irresponsibly on a concept with many loopholes, flaws, contradictions, uncertainties and lies!'

Andrew scrolled through his phone quickly.

'This is what a famous mathematician and astronomer said about the probability of evolution,' continued Andrew, '"The likelihood of the formation of life from inanimate matter is one to a number with 40,000 noughts after it ... It is big enough to bury Darwin and the whole theory of evolution. There was no primeval soup, neither on this planet nor any other, and if the beginnings of life were not random, they must therefore have been the product of purposeful intelligence." [124] Yet evolutionists are still trying to reason away the true origin of man and the universe – it's an outrageous consideration! It flies in the face of reality, mocks in the face of sanity, and spits in the face of Divinity. Will it not eventually turn its serpent's head and sink its fangs with fatal consequences upon the souls of those who tread with scorn the Creator's glory? You don't think of it that way, for you erase the hand that writes the laws and firmly holds the sceptre of rule, as though it were but the imagination of fools and the weak of heart!

'You have a little one arriving in less than 3-months' time. You're proud when you consider this little being that *you* have made! Yet what have *you* actually done? I mean no disrespect, but what have you actually done other than engage in a pleasurable act? You cannot make that little being! It is something, a profound thing, that is within the makeup of man that enables him to create such an amazing being. The psalmist, David, writes, "For you (God) created my inmost being; you knit me together in my mother's womb. I praise you because I am fearfully and wonderfully made; your works are wonderful, I know that full well." [125] If there is a God who has given us a body, life and abilities, why would we not want to serve and praise Him? And if there is a Redeemer who has paid our ransom, restored us to our Maker, cleansed us from sin and through the Holy Spirit, renews us, teaches us, guides us and helps us do right, why would we not want to accept Him, serve Him and honour Him? Unless it's as John said, "Light has come into the world, but men loved darkness instead of light because their deeds were evil." [122] Consider your little girl, Loris! I pray that she's born to you healthy and strong. And when you, in joyous spirit, hold that tender bundle in your arms, who will get the glory for what has been created – rocks, pond scum, man or the true creator, God?'

'The truth of the matter,' spoke up Loris, 'is—'

'The truth of the matter,' interrupted Andrew swiftly, 'is that there can only be one way; the paths can never merge. They're on different tracks, going in different directions, seeking different purposes, hailing different sources and culminating in different results. You're the one who has to decide, for you're the one to bear your consequences. Yet, note that your very decisions will influence many others, most notably Sarah and particularly your two precious little girls and soon a third – a strong burden to carry for life and eternity should you be the cause of your loved ones' eternal sorrow and torment! Your girls who cried out in anguish for you in the lake will stand and continually curse you to your face in the lake of fire, should you lead them to damnation through a lie.'

Loris could not retaliate, he suddenly felt muted and unable to utter a word even if he tried, as though something was stopping him. He could just listen, Andrew's words piercing his eardrums and penetrating through his conscience, deep into his heart and soul.

'In the book of Luke,' continued Andrew, 'it's recorded that Jesus said to His disciples, "Things that cause people to sin are bound to come, but woe to that person through whom they come. It would be better for him to be thrown into the sea with a millstone tied round his neck than for him to cause one of these little ones to sin. So watch yourselves." [126] Now that you've succeeded in your task, you will stand up before the world and declare your discovery. They will look up to you with awe, not disdain; showering you with praise, not cursing; declaring your brilliance and scientific genius, not spurning your work; you will be welcomed, not shunned; and your wisdom sought and followed, not relegated to the trashcans belonging to fools and fops. Because you claim that you can see, you, like the Pharisees in Jesus' time, stand guilty, for it's all present before your very eyes, but you're not prepared to see and acknowledge it! You'll go into that press conference with your eyes shut in the face of your discovery! Answer me this, what more would you have done than just discover that which is already there, that which has already been created? It's madness to comprehend the cold and callous mind of man – his proud and self-important folly, whereby he elevates himself to the status of God! Yet he stands on nothing less than a foundationless cloud and rides on the puff of a wind – both of which, be it ever so trivial, his hand never made either!'

Loris seemed to withdraw in himself, although he looked disrespectfully at Andrew.

'Let nature rebuke you,' said Andrew, pulling up another scripture on his phone. '"But ask the animals, and they will teach you, or the birds of the air, and they will tell you; or speak to the earth, and it will teach you, or let the fish of the sea inform you. Which of all these does not know that the hand of the LORD has done this? In His hand is the life of every creature and the breath of all mankind." [127] Look at society today! It supposedly seeks respectability, but places itself in the hands of man. Man believes that he's naturally good but he isn't; he's naturally evil – and this has been clear right from the beginning, with the killing of Abel, Cane's brother.[128] In Genesis 6, God was already grieved that He had made man, and His heart was filled with pain! If you want respectability, pursue a path of repentance and gain forgiveness, true life and respectability in God's sight. In hell there is no respectability, only regret and sorrow and the continuous reminder of one's foolishness in spurning so great a gift given by God through His Son, Jesus Christ – through whom the universe and man were also created! The fool says in his heart, "There is no God."' [129]

Andrew's face was still glowing bright with a righteous anger and his demeanour strong and purposeful. This was one of the few times that he let his emotions mix with his discourse, and it proved a formidable blend not to be trifled with through response or argument.

Loris stood speechless, just looking at Andrew with disgruntlement unashamedly displayed on his face. Although he still felt muted, he reasoned it unwise to respond further in light of Andrew's displeasure, but then he knew that he would only prove himself the very fool if he tried, for he did not have a purposeful or profitable answer to give. He knew that he could not, for if there truly was a God, which he did not believe, Andrew's words would ring clear and true of every man, woman and child who dismissed and rejected the hand of the Creator. He also knew deep down in his heart that evidence to prove there was no God rode along with man on that same foundationless cloud being driven by the wind of pure speculation and nothing other.

Andrew stared at Loris momentarily, silence slicing surgically through the strain between the two scientists.

'I'll see you on Tuesday, Loris,' said Andrew, an air of disappointment in his voice as he turned and headed for the exit. 'Give me a call if you need assistance with anything. You know I'm committed to this work.'

Andrew did not wait for an answer from Loris nor received one. He promptly left the lab, leaving Loris standing in stunned, stony silence!

Chapter 40

Origin of origins

LORIS watched Andrew leave, staring at him with great displeasure and a bitter resentment in his spirit, yet he could not dismiss what he had said. His head was ringing with what Andrew had spoken, and his mind raced with thoughts, all shoving for supremacy. Loris' own thoughts tussled with Andrew's words, and within the quietness of Pepe, he had an internal battle. He eventually heard in the distance a vehicle come to life and leave the premises, but it did not register in his thoughts straightaway.

Loris suddenly realised that he was alone and looking at his watch, came to his senses. Pushing aside all thoughts, he got on with his task of backing up all the data. He worked carefully but wasted no time, desiring to get out of there as fast as possible. Loris finished up, switched off everything and exited Pepe. He made a beeline for his car, greeting security on his way past with little interest, and was swiftly out of the parking area and heading towards home, the tussle between he and Andrew having resumed full force in his mind. Loris was halfway home when he suddenly changed course and headed for the harbour.

The sun had dipped behind the horizon, with only fragments of its life and beauty gasping for a last breath before being sucked below the surface of the distant sea. The moon was visible but only as a weak sketch upon the darkening blue face of the sky, while stars were still hiding in their chambers.

He arrived at the harbour, parked his car and promptly climbed out. The icy wind blowing in off the sea hit him face-on, instantly chilling his nose and ears and causing him to quickly zip his thick jacket up to the neck. He was not put off however and made his way purposely down to the pier. Loris sat down on one of the large weather-worn rocks by the water's edge, his demeanour glazed over with contemplation.

The world was dead to him, only nature being able to induce some interest as he looked out over the sea into the distance. Its waves were restless, much like Loris' spirit within him, with the wind whipping froth from the tops of the waves, and yeasty foam being constantly washed up onto the shore before him. The sight before Loris drew him deeper into thought, and he considered the bubbling primordial waters that he was sure had had a central role to play in the birth of his forefathers. As he dwelt on this, Andrew's words, "Consider your little girl, Loris!" spoke so loudly to him that he turned around to see if someone had actually spoken, but he was alone. There were only fishermen a fair distance away folding up their nets, pulling in their boats at the slipway or washing down their equipment, their general conversation muffled apart from the occasional roaring belly laugh that deeply penetrated the surrounds.

Loris considered his yet unborn girl and the sonar pictures that he had seen when accompanying Sarah for her scans. Her delicate features and fragile frame, was this the work of an

Almighty God or was it the haphazard work of some random occurrence in a natural cauldron of chemicals? He felt that Andrew was at least right regarding one aspect, that although the little girl was his and came from his body, he could not lay claim to the amazing wonder of how she was being made – this was a phenomenon in itself. He considered his two daughters and marvelled at their simplicity, innocence, youthful beauty and his influence in their lives. Loris switched his thoughts and considered the recent discovery and the findings attached. He thought long and hard, running through it all again and again in his mind. He was feeling the pressure, self-inflicted pressure, but it was also partly due to Andrew's response to him that very afternoon. Was there something that could overturn Andrew's apple cart, was there something he was missing?

'There must be something additional!' exclaimed Loris to himself. 'There must be something that I'm also not seeing! There just must be!'

He felt that the sureness of answer must be there in what they had found, which would tip the scale and bring about a victory and end to the present clash. Loris felt his body tighten from strain as the night blackened quickly before his eyes. His sponsors and support were relying on him for answers, the world would soon be waiting for a verdict from him, his family was depending upon him for direction, and above all, his conscience was now counting on him for truth!

Loris looked up at the grim moon, half wasted away due to its current phase. Its sickly-yellow colour yielded no delightful sight and cast no pleasant silvery hue across the troubled waters. The stars too seemed lacklustre, and Loris gave no thought to them, his mind remaining focused on his present concerns. He looked at his watch, jolting when he saw the time and that he had been sitting there for nearly two hours. Loris looked about and realised that the fishermen had disappeared, having cleared away all trace of their day's fishing activities. People were now filling the handful of restaurants along the pier.

He leapt to his feet and promptly made his way to his car, his thick, curly black hair, ruffled from the stiff breeze, more wild than normal. Loris jumped into his car, phoned Sarah to inform her of his plans and headed back to the lab.

Upon entering Pepe, Loris switched on the lights, having first visited the staffroom and made himself a strong mug of coffee. He gathered all the written files and opened the computer files that he and Andrew had created on da Vinci. Loris sat paging through all the details as he sipped his coffee, searching, searching, searching for something that he may not have seen until then. He scrutinised all the photos, going over them multiple times, trying to look at areas that may not have been the focal point when they had first investigated them, but he found nothing.

A little disappointed, Loris went to make himself another mug of coffee. He returned and promptly began watching the video that he had made of the discovery and capture of da Vinci, including additional filming they had done. He played it over and over, slowing it down, speeding it up and pausing it at various timed intervals. After a couple of hours, Loris stood up and approached the large high-definition monitor on which he was playing the video. He looked closely at a still of da Vinci, having paused the video, and examined it carefully. He played it once more, still standing up close, and then paused it again, intently examining the "little guy". An amazed look came over him, and he cupped his hand over his mouth, hiding his smile.

Loris got on his knees before the monitor and bowed his

head to the ground. He straightened and, while still on his knees, lifted his hands heavenwards as his vision clouded. He had obtained his answer, it was there all along, he was just not seeing it. He now knew what to say, and the whole world was going to hear it, including Andrew, George, Professor Stanley Burg, Mark Marsh, Rabbi Noah Arkesden and particularly Sarah! Loris got up off his knees and quickly went to his desk, where he made his notes. He finished up, and with an air about him, switched everything off, closed up and headed home satisfied!

'So, Loris,' said Professor Smyth merrily, holding out both his hands to greet Loris, who had just entered his office, 'all ready for the press conference this afternoon? It wasn't easy, but we've managed to get everything in place!'

'I'm pleased to hear it,' said Loris with a smile, heartily shaking Professor Smyth's hand. 'Apart from a few things to sort out, I'm as ready as I'll ever be!'

'The world awaits!' said the professor joyously. 'We managed to get the whole world linked to this announcement, with many of the major news casts sending reporters.'

'The whole world?' queried Loris, quite taken aback by what Professor Smyth had told him. 'On such short notice? I expected it to be widespread, with links through satellite to go to many nations, and for it to be spread from there, but not that we would have a large turnout at the press conference itself!'

'Yes,' replied Professor Smyth. 'Although it wasn't easy going, after your discovery of Midge, we gained a much better response from those contacted. Late last night we had to move the venue to the Boulevard Inn because the university's PR facility is too small. We've got a whole pack of reporters from major newspapers and television broadcast stations as well as a satellite link and online connection. This is a historic occasion for the university – for everyone! I knew I could count on you, Lori, and the dean sends congratulations too! We've ousted our critics and beaten our opposition! The news yesterday morning of your discovery has made me so excited, I cannot tell you. I could hardly sleep last night in anticipation of today!'

'That's incredible!' exclaimed Loris, quite surprised at what the professor had managed to pull off so quickly. 'Well, they're going to hear it!'

'And the sooner the better!' responded Professor Smyth excitedly, his penetrating voice getting louder. 'It's what we need to hear! It's what the world and science needs to hear, what religion needs to hear! It will be a major turning point for sure in the circles of science!'

'It'll at least be a major talking point,' joked Loris, 'that's for sure!'

'You joke well, my dear colleague,' responded the professor, his laughter booming through the walls of his office, 'but don't be modest, man! This is something to be proud of, to tell to the world confidently. I wish our dearly departed colleague, Professor DeRoach, was present to hear you!'

'So do I, in fact,' affirmed Loris, sadly. 'I have the answer and know exactly what to say! Creationists are going to be shocked and taken aback by what I present! They will not be expecting it. It's going to knock the socks off everyone! Andrew will be behind me when I speak, but I would love to see his face. He'll not be ready for it!'

'I'll be sitting next to him,' said Professor Smyth, 'so I may get a glimpse of his expression. If I do, I'll let you know. Gone are the words, "The fool says in his heart, 'There is no God.'"" [129]

'You're absolutely right!' said Loris thoughtfully. 'I've heard them spoken to me too often. Well,' said Loris, looking at his watch, 'if we've changed venues, I need to head off and sort a few things out at the Boulevard Inn. I'll see you this afternoon.'

'I wouldn't miss it for the world!' exclaimed the professor, accompanying Loris to the door. 'I'll be on my way to the Inn shortly as well, but if there's any issue before I get there, you let me know.'

'Thanks, Kenny,' said Loris appreciatively. 'The support and effort you've provided throughout has been huge.'

Loris shook Professor Smyth's hand and promptly left, focusing quickly on the concerns and tasks that he had to attend to before the press conference began at 3 p.m. that afternoon.

Time rushed forward and soon hounded the organisers of the press conference as they put the final touches in place. Andrew, having not been required for anything, arrived half an hour beforehand, smartly dressed and ready for the occasion. Loris was already there, also smartly dressed, with his thick mop of black curly hair brushed and bouncy. A general greeting took place between the two microbiologists, but there was no excessive friendliness, partly due to the confrontation less than two days before, and partly due to the immensity of what was before them, with Loris' attention being constantly required by the organisers.

When the doors to the conference hall were opened, it filled up quickly with reporters and guests, who had been idling about outside for some time. The ambience was electric, with excitement and eager anticipation flowing liberally amongst those gathered. The cameras were manned, lighting on, microphones operational and everything in place in time.

The chairs for the attendees were in arcs, around a small raised platform, which had a lectern with the Inn's logo on the front of it, and a number of chairs were placed in a row against the wall at the back of the platform. Andrew, Loris, Professor Smyth and Dr Whyte were seated there, while the master of ceremonies, who was from Ailensbury University's PR department, took the stand.

On the stroke of 3 p.m. he welcomed the guests and reporters, gave some background information and introduced the four gentlemen behind him on the stage. He was professional and got on with business, soon calling Loris to come forward.

Loris stood up and, to the loud applause of the audience, made the few steps it required to the lectern. The strong lights glared upon him as he looked out at the people before him while waiting for complete silence, which was soon afforded him.

'Ladies and gentlemen,' began Loris, his heart beating strongly, not being familiar with making such addresses, and concerned about the outcome, 'fellow microbiologists and scientists, guests and reporters who have kindly gathered. It is my privilege to present to you this day a great discovery that myself and my colleague, Andrew Renshaw, with the assistance and support of Microlab Industries, Ailensbury University and also Bramford University, managed to achieve on Christmas day after months and months of research. It was an investigative research into the origin of origins.'

Loris stopped and turned around, looking at Professor Smyth and then at Andrew. Andrew looked directly at Loris, and for a brief moment their eyes locked, like gunfighters in a duel. Andrew maintained a deadpan look, an intense indifference, for there was nothing more he could say or do. He played the supportive role, irrespective of what he managed to achieve. Loris headed the project, and what he would say the world would run with and be influenced by. His heart, however, went out to Loris, for he had grown fond of him as a colleague and close associate, despite their differences.

'I would firstly like to acknowledge Professor McKenzie Smyth,' said Loris, turning back to the audience and cameras, 'who placed confidence in me and made this investigation possible by opening up the channels for investigation and research. He was always a strong support. I would also like to thank my colleague, Andrew Renshaw, who was a big part of the contribution and success, to a degree and magnitude he will never fully know.'

Loris stopped speaking, the audience applauding the two men.

'I've been through the data,' said Loris, continuing after the applause had subsided, 'over and over again. I've seen enough, I'm truly convinced, and the world can now be too!'

'So have you discovered the Origin of origins?' called out one of the reporters eagerly, not waiting for Loris.

'Yes,' replied Loris, a little surprised by the interruption, 'I believe I have.'

'What was in the beginning?' questioned another hasty correspondent. 'Tell us!'

'I have every intention to tell you,' responded Loris, his usual calm manner holding steady this time. 'In the beginning – In the beginning God...'

Enjoyed this book?

WHILE I hope you found this book enjoyable, I also hope that you found it insightful, thought provoking and even challenging.

For information on available titles, please visit:
www.thehumblesaint.com

Publisher contact:
www.thehumblesaint.com/contact/duke-of-valmary

Author contact:
www.thehumblesaint.com/contact/judson-mccawl

About

GOD, through the saving grace of Jesus Christ, has almost always been a part of my life. My mother sat quietly with me one day at her bedroom window in the warmth provided by the sun and explained with the aid of an illustrated book the salvation that we can receive through Jesus Christ. My young mind comprehended what was being told, and at the tender age of two and a half, I asked Jesus into my heart through His Holy Spirit, praying without my mother's directive in the Name of the Father, and of the Son, and of the Holy Spirit.

The principle of Law and Grace was also taught to me by my mother, as a foundational teaching, and the concept of placing it in a descriptive way through book form first presented itself to me late one night as I was about to go to bed.

Having never been an avid reader, let alone a writer, I climbed into bed thinking that it would be grand to be able to put pen to paper and create a practical, complete and detailed story around the Law and Grace principle but mentioned to the Lord my prior struggles at school just to manage the required word count for English exam essays. I've been one to admire the skill and ability of writers, particularly fiction. The art of creating a story and descriptively presenting it in the various scenes has captured my interest and respect. Numerous times I have asked the question, how do they manage to do it? Nevertheless, the thought came to mind that I should at least try – who knows!

Suddenly, as I contemplated some of the potential scenes, what I would term a flood of descriptive writ loomed large and clear in my mind. I was quite taken aback, and although tired and ready for sleep, I opened my eyes and climbed out of bed. I headed to my work desk in the room next door and promptly jotted down on a notepad some of the words and sentences to describe the scenes that had flashed through my thoughts.

Although it was all taken cautiously, knowing that a few words does not produce a book, these notes were steadily worked on.

Little did I comprehend at the time that the specific work I set out to complete would be achieved and further blossom into a series. The four works produced thus far are for me nothing less than miraculous for which I give the Lord thanks.

References

1. Ecclesiastes 12:13b,14

2. Isaiah 65:16

3. Hebrews 6:18

4. Luke 12:5

5. Hebrews 4:12

6. Isaiah 45:23

7. Philippians 2:8–11

8. Romans 5:12–21

9. Proverbs 14:12

10. Hebrews 12:14

11. Stuart Burgess, 'Expert engineer eschews "evolutionary design '", Creation Ministries International, Creation.com, article from Creation 32(1):35–37, January 2010, Philip Bell interviews Stuart Burgess, as at April 27, 2020.

12. Steven Vogel, Duke University, USA, *Cats' Paws and Catapults*, Penguin, 1998.

13. Steve Jones, University College London, *Darwin's Ghost*, Random House, New York, 2000.

14. Westneat et al, Proc Royal Society B (2005) 272, *Evolutionary Explanation of Fish 4-bar Mechanisms*.

15. Stuart Burgess, *Inspiration from Creation*, Creation Ministries International, DVD.

16. Acts 4:12

17. Isaiah 64:6

18. Romans 10:3

19a. Philippians 3:9

19b. 2 Corinthians 13:5 (KJV)

20. Genesis 2:16,17

21. Exodus 20:1–17

22. Deuteronomy 27 and 28

23. Acts 17:30,31

24. John 14:15

25. John 15:14

26. 1 Timothy 2:4

27. 2 Peter 3:9

28. Romans 6:23

29. Isaiah 1:18–20

30. Barry Stagner, 'As in the Days of Noah', YouTube: The Truth About God – Barry Stagner, Published on May 1, 2019, as at April 27, 2020. https://www.youtube.com/watch?v=6V9-vwuzIz4

31. David Pawson, 'Unlocking the Old Testament Part 2 – Genesis 1', YouTube: David Pawson – Official, Published on January 12, 2015, as at April 27, 2020. https://www.youtube.com/watch?v=TdKe0NNHWmY

32. Daniel 12:4 (KJV)

33. Isaiah 46:10

34. 2 Peter 1:19–21

35. *Isaiah 44:6*

36. *Psalm 90:2*

37. *Based on 2 Timothy 2:18,19*

38. *Genesis 1:1*

39. *Kent Hovind, 'Debate #19: Three on One', YouTube: Kent Hovind OFFICIAL, Published on November 17, 2013, as at April 27, 2020. https://www.youtube.com/watch?v=PqHgrUu4ZWg*

40. *John 1:3*

41. *List of creation websites:*

Creation Ministries International: https://creation.com/

Answers in Genesis: https://answersingenesis.org/

Institute for Creation Research: https://www.icr.org/

Biblical Science Institute: https://biblicalscienceinstitute.com/

Creation Research Society: https://www.creationresearch.org/

Creation Science Evangelism: https://drdino.com/

42. *Esther 8:17*

43. *Genesis 17:5; 15:5; Romans 4:16–18*

44. *Amir Tsarfati, 'Amir Tsarfati: Who are the real Jews?', YouTube: Behold Israel with Amir Tsarfati, Published on September 18, 2020, as at December 22, 2020. https://www.youtube.com/watch?v=RRFW0Z7iE4E*

45. *Romans 11:1–24; 9:6–9*

46. *John 3:1–15; 7:50,51; 19:39–41*

47. *Acts 2:36 (KJV)*

48. *Proverbs 30:2–4*

49. *John 3:3*

50. *Zechariah 12:10 (KJV)*

51. John 3:16; 14:9b,10

52. Genesis 1:26,27

53. Acts 2:36–38

54. Jeremiah 31:31–34; Hebrews 8:8–12; 10:16,17

55. Jeff Miller Ph.D., 'The Five Manifestations of Natural Phenomena', Apologetics Press, as at April 27, 2020. http://www.apologeticspress.org/APContent.aspx?category=129&article=751

56. Psalm 19:1,2

57. Isaiah 40:25,26,28

58. David Pawson, 'Unlocking the New Testament Part 5, John Part 1', YouTube: David Pawson – Official, Published on February 4, 2015, as at April 27, 2020. https://www.youtube.com/watch?v=XFXTBYMFrYI

59. 2 Timothy 3:16a

60. Matthew 24:6,7

61. Hebrews 4:12

62. John 8:32

63. Job 38:1–7

64. Job 28:23–28

65. 2 Peter 3:3–6

66. Hebrews 9:27

67. Jeremiah 18:1-12

68. Jeremiah 18:12

69. Exodus 3:19; 7:13,14; 9:34,35; 10:1

70. Numbers 14:11,27a,29a (KJV)

71. Psalm 95:7b,8a

72. *Romans 12:2*

73. *Dr Jason Lisle, 'The Secret Code of Creation' ('Dr Jason Lisle – The Physical World Obeys God's Math (Fractals)'), YouTube: 2028 END, Published on December 2, 2014, as at April 27, 2020. https://www.youtube.com/watch?v=NaDvPeWjBuY*

74. *Isaiah 40:28*

75. *Genesis 3:15*

76. *Luke 2:10*

77. *Romans 5:12*

78. *Isaiah 53:6a*

79. *Isaiah 7:14*

80. *Matthew 1:20–23*

81. *Acts 17:30 (KJV)*

82. *Luke 15:10 (KJV)*

83. *Mark 8:36 (NKJV)*

84. *Matthew 10:28b (NKJV)*

85. *2 Corinthians 6:2 (KJV)*

86. *2 Corinthians 5:17*

87. *Malachi 4:2*

88. *Ephesians 2:5*

89. *Colossians 2:14*

90. *Hebrews 9:27*

91. *Psalm 9:17 (KJV)*

92. *Psalm 8:3,4*

93. *Ezekiel 33:11*

94. *Ezekiel 18:30–32*

95. *Colossians 2:15*

96. *2 Corinthians 6:2*

97. *Isaiah 55:6,7*

98. *John 5:11,12*

99. *Psalm 4:2*

100. *R Dawkins, The Blind Watchmaker, W.W. Norton & Company, New York, USA, p. 1, 1986.*

101. *R Dawkins, Now, 3 December 2004, PBS Network, 'Battle over evolution' – Bill Moyers interview with Richard Dawkins.*

102. *Stephen Hawking and Leonard Mlodinow, The Grand Design, New York: Bantam Books, 2011, pp.159-162.*

103. *Sir Fred Hoyle, 'The universe: past and present reflections.' Engineering and Science, November, 1981. Pp. 8-12.*

104. *Spike Psarris, What You Aren't Being Told About Astronomy, Volume 3, Creation Astronomy Media, 2016.*

105. *John Horgan, 'Is speculation in multiverses as immoral as speculation in subprime mortgages?', Scientific American, January 28, 2011.*

106. *Tim Folger, 'Science's alternative to an intelligent creator: The Multiverse Theory', Discover Magazine, December 2008.*

107. *Brian Greene, The Hidden Reality: Parallel Universes and the Deep Laws of the Cosmos, New York: Vintage Books, 2011, pp. 11-12.*

108. *Bernard Carr, Cosmologist at Queen Mary, University of London, as quoted in Tim Folger, 'Science's alternative to an intelligent creator: The multiverse theory', Discover Magazine, December 2008.*

109. *Isaiah 45:9,12*

110. Psalm 2:1–4

111. Psalm 104:24,25,27–30

112. Nasa Science, 'Oort Cloud, In Depth', page updated: December 19, 2019, as at April 27, 2020. https://solarsystem.nasa.gov/solar-system/oort-cloud/in-depth/

113. Psalm 19:1–4

114. Romans 1:18–20,22,25

115. Isaiah 47:10b

116. Isaiah 42:8

117. Matthew 5:36

118. Romans 1:21

119. John MacArthur, 'When God Abandons a Nation', Grace to You, Code: 80-314, August 20, 2006. https://www.gty.org/library/sermons-library/80-314/when-god-abandons-a-nation, as at April 27, 2020; YouTube: Grace to You, Published on March 24, 2017. https://www.youtube.com/watch?v=Cz8AA_Oa0EU

120. Ecclesiastes 3:11b

121. 1 John 1:5b

122. John 3:19

123. Jerry Bergman, 'Do any vestigial organs exist in humans?', Creation Ministries International, Creation.com, article from Journal of Creation 14(2):95–98, August 2000, as at April 27, 2020. https://creation.com/do-any-vestigial-organs-exist-in-humans

124. Fred Hoyle, 'Hoyle on Origin of Life', Creation Ministries International, Creation.com, as at April 27, 2020. https://creation.com/hoyle-origin-of-life

125. Psalm 139:13,14
126. Luke 17:1,2
127. Job 12:7–10
128. Genesis 4
129. Psalm 14:1